Constantinople: Birth of an Empire

Books by Harold Lamb

BIOGRAPHICAL NARRATIVES

Babur the Tiger: First of the Great Moguls (1963)
Cyrus the Great (1961)
Hannibal: One Man Against Rome (1959)
Charlemagne: The Legend and the Man (1954)
Theodora and the Emperor (1952)
Suleiman the Magnificent (1951)
Alexander of Macedon: The Journey to the World's End (1946)
Omar Khayyám: A Life (1934)
Nur Mahal (1932)
Genghis Khan (1927)

NOVEL

A Garden to the Eastward (1947)

HISTORICAL NARRATIVES

Constantinople: Birth of an Empire (1957)
New Found World: How North America was Discovered and Explored (1955)
The March of Muscovy: Ivan the Terrible (1948)
The City and the Tsar: Peter the Great (1948)
March of the Barbarians (1940)
The Flame of Islam (1931)
Iron Men and Saints (1930)
Tamerlane (1928)
   Tamerlane AND *The March of the Barbarians* WERE LATER COMBINED
   AS *The Earth Shakers; Iron Men and Saints* AND *The Flame of Islam*
   AS *The Crusades.*

FOR OLDER CHILDREN

Chief of the Cossacks (1960)
Genghis Khan and the Mongol Horde (1954)
Durandal (1933)
Kirdy (1931)
White Falcon (1925)

Justinian and his retinue presenting offerings.

MOSAIC DETAIL FROM THE APSE WALL OF ST. VITALIS AT RAVENNA,
COMPOSED ABOUT A.D. 547.

CONSTANTINOPLE

Birth of an Empire

by Harold Lamb

Alfred A. Knopf

NEW YORK · 1966

L. C. catalog card number: 57–12072

© Harold Lamb, 1957

This is a Borzoi Book, published by Alfred A. Knopf, Inc.

Published October 21, 1957
Second printing, September 1963
Third printing, September 1966

Contents

Maps

BY RAFAEL PALACIOS

List of Plates

Constantinople: Birth of an Empire

"Men who saw night coming down about them could somehow act as if they stood at the edge of dawn."

LETTER OF A CONFEDERATE SOLDIER,
WRITTEN SHORTLY BEFORE HIS DEATH

FOREWORD

THIS IS THE STORY of a city built by survivors. As often happens in a great disaster, these survivors were not one people ethnically, but a fusion of many peoples. They gathered together to defend not so much their lives and property as their way of life. In so doing they displayed a certain perversity; they refused to surrender their city. They kept on refusing for nearly a thousand years. History has named them the Byzantines.

They were alone in their survival. In the West a long twilight fell on the Roman Empire during the centuries between A.D. 200 and 450. It ended in the darkness of the first Middle Age. In the East, however, the inhabitants of this city learned the hard lessons of disaster, and they managed to hold back the night.

Their city bore many names, including Constantinople and the Guarded City, before it became known to everyone as Byzantium. Like its people, it had a certain peculiarity. It lay on a small promontory between the tideless inland seas, where the three continents of Europe, Asia, and Africa came closest together. Ancient caravan routes tended toward it, and great rivers led away from it. So the waters that gave access to the hinterlands of the continents also served to protect the point of land on which Constantinople stood. Probably nowhere else could the ancient civilization of the Mediterranean have been preserved.

Its preservation was the work of many men through long lifetime spans. Our story is concerned with one century, the sixth century of Our Lord. The greater part of this time is known for good reason as the Age of Justinian. It was by no means a so-called golden age; it was shaped by intense effort to hold to values in human life. Out of that effort came something unforeseen, and too little understood until now.

The men of Constantinople managed to change the twilight on their horizon into the dawn of a new age, the dawn before the light of modern times. We are the heirs, not of a glory of Greece and a grandeur of Rome, but of their effort in that city between the seas fourteen centuries ago.

I END OF AN AGE

THE FIRST CIVILIZATION of our ancestors in western Europe arose in the towns. There it stayed. It passed in the obscurity before history from the porticoes of a Knossos to the piled rocks of a Mycenae, and to the tawny height of an Acropolis. Minoan-Greek man was shaped by his city state, unaware at first of the vastness of the world beyond it.

Minoan-Greek civilization was sea-borne, taking refuge in the protecting walls of ports. Perhaps the Middle Sea, the Mediterranean itself, became a cause of this compartmentation of separate city-states. For it offered no single passageway by water, at least to primitive navigators in open boats. Peninsulas and island archipelagos divided it; contrariwise, its arms and bays stretched inland, so that early explorers knew it as a collection of smaller familiar seas, the Aegean, Ionian,

Adriatic, and so on to the far Euxine (Black) Sea. Those explorers, venturing into strange waters, came home with tales of wonders seen. The dim tradition of the Argonauts bears witness to temptations of strange sirens and perils of unknown, clashing rocks on their voyage to the edge of darkness at the cloudy Caucasus, where Prometheus reared in eternal chains.

Although divided in this manner, the Middle Sea offered a life-giving boon to its inhabitants. Its warmth kept the small rivers free from ice and the fertile, forested land drenched with rain. The seafaring Carthaginians were the first to girdle most of its coasts with trading posts; the Romans first gained power, with acumen, by building a fleet, and, with ruthlessness, destroying Carthage, mistress of its waters. The power of the Caesars never managed to progress far inland beyond the line of the two rivers Danube and Rhine in the north, and the Sahara in the south. Or if it did so, it came to regret the feat in one way or another.

This same power of the city on the Tiber had arisen in the first place by breaking down another compartmentation, that of human superstition. These ancient city-states of the west had all formed around sanctuaries where a sacred fire usually burned. Each sacrificed to gods of its own, and to ancestors buried in its earth—to ancestral spirits of the misty underworld which might give help or harm to their descendants, the human beings.

Even in its golden age in the fifth century before Christ the city of Athens heeded its invisible rulers, the deities who made known their will through omens. As for the ancestral spirits, they endured stubbornly, to become the *manes* or household habits of Roman families. Hardly less than the authority of these unseen guardians was that of the municipality itself over its citizens. They were no more than slaves of the state. Even Plato argued that children belonged less to their parents than to the city.

And on the Italian peninsula the influence of the *manes* held like bands of steel. Each father, as priest of the family, served the household gods; each gens guarded its walled community, calling outlanders *pagani*—pagans—and strangers *peregrini*—wanderers. These might find shelter outside the walls, but could not participate in festivals or sacrifices. The mysteries of the civic sanctuary were kept as secret as the Sibylline Books of Rome. In this *Roma Dea*, where ancestral temples surrounded the guarded sacred fire, the power of the father over his family, of the gens over its collected families, and of the *civitas*, the united city, over all held steadfast for a long time. Yet, oddly enough, this religion of the early Romans was not a true municipal religion. And from that came the city's first strength.

Because her walls enclosed differing peoples more numerous than her seven hills, the temples around that earliest forum sheltered as many gods. There was a Jupiter from Praeneste and a Venus from the Sabine hills. If there could ever be a melting pot of deities it was here in the Pantheon, to serve all vanquished peoples. Accordingly her laws made room for the laws of Etruria or Latium. In this way *Roma Dea*, unlike a single Greek polis, developed the power of a cosmopolis. In her last days the poet Claudian could exclaim that within her borders "the stranger walks in every land as if it were his own; he drinks at will the waters of the Rhone or the Orontes, for the whole earth belongs to a single people."

Claudian's last phrase, however, was not true.

To this original strength was added loyalty to tradition. In the unpredictable city-states of Hellas, a Socrates might argue for a man's conscience against the tyranny of tradition. Certainly, as enlightenment came to them, the imaginative Hellenes shifted their devotion from their native cities to other things, a political cause or a social class. Thereafter men fought for such things within the city. A Theban might find the leader of his cause in a Macedonian invader. The last bitter strife of Athens against Sparta was not so much a war between cities as a struggle to the death between a democracy and an aristocracy.

Nothing of the kind transformed Rome. As Roman power derived from her municipal melting pot, it endured by the inexorable will of the state, at first given voice by the *princeps*, the first citizen, supreme magistrate and archpriest of the gods as well. Moreover, as the state gained supremacy over others, the privileges of Roman citizenship enlarged vastly, to much more than dictatorship over laws and freedom from taxes. Citizenship not only conferred superiority over other men, but brought also increasing comfort in living as if from the peculiar favor of a goddess confined within its walls, Abundance. Under such conditions the lower strata of humans might not reverence tradition as much as the *potentiores*, but, by and large, were content to enjoy their ease of life in the shadow of the wealthy. Spasmodic revolts by one class, gladiators or slaves, did not seriously alter this traditional way of life. Later on, a tenement dweller who lived on the dole might not sit beside a patrician who had his seat reserved in the theater, but both of them saw the same show. Both of them had been raised to the same ease of life by slave labor; barbarian gladiators provided the entertainment, and the food ration of the city came from remote provinces.

Revolt did not arise in those conquered provinces to threaten the reigning city. Rome was tolerant, at first. Her satellites kept their councils, and—what was more important—their customs. Then, too, their local gods might well be among those honored in the Pantheon by the Tiber. But tolerant *Roma Dea* grew into the all-conquering *Roma Aeterna*. All privileges belonged, henceforth, to her citizens; all labor fell upon the slaves or the other classes.

Aware of this peril of empire, St. Augustine wrote in his book *The City Of God*: ". . . is it well for good men to rejoice in extending an empire? If human affairs had been happy, without war being waged, all kingdoms would have remained small. Many kingdoms of nations would have rejoiced . . . together, like neighbors within a city." Even this bishop of a small African port, confronted by the collapse of an empire, still uses the simile of neighbors *within a city.* (Although he is aware of something new intruding: *nations.*)

Nor was the Roman Empire challenged by a strong enemy. The cosmopolis had made its great effort in destroying Carthage and mastering the whole of the Middle Sea. After that, conquests went on according to plan. The citizens of *Roma Dea* learned to stage with splendor the triumphal return home of her emperors. As early as the Augustan age, Vergil could put it that her mission was "to rule with peace the vanquished foes." (Augustine put it differently in A.D. 400, saying that the Romans held that "liberty was not enough unless domination should be added to it.") Yet the moody Hadrian was not happy within the city walls, and the restless Trajan sought new frontiers beyond sight of the Tiber. On his triumphal column in the forum built for him there is one scene still visible, a miniature of Roman achievement.

Touched with rare artistry, it reveals the dynamic Trajan about to step into a longboat on an unknown frontier river. Men of the countryside will row the boat. Behind them rise the symbols of empire, the revered standards of the legions, the fortified gate of a town already possessed of an amphitheater and temple. Curiously enough, the soldier-emperor wears a civilian toga. Not yet did the emperors display themselves in war's uniform. In appearance at least Trajan remains the first citizen of the ancient city, the archpriest who had been *pontifex maximus* of *Roma Dea.*

By that time (A.D. 117), however, the city had become the nerve center of the great western Empire. No rival power roused the energy of its people. No rival culture stirred the lethargy of the Hellenic-Roman. In proof, the mechanical wonder of aqueduct and highway reached to the *limes*—forti-

fied zone—of the frontiers. At the desert's edge a garrison
town like Timgad had its municipal baths and theater.
Within its guard towers a garrison soldier off duty might read
the roll of a book while he sipped his bowl of wine; outside
wandered shadowy people, primitive or pagan. So far had
stretched the limits of the city of Romulus.

And no farther extended the culture of the Romans, which
knew neither missionaries nor wandering philosophers. For
the Romans did not share the curiosity of the Greeks about
lands beyond their horizon. They did not explore after Trajan's
day. Their one recorded world map is a road map of the
Empire itself, ordered made by Agrippa, the builder of the
Pantheon. The only truly Roman geography gives merely
the distances between the towns. (Claudius Ptolemy, the
astronomical-minded cosmographer, was an Egyptian, and his
plotting of the sphere of the earth attracted little attention
for five centuries.) The best-trained physical scientists worked
as road surveyors. They never managed to follow imaginative
Greek thought toward outer space. This complacency took its
toll from them. The world proved to be larger than they
thought.

In buried Pompeii there survives a wall painting as real as
a candid camera likeness of Roman tradition. In the luxurious
Villa Boscoreale the living room imitates a verdant outdoors.
And there, watching the ritual of the Roman home, stands a
solitary philosopher, gnarled and beggarly, leaning on his staff.
He may have been a Greek Cynic, hired to tutor the children
of this unknown wealthy family. Or he may have been one of
those preachers from the East, a Christian who appealed to
credulous women and slaves. In Rome itself the Christians left
their earliest picturings only underground in the network of
the catacombs. Above ground the monuments and the mural
paintings were those of pagan Rome.

This vast apparatus for comfortable living remained intact

for a long time. The Romans never realized what they had
destroyed for the sake of utility. The gay Greek spirit had
taught them only amusing games, just as Greek music had
been made to enliven their banquets. Out of the research
of an Aristotle they gleaned only what was useful to them—
turning an embryo invention of steam into an excellent
pyrocaust for heating floors. Vergil, their propaganda poet,
cried that they left to others "to map the stars . . . or, with
happier grace to evoke from bronze a living face."

Yet already within this vast housing of Roman engineering
human vitality was failing.

The life now flowing into the great gates of the city was
that of the Mediterranean over which it had ruled. "The
waters of the Orontes flowed into the Tiber." While Greek
rhetors tutored Roman youth, Cretan fishermen brought
rarities of the sea to the tables of magnates and Syrian
merchants carried silk to ladies in patrician atriums. The
ghosts of earlier Mediterranean cultures had been made useful
to the Romans. Berber caravans fetched ivory for ornament
and black slaves for labor from the deserts, and Ethiopian
seamen, instead of Roman shipmasters, brought the luxuries
of India from remote seas. The only Roman fleets were the
grain carriers making the seasonal run to Africa and the coasts
of the Euxine. As for manufactured articles, they were better
made by now in the provinces, to be imported to the city
on the Tiber, where the wealth sufficed to pay for imports—
until the supply of gold failed. So recruits for the armed forces
were drawn from the barbarian peoples settled in the provinces
—until the armed forces were sustained only by barbarian
manpower.

These happenings brought a certain awareness of danger.
Efforts were made to return to the well-being of the early
Empire by re-enacting the past. Sacrifices to the ancient gods

of the Pantheon became ritual. Within the city the old ruling order of the *Senatus populusque Romanus* was invoked in speeches, if not in reality. It is clear today, but it was not so evident then, how all that had changed, never to be the same again. The senatorial order opening its ranks to wealthy commoners and then to military strong men—the Latin farmers yielding to sharecroppers, then to slave labor—the very agricultural and mining machinery no longer furnished slaves by absentee landowners. The vast city becoming a parasite, drawing its strength from the provinces and captive labor—without vision to rouse the energies of its people.

As for the *populi Romani*, they were becoming merely the population of the city of Rome, numbering very nearly one million. This society did not feel itself threatened for the simple reason that it was securely protected. The moribund city had no premonition of inward collapse. This came after the glory of Trajan and the long peace of the Antonines (A.D. 138–192). During the third Christian century the entire structure of the Empire broke apart in civil conflict and ensuing wars.

The wars gave no anticipation to the populace of *Roma Aeterna* that its civilization would come to an end. The weakening of the Empire was more apparent to barbarians outside the frontiers.

After the inward shock of the third century came the invasion of the outer peoples. In the east, desert folk defied the Caesars. From the cloudy north, nomadic folk pressed over the frontier rivers. The Romans were suffering now from their lack of curiosity about the rest of the world. Yet they understood military peril and reacted sharply to it. The city, you might say, felt itself besieged. Aurelian (A.D. 271–5) restored the battle fronts, and built around the city a wall meant to be impregnable. It stands today. But Aurelian was murdered by an officer clique.

Then, as the internal stress increased, came a third impact.

Roman military complacency felt the force of strange religions of the East.

Now the Romans of late had looked upon that East as a frontier, the *oriens.* But there beyond their guard posts stretched the vastness of Asia. They no longer sent soldiers or merchants to explore the hinterland as in the Augustan age or Trajan's day.

In Asia great cities had fallen, but their cultures had endured. Tyre had gone the way of Nineveh, yet had left a heritage for others to enter upon. More than that, the downfall of an empire had not ended a civilization. Why that should have been is not entirely clear today. Perhaps the nations of Asia had learned more from each other than we realize. Perhaps a physical city meant less to their welfare. The people of Moses had departed from the fleshpots of Egypt to seek a land of their own. Certainly the great religions of the East escaped from the boundaries of the political states. Into dominant, pagan Rome, these religions had entered only in clandestine fashion. But as distress intensified, ordinary folk sought solace in mysticism. The ancient city gods no longer answered their questions. Nor did reason suffice. Educated Cynics might explain the causes of disaster, and Stoics argue the need of new values, but the illiterate longed for help.

It came from the clandestine faiths, not from Agrippa's Pantheon. It brought hopeless people to pray in cave or crypt or synagogue, whether to Mani or Mithra of the sun, or Yahveh, or Jesus. Those who prayed felt a hope unknown before.

There could be everlasting life.

Christians left traces of their rejoicing on the dark walls of the catacombs. They whispered their messages as evangels —"good tidings." Among their rude paintings the most common is a woman lifting both arms toward an unseen heaven. At times men are traced gathered about a table without visible food. Evidence tells us that their earliest singing was an *alle-*

luia—an exultation without words—more than the measured song of an ancient hymeneal or celebration of the Dionysian mystery.

This wordless hope reached the armed forces. The soldiers —the legionaries were vanishing from the scene—were weary of Roman discipline and stunned by defeat. They listened to the rumors of a new kind of life. The change in the army came slowly, but presently the commanders found that their men were no longer the recruits of a province like Illyria or Thrace, but the followers of a Mithra or Yahveh. More than that, the hardiest barbarians brought in with them strange myths of a Sky Father or a Great Earth Mother. Aurelian, the soldier-emperor who made a stand against disaster, worshipped a sun god.

At some unrecorded point in time the Roman armed forces began to obey obscure prophets instead of their commanders. Men even consulted their own consciences in carrying out an order. That was the end of the cadaver discipline of the early Caesars.

There were leaders who realized that as the people changed, the rule itself must change.

In the bloody convulsion of the third century's end a low-born Dalmatian saw clearly what lay ahead—the doom of the Roman state. Ruthlessly this Diocles acted upon his foresight, cutting his way with his sword to reach the throne as Gaius Aurelius Diocletianus (A.D. 284–305).

Diocletian made himself an architect of survival. The superior civilization of his world-state still gave it the know-how to beat back physical invaders. If force could be added to intelligence, if one trained mind could direct the defense against the varied barbarian peoples. . . . Diocletian seemed half mad to observers within Rome. He cast the government into military semblance, made officials his servants. Secluding himself from approach, wearing the shimmering silk robes of the East, forcing visitors to prostrate themselves at his feet, he took on the appearance of an Oriental despot.

Yet even while he hewed the state apart Diocletian held to some ancient traditions. He claimed for himself only the ancient title of dominus. When he proclaimed his will to be divine, he re-enacted the divinity of the early Caesars. When he levied the great emergency tax—and made it permanent— he gave it the name of the half-forgotten goddess Annona, protectress of the grain harvest. Setting up operational bureaus to get things done, he called them *officia*, the services. He bound working men—sons after fathers—to their trades, soldiers to their regiments, and the remaining peasants to their land—all by due process of law. Roman citizens became subjects.

It was not enough.

Soaring prices were fixed at a maximum by new laws, and the sinking coinage regulated—until regulation broke down. Rome was still the market place of diminishing world trade, and the black markets of the city could not be controlled. The city grieved audibly when Diocletian tore down the barracks of the Praetorian Guard, a figurehead force without meaning, yet symbolic of the city's ancient glory. Diocletian built his immense baths near the site.

Diocletian seldom saw his imperial city. The new Dominus shielded himself by an armored bodyguard, remembering the fate of Aurelian. Throwing the old provincial armies into one mounted field army, he ranged the menaced frontiers, alert to the hour-to-hour warnings brought in by his *agentes in rebus*, his secret service of information. On new-built swift galleys, he took short cuts across the seas from the palaces of Ravenna to a port of the East, Nicomedia (modern Izmit). By his ruthless reshaping he restored the authority of the state and reduced the human beings within it to serfdom.

Precisely for those reasons, the clandestine religions gained firmer hold upon his people. Diocletian foresaw danger in the religion that spoke of rendering to Caesar only the things that were Caesar's. Yet his merciless persecution did not weaken the invisible Church of the Christians. Perhaps he half hoped that his people would turn back to the ancient worship of the Pantheon. It did not happen that way. Execution of soldiers who had refused to bow to the commands of their Emperor lingered in the memory of the people as the martyrdom of a St. Sebastian or a St. George of Cappadocia.

In the end, exhausted by his efforts, Diocletian shut himself up in his new palace, built on the plan of a vast Roman camp, near Salona, which had been his home on the Dalmatian coast. To give permanence to his system, he named another as co-emperor, and appointed two Caesars as vice-emperors.

It was not enough.

The plan for succession broke down in a welter of strife among rivals for the throne. The man who won the last victory was a Balkan bastard, Constantine by name.

Constantine (311–37) had more than Diocletian's brutal force and a greater sense of realities. He abandoned the fiction of a dominus ruling from Rome. He gave up the attempt to purge the new army of religion. After puzzling over the strange cult of Mithra, he announced that he was the protector of the Christians. This religion appeared to him to be favored by the best of the remaining armed forces.

And, without making announcement of his intention, Constantine abandoned the senate and had his portrait carried through all the villages to display to the inhabitants the likeness of their solitary new emperor (*imperator*). Before his mobile headquarters a larger propaganda painting on panels was displayed, revealing Constantine Imperator standing in triumph over a stricken dragon at a battle's end. What the dragon represented remained a question. But in the sky over Constantine a cross was clearly painted.

Probably the man from the Balkans had no realization of what might come from his recognition of Christianity. Yet he called a council of its patriarchs and bishops, thus granting authority by imperial consent to its Church—a proceeding that would have unanticipated consequences in the coming centuries.

As far as the senate and the population of Rome were concerned, they foresaw no lessening of their rule in "the citadel of peoples," as they called it now. On the occasion of Constantine's official entry they hastily improvised a triumph in the manner of the early Caesars. They built him a new triumphal arch overlooking the ancient Forum. Having little time or artistic skill for the work, the builders stripped many carvings of Trajan's day from remote walls to ornament the arch. And Constantine, inspecting their creation, made no objection to the invocations to Jove among the inscriptions. He did remark that tributes to Trajan were like so many "weeds on the walls"—a remark that could be interpreted in different ways. He discarded the laurel wreath of the early Caesars for a gold headband, the diadem of a great king of the East.

Just then propaganda painting flourished, in the portraits of great men, the picturing of omens and events. For the Romans no longer had the means to construct the mosaic-studded vaults of Caracalla's day. Cheap paint could transform a wall under the hands of workmen who did not dream of the magic of Pompeii. Perhaps Constantine brooded over such a wall in Ostia, the half-deserted port of Rome. It revealed a band of small boys marching, wreathed for sacrificial rites, carrying a banner surmounted by the busts of mighty early emperors, dragging after them a model of a ship. Small boys trained to march—toward what?

For Constantine understood what his eyes perceived, the stagnation in the western towns, the weeds in the paving. From Milan to far Cologne ("the Colony") those towns had not

been built by native hands, but by engineers to house military
and commercial traffic. When that traffic dwindled like a
drying river, the towns died. And the seaports of the West became ghosts of broken quays.

Impelled by a reasoning he never explained, the implacable
Constantine abandoned the attempt to hold the world empire
together. There was no longer an eternal Rome served by subject peoples. There could only be salvage.

His decision to build a new city in the East can be explained quite logically. But Constantine's was not a logical
mind. Even the eccentric Julius Caesar had planned just
before his assassination to march his legions eastward. Then
by necessity for a long time the soldier-emperors had made
their headquarters at Milan or Ravenna, close to critical
frontiers. Diocletian, while building the palace on Adria's sea
(Adriatic) had operated chiefly at Nicomedia, port of the eastern Propontis (Marmora). He had sent one Caesar to Sirmium (now Mitrovica) on the embattled Danube. And Constantine had been born in Sirmium, secure within its mountains. Apparently he thought for a time of returning there.

For military reasons it might have been wise to do so. From
the Dalmatian coast and the Balkan valleys came the most
dependable recruits to the hard-pressed field army.

Then, too, on the eastern coasts still-wealthy ports existed,
Alexandria, Ephesus, mighty Antioch. Rome itself had been
sustained by supplies from their hinterlands and from the
African coast. It would be wise, beyond doubt, to move his
capital to the center of eastern trade, beyond reach of the tides
of invasion. For a while Constantine explored the hill of
Ilium, where services still went on at the hallowed graves of
Troy, traditional home of the Romans—so the poets proclaimed.

Constantine never explained why he turned away from Troy
and ignored luxurious Antioch. He had put to death the most
promising of his sons; he had listened to the wailing of the

boy's aging mother, Helena, and had ordered his own scheming, aristocratic wife Fausta to be slain in her bath. Did he
reason clearly at such a time?

He embarked in a boat and crossed blue water to a windy
headland. On its miniature sea, it lay between the two great
seas, and it was near the scene of his last victory.

The city on this wooded point was Byzantium. It had never
played a part in the growth of the Roman Empire.

It is said that Constantine wished to make a symbolic
move from Rome with its pagan monuments to a city of
Christian tradition. That may be. Yet the Byzantines had
been known as a peculiar folk, trading along their waterways
while keeping stubbornly apart from others. Alone, as it were.
They had in fact presumed to resist military dictators, from
Philip of Macedon to Constantine himself.

Of course observers soon found omens to relate—how eagles
had swooped down to pick up measuring tapes and fly across
the water to Byzantium. It was said that Constantine had been
influenced by a dream, but he himself never said that.

His actions during the building of his new reigning city
indicate a troubled mind. He walked around the excavations
with a pagan philosopher, Sopater; he ordered an immense
porphyry column to be shipped from the Nile, and people said
that he buried beneath this column in his half-built Forum
of Constantine the sacred Palladium image, taken secretly
from Rome. Certainly he had a shrine erected to the goddess
Fortuna, although later a cross was fastened to her forehead.
As for his own statue, a gigantic figure of Apollo was set up.
Constantine's head was put on the decapitated god, and rays
of the sun were added to it.

In his feverish haste to erect the structures of his new
city the brutal Balkan stripped statuary and columns from
hallowed foundations, taking even the serpent column from
the Delphian shrine. He paced out an unbelievable distance
for the new city wall, claiming—so the rumor ran—that seven

hills lay within its circuit, as at Rome. Anyone could see there were only three ridges of land that might be called hills. The buildings themselves were thrown together out of rubble and rough marble adorned with spoils from Rome.

When it came to dedicating the wall, after ancient custom, Constantine selected a day of the 276 Olympiad (May 11, 330) when the sun was in the sign of the Archer. And according to observers from Rome he gave his half-finished city the almost forgotten name of Anthusa, the ancient cult name of Rome itself. However that may be, he soon spoke of it as *Nea Roma.* Yet the whole thing was such a muddle that everyone began to call it Constantine's City, Constantinopolis. Beyond doubt, it was not and could not be a New Rome.

"Constantinople is dedicated," that caustic critic St. Jerome wrote afterward, "while almost all other cities are stripped bare."

However, there was no mistaking Constantine's determination to move his rule to the new site. The senate building on the old Byzantine acropolis rose within a forest of familiar statues; residences raised for the elite of the Roman families, across from the hippodrome, had garden courts copied from those in their Roman homes. Yet few senatorial families moved over to their new quarters. Other emperors had had such mad ideas. And it was madness to fancy that Constantinople—the name had a Greek twist to it already—could become a second Rome of the Caesars. Besides, where in this eastern settlement could be found a cool Praeneste, a delightful Baiae?

True, much of the rabble deserted the alleys of Rome because the mad Emperor offered an abundance of bread, oil, wine, and both pork and beef in his new quarters. Then Constantine surprised the best-informed people by asking for Christian rites at his death in 337. At that moment he called himself "God's man."

No one realized, and Constantine himself could hardly have

known, that he had brought about something startling and quite new. He had founded a Christian imperial city to be ruled after him by his sons.

As the wisest observers predicted, only disturbance came from the rule of Constantine's weak sons. Into this chaos pressed the outer barbaric peoples, until Julian, of the ancient Julian-Claudian family, gained victories over the Franks. Being a scholar as well, this Julian ("The Apostate," 361–3) restored the worship of the old gods. Fate, however, intervened to end his life abruptly on a march into the East, at the Euphrates River.

This seemed, to the most influential senators of elder Rome, to be the working of immutable destiny. By that destiny *Roma Aeterna* had ruled the world for more than four centuries from the seven hallowed hills on the Tiber. These senators could not believe that the co-emperors residing in the makeshift city on the ox-ford—the *Bosporus*—would prove to be stronger than Fate. That was clearly to be seen, barely a decade after Julian, when Valens the co-emperor in the East died under the swords of the Goths at Hadrian's City (Adrianopolis). Whom the gods would destroy they first make mad. The pagan senators offered ritual sacrifice at the altars of both Fortune and Victory.

As if in answer to the sacrifices, Theodosius appeared. A hulking Spaniard, hailed as imperator by the troops at Sirmium, Theodosius fought off sickness while he gained victories as of old, far from Rome. Constantine's family line had ended with Julian, and it seemed as if the fortunate Theodosius would end Constantine's mad endeavor as well. He rode back into the West. By enlisting Germanic tribes, he held back the farther barbarians. For a decade of years this one Imperator commanded and the Danube, if not the Rhine, became the *limites* as of yore.

Yet something that had affected Constantine also influenced

the taciturn Theodosius the Great. He bowed his head before the objurgations of a bishop of Milan, one Ambrose. He
did penance, as if an Augustus and imperator could be a sin-
ner—after a massacre of rebellious subjects in a circus. By so
doing he acknowledged the primacy of orthodox priests, and
particularly those who acted as the successors of the Apostle
Peter, tending the apostle's tomb on the small height across
the Tiber. He challenged Fate by abandoning the Roman cavalry standards for the new *labarum*—a barbaric word—a cross
with a purple banner bearing initials of the name of Jesus, a
condemned man. His Germanized army followed this labarum
standard, as if Christianity had become the Empire itself.
Imagine an empire made up, not of Roman citizens, but of
orthodox believers in a religion! Men of the best families
could not imagine it, but they feared it.

One of them, Quintus Aurelius Symmachus, made a notable
speech against the new order before the packed senate. Symmachus, of the Aurelian gens, owner of fifteen estates in Italy,
was speaking in defense of the ancient temples of Victory and
Fortune. "Every nation has gods of its own . . . then leave
to us the shrines upon which our oaths of allegiance have been
sworn for so many generations, and by which we have
gained so many triumphs. Leave to us the system which has
brought, for so many years, prosperity to the state." Symmachus spoke as a true patriot, with all the eloquence of
Vergil and due heed for the wealth guarded in the historic
shrines. "Our treasury must be refilled, not by taking the
wealth from our shrines, but by taking spoils from our enemies."

Symmachus was a good man who never understood that his
generation would be the last of its kind. Even when his carriage and its running slaves had to turn off the highway to
Milan to avoid thronging Gothic cavalry, he could not imagine that his city of Rome would never again take spoils from
her enemies. When his eldest boy was initiated to public life as

praetor, Symmachus spent half a million solidi on public games to honor the occasion in the best ancestral tradition. He ransacked the provinces to import crocodiles from the Nile, swift horses from Spain, racing drivers from Sicily, and Saxon gladiators from the Rhine frontier. He fell into a rage when the Saxons strangled themselves to death rather than provide a show for the Roman populace. In another generation Saxons would make their way into the province of Britain, Goths would close the transalpine highways to Gaul, and the Spanish province would be lost.

Theodosius the Great died of dropsy in 395 by the Christian calendar. After his effort at unification of the Empire, the frontiers ceased to be. A human flood of Hunnish and Alan folk came between the Rome of the West and the city in the East.

From this *pars orientalis* the tidings became fewer and fainter, like signals from a storm-driven ship. A boy had been crowned, a second Theodosius, taking his father's name. His stubborn sister Pulcheria tried to carry out the task of ruling, while a minister built a Cyclopean wall—a triple wall, over a waterway—about Constantinople as a last-ditch defense. How could a child and a woman and an engineer take the place of the great Theodosius? The city on the Tiber relied on astute masters of soldiers like the Vandal-born Stilicho to lead forth new armies. The distant Pulcheria sent to Palestine to the border town of Jerusalem for protection; she gave to the Constantinopolitans a painting of a Virgin called "Guide to the Way." In time of disaster—frequent enough in these days— Pulcheria had the "Guide to the Way" carried through the main street in procession. Her weak brother was known as the Penman, being obsessed with books. They wrote out for him a code of the laws, made up of all the decrees of past emperors, as if writing down laws could help them in ruling. The great emperors had spoken their minds, and their words had *become* the laws. . . .

Pulcheria, who seemed to be a sensible girl, succumbed to the allure of incantation; she worried the ministers into setting aside auditoriums to make what they called a university. Here it seemed that Greek rhetors intoned Homer and explained Aristotle. That had been tried for generations at the Porch in Athens without any visible profit to the Athenians. . . . No, all in all the tidings from the tenement city in the East did not make clear sense to the home-abiding Romans.

Judging by the records they left, these senators and *potentiores* felt no awareness of coming doom. Least of all were the good Symmachus and his fellows aware that they themselves were a cause of the downfall of their empire.

Rather, the society of this last age flattered itself that it revived good taste as well as the clean living of ancestral tradition. Who among them, they asked, indulged in the perversity of the early Empire? They indulged in no epicurean rarities like pheasants' eggs or Lepidian feasts. Who nowadays invited the Vestal Virgins as dinner guests to watch the antics of the naked dancing girls with the men? Nor did their women indulge in dancing to barbaric music, as in the time of the great civil wars. Now the women liked to curl their short hair in masculine fashion, although they still made up their faces in coloring and even in shape.

When they drank the red wine of Cyprus, the elite of society watched the sails of the corn ships from Africa coming up the Tiber. On every side they beheld security. Rome itself had never been more impressive. Within the fourteen gates gleamed the splendor of brazen towers, of sky-scraping "islands" of apartments, of victory columns rising from the forums of the emperors. Palaces crowded on the Quirinalis revealed by their very ugliness that they were built for eternity. Vaults of the newest public baths expanded into sun terraces and gymnasia for sports—filled with the perpetual melody of mechanical lyres. Down the course of the Greatest Circus the chariots flashed with increasing speed owing to better breeding of race horses.

The racegoers had never enjoyed greater comfort than now, under the silk canopies of blue and green, the colors of the factions. Each spectator was provided with oil, wine, and meat in addition to the old-fashioned dole of grain.

Never had the standard of living been raised so high for the city-dwellers. One of them, Rufus Avienus, described a day in his country retreat. "At sunrise I make my prayer to the gods, then go over my grounds with the servants, to show each of them his task. After that I read, calling upon the Muses, until it is time to oil myself for exercise in the sand-covered exercise space. Then in a happy humor, thinking not at all about money affairs, I bathe, and eat, drink, play, and rest. While my small lamp burns, I write these lines with a prayer to the nymph who may watch over my fountain at night."

One veteran from the East front, it is true, distrusted this comfort amid splendor. "Two things are craved above everything," Ammianus Marcellinus wrote. "Bread and circuses." He saw the sensual vice in the dark corners of the baths, the energy of the multitudes exploding in arguments over charioteers, the agility of footloose boys banding together to snatch and stab in the streets, the cunning of spies lurking for payment against bringing charges of treason, while judges waited to be paid before giving judgment. Marcellinus distrusted most the pantomimists who imitated in dances the indecencies of the underworld.

But the Senate and the Roman People—the old phrase was still used in speeches—could imagine no change in that state of affairs. There would be other Caesars, and Rome would rule as before. Because there existed nothing else capable of ruling. . . .

When Alaric's tribal horsemen entered the Salarian Gate, after bribing the gatekeepers in 410, the outward aspect of the city did not change. The immense buildings sheltered the multitudes as before. The worst fires swept the residences on the Aventine, but their owners had fled to country villas after burying the most valuable art works. Alaric's Visigoths stayed only three days to gather their loot.

Rutilius, the prefect who took office after the sack of Rome, worried chiefly that the grain ships might not arrive from Africa in time, thus causing the populace to riot and injuring the fame of the new prefect. When Rutilius' ship—he came from ravaged Gaul—anchored in the Tiber, he was reassured to behold the gilded roofs of the ancient temples standing unharmed, and to hear the familiar cheering of the circus crowd. He saluted with deep feeling "his fair mistress of the world."

There came, however, a grieving letter from a former citizen of Rome. From his cell in Bethlehem, whither he had retired to work, St. Jerome wrote: "The great city is captured which had taken captive all the world . . . the Roman world is sinking into ruins, and still we hold our heads erect."

In his remote cell, in the desert by Bethlehem, the catastrophe was clearly evident. It is not in the civic center that the mortality of a city becomes known. Moreover, letters from fugitive patricians reached Jerome. Many of them were seeking their *latifundiae*—their broad acres—in tranquil Africa. One lady, Demetrias, daughter of a consul, wrote that she had managed to ransom her grandmother from the Goths in Italy and to charter a vessel for Africa. Yet when the noblewomen landed on African soil they were forced to ransom themselves again from the local governor, a Count Heraclian who happened to be the murderer of the military commander Stilicho. Count Heraclian amassed gold during the crisis by selling fugitive Roman girls to a gang of Syrian slave-merchants.

Only by degrees did the refugees realize that once-stable Gaul no longer had Roman masters, and that Huns were feeding their horses in the estates of Venetia. There was no longer communication with Spain or Britain. Still, the smaller isles of the sea offered shelter in farms and fishing villages. When his ship, outward bound, passed the rocky isle of Igilium, Rutilius Namiatianus saluted it as the shelter of the Romans with a verse: "So near to Rome, yet so far from the Goths. . . ."

Rutilius noticed that Vandal fleets moved over the sea. But it did not occur to him that his civilization was dying. It lived on only in the minds of a few men like himself.

There were so few with vision. Where lights still shone in the ports of the African coast, a rumor passed from Spain. A barbaric people, the Vandals of Gaiseric, were crossing in rude log vessels with their families and animals to this sheltered shore. On that shore one man awoke in a morning to feel eternity near him. St. Augustine found words for his thought and wrote them down. Rome would cease to be; the earthly city of Christians would perish, and they would become wanderers in search of an abode.

"For here we have no lasting city, but we seek one that is to come."

II

THE
GUARDED
CITY

BEHIND THE GOLDEN GATE

THE MAN who would become Justinian the Emperor
came out of obscurity. This obscurity seemed to follow him
as he went his way without attracting attention, almost to the
hour in which he set his hand to the making of a new order of
things. Because of that, a certain mystery attached to his life.
Perhaps he intended it so.

Nobody except his uncle paid any particular attention to
Petrus Sabbatius at first. His questioning gray eyes, his ruddy
flesh and heavy frame were common enough in the bare Macedonian valley out of which he journeyed to the city. At that
time, about the year 500 of the Christian calendar, he may
have been eighteen years of age, young enough to be excited
by new surroundings, too old to change much inwardly.

And that proved to be important. Peasant-born, Petrus carried with him a core of his homeland, the rock heights and quiet pastures of Macedonia, a home where every person labored with few tools beside the surging Vardar River. He had determination as hard as the gray, eroded rocks, and he had imagination as well, to think of what might lie behind the ridges.

It is clear that from his valley Petrus Sabbatius brought away—besides the letter of his uncle—a devotion to the name of Rome, a memory of silence. He remembered, too, the fear of the older folk of the raiding of Attila's Bulgar-Huns. He had a remarkable memory. Except for that, he showed no sign of ability to make a name for himself in the city of Constantine.

Already the city had gained repute of an odd nature. Wayfarers said that it sheltered the *melior pars generis humani*. But who were the better part of human beings? Monks of the mountain trails repeated it was "the city guarded by God." Yet how could one city be so guarded?

Petrus must have had his first glimpse of strangeness where the cart road of the Vardar River reached the coast of Macedonia. There to the east stretched the paving stones of the Via Egnatia. Beside this imperial highway reared milestone markers. From it galloping couriers, streaming feathers on their heads, turned in to post stations; swift carriages glinting with silver trim emerged from taverns shaded by grape arbors. And then the road touched the shore of the dark, tranquil sea where the red sails of a ship moved like a harbinger toward the rising sun.

Certainly the Macedonian peasant must have felt the strangeness of this coast, of ancient headlands stark above an unchanging sea. Nor did the city come into sight like a familiar highland town of gray stone among grazing herds. The first of it, the suburb of Hebdomon, thrust shade trees upon the road. In an empty drill-ground girls danced a ring-around by a pavilion of purple stone where a bronzed monk shouted: "Now enter upon your heritage—nourish the beggars and escape the torments of Hell." People feasting in houseboats drawn against the shore threw new pennies toward this advocate of blessedness.

Even where the highway ended in a triple gate, the city itself could not be seen. An apparition stood there: threefold walls, white under the sun, rose against the sky. The last towers stood ten times the height of a man, and the terraces between them hung over deep dry moats that could be flooded from the aqueducts passing overhead. Seventeen miles this rampart stretched around the guarded city, and for most of the way the sea lapped against the wall.

One step within it, and the wayfarer was blinded by the glare of polished marble walls leading him to the inner portal. Through the gate streamed farmers' carts and merchants' mule trains with swaying packs odorous of spice and sandal, while the drivers cried out in the tongues of unknown lands. Above this portal of the Golden Gate poised a statue of the Theodosius who built it, with emblems of the new city—a bronze two-headed Roman eagle and a winged woman who might have been Victory or simply Fate. Beneath them in letters of gold there was a legend: "He who built this gate of gold will bring to you an age of gold."

No doubt it had been meant to impress visitors, and the street within had been named the Triumphal Way. However, people called it simply the Middle Way, and it was lined by shops in which the owners worked silk from drawlooms, or set pieces of jewelry, or produced rareties from purple dye to elephants' teeth. Within curtained booths money changers waited by their scales; soothsayers of the old-fashioned kind burned incense before a client and cast powdered alum on the embers to seek a message in the ashes.

For this city of Constantine did not resemble the monolithic older Rome; it had little splendor as yet. It served as a thoroughfare of trade, an abiding place of wanderers; it offered small-domed churches to congregations. True, Roman engineering skill had created vast cisterns, some of them covered, at the ends of the aqueducts. Sewers deep in the earth drained refuse into the sea. A lofty statue, called the Slave of the Winds, moved with the wind; there was a municipal hospital built by a benevolent man named Samson. But the marks of pioneering still showed. No more than a giant chain guarded the harbor, open to all the inland seas, and this harbor was no more than the odd, curving inlet that glowed under the sunset and so gained its name of the Golden Horn. As yet the city consisted chiefly of the multitude of people gathered within the mighty circuit wall.

Beyond the rolling uplands of the peninsula danger waited. The year of Petrus' arrival, public criers emerged at evening in each district. They shouted their message to the doorways: "By command of the Emperor, Ever August—all stonecutters, all masons, all partisans of the Blue, the Green, and the White demes, will march after the hour of Prime to the Long Wall. Aided by God, obey the command of the Emperor!" The Blues and the Greens were the popular parties—the democracies—of the city.

It appeared that forty miles from the Golden Gate, a new long wall was being built in haste across the peninsula to bar the advance of barbaric Bulgar-Huns who had broken through the frontier armies of Thrace. More workmen were needed to raise this barrier in time to check the invasion.

Petrus Sabbatius mingled with the multitude. They say he fell into talk with all comers; having a straightforward mind, he believed at first the tales that were told him; he could be taken in by sophistry—and experts in deceit thrived within the crowds. Moreover, knowing only Latin and his uncouth Macedonian dialect, he had trouble understanding the Greek patois, the chanting Persian, and harsh Armenian of the market places, and the guttural orders of the soldiers, who came as a rule from Germanic or Isaurian stock.

Perhaps for this reason he found a welcome refuge in the

Studion. Near the Golden Gate this old church and herb garden with a barrack of a monastery offered shelter without question. One who knocked at the visitors' door could have soup
and bread and olives and a pallet bed. He would not be bidden
to the church when the wooden clapper was struck for an office. Yet wherever he rested, he would hear the rise and fall of
a single voice and the full chant of the monks in answering
tones. Through the darkness this singer sang his praise, candle
in hand, until another came to relieve him. The singers were
called The Sleepless. They claimed that a certain Studius,
once a consul of fame, had built this oldest of the churches,
and that another potentate named Alexander had brought the
monks hither. Alexander had withdrawn to seek peace in a
monastery of Asia, where he had been given the four Gospels
to read. When he had read them many times with care, he
asked, over and again: "Is all this true?"

True indeed, he was told, being the very words of Jesus
Christ.

"Then why don't we do as he bids us?"

After that Alexander went forth to live in a cask by a river,
the Euphrates. He labored with his hands for other people,
not to be a slothful servant; for himself, literally, he took no
thought for the morrow. After a while followers joined him to
live in the same manner, and Alexander led them away in
search of a home. But no abbot or archimandrite did they find
to take in a throng of hungry wanderers.

"Not until," the monks told Petrus with smiles, "he came
to the Studion did Alexander escape arrest for disturbing the
peace! In his name we keep up our song and keep our doors
open."

The quiet hours in the monastery appealed to Petrus. Here
he found order maintained by unwritten laws. He had nourish-
ment enough to enable him to work, and no one asked why he
worked with books of his own instead of laboring in the common kitchen garden. The Studion left its mark on him.

These same merry monks of The Sleepless had a question
of their own to ask him: "Is not Michael Archangel the protector of human beings—has he not power to heal sickness and
preserve life?"

There could be only one answer: yes.

"Well, then," they asked, "why do you labor at bricking up
walls and carrying spears to safeguard the city? Cannot the
power of Michael Archangel do that?"

When Petrus thought about that, he answered: "It is needful to do what we can."

"Then do you pray," the monks retorted, "for that is the
most needful thing."

Now it became clear why The Sleepless found no favor with
the authorities. They would not abide by ordinary laws. But
other inhabitants of the city also followed ways of their own.

❀ ASPECT OF THE CITY

These inhabitants numbered more than 700,000. They dwelt
in fourteen districts, each with its curator and public crier and
patrol of police who carried only spears and wore polished iron
caps and had a purple eagle stamped on their leather jackets.
Yet by the time of Petrus' arrival there seemed to be fourteen
different peoples making their homes in communities of their
own. The oldest streets—of Constantine's original town—
were darkened by wooden tenements that edged outward with
flimsy stairs and window bays, infested by the families of freedmen workers. In the Place of the Ships across the teeming
harbor half-naked fishermen from the Greek islands sunned
themselves and dried their nets on stone nymphs that had
been ornaments of the waterfront. These watermen had a
shrine. It covered an ancient galley's prow. The figurehead on
the prow stared out majestically to find its way upon the sea,

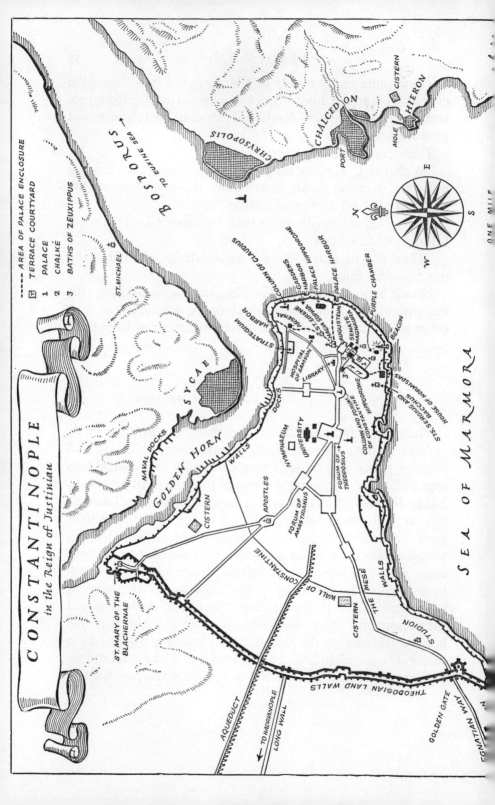

CONSTANTINOPLE
in the Reign of Justinian

----- AREA OF PALACE ENCLOSURE

⊞ TERRACE COURTYARD

1 PALACE
2 CHALKÉ
3 BATHS OF ZEUXIPPUS

ONE MILE

BOSPORUS

TO EUXINE SEA →

CHALCEDON

CHRYSOPOLIS

PORT

MOLE   HIERON

CISTERN

N E S W

ST. MICHAEL

SYCAE

NAVAL DOCKS

GOLDEN HORN

DOCKS

WALLS

CISTERN

APOSTLES

NYMPHAEUM

UNIVERSITY

FORUM OF AMASTRIANUS

ST. MARY OF THE BLACHERNAE

AQUEDUCT

TO HADRIANOPLE

LONG WALL

FORUM OF CONSTANTINE

THE MESE

WALL OF CONSTANTINE

CISTERN

STUDION

THE WALLS

THEODOSIAN LAND WALLS

GOLDEN GATE

EGNATIAN WAY

SEA OF MARMORA

STRATEGIUM

HARBOR

COLUMN OF CLAUDIUS

GARDENS

ARSENAL

ST. IRENE

ST. SOPHIA

AUGUSTEUM

SENATE

MAGNAURA

PALACE HIPPODROME

PALACE HARBOR

PALACE HIPPODROME

PURPLE CHAMBER

BEACON

HOSPITAL OF SAMSON

LIBRARY

HOUSE OF HORMISDAS

STS. SERGIUS AND BACCHUS

COLUMN AND FORUM OF CONSTANTINE

FORUM OF THEODOSIUS

FORUM OF AMASTRIANUS

and it could have been Neptune himself. "No," the seamen said, "it is the spirit of the city."

At sunrise, before the porters in padded coats picked up their loads, the boys of the Thracian farmers hurried their grass-strewn baskets of grapes or figs from the carts to sell in the streets. The son of Sabbatius, purchasing his morning fruit from one of them, asked: "Who rules the city?" Boys would always tell their thoughts, while their work-dulled parents had little to say.

"The Three," the youngster explained, fisting his copper coin and beckoning toward the narrow height where the Horn joined the Bosporus. Against the sunrise gleamed the domes of the palace and the gilded wooden roof of the great church, near the dark bulk of the hippodrome.

"The palace belongs to the Emperor," the boy chanted, "the church to God, and the racing place to us. Didn't you know that all three rule, and three is the best number?"

The great structures did stand apart from the streets. But Petrus sought out the library, where the pillared darkness of an old basilica was banished by hanging lamps. The walls were solid with books lying in their niches, their parchment edges marked with such names as the poet Juvenal, or the saintly Chrysostom, the Golden Tongue, who had castigated the city and never forsaken it, or the somber Marcus Aurelius. The guardians of the books explained that the pagan Julian had gathered here the first 150,000 *volumena*, or rolls. And although Julian had been accursed, his books had been kept. Here, they said with pride, was the true treasure of the city. Most of the students at the reading stands wore the short Greek chlamys and kilt. And they pored over the innumerable edicts of past emperors, grumbling audibly.

Over the stir of the library resounded a faint musical beat. Behind the building wound the Street of the Bronzesmiths, the makers of fire-wrought metals. These bearded giants of the Cappadocian mountains had a trick of chiming their hammer

blows on a single forge in cadence. They had a jest—that
Pythagoras had invented music when he listened to the ringing
blows of the smiths.

At the Vespers hour the chiming of the hammers ceased
and the workers filed out to their chosen shrines. None of
them threw on the folds of a Roman toga, because that was
restricted to the palace officials or a rare visitor from ancestral
Rome. In the Street of the Silversmiths slender Egyptians
shaped precious vessels with deft fingers. They coaxed supple
gold into patterns to receive dark enamel while the artists of
Alexandria painted portraits in gold wash, to be covered by
molten glass. They kept their secrets jealously to themselves
because their skill transmuted materials of base value into
precious wares. Carefully they locked iron grilles across their
work stalls in the evening.

A sense of danger lay beneath the jesting of the artists. At
any moment they might hear the clanging of the district's
alarm bell. They did their work, uncertain what the next day
might bring. Petrus had known that uncertainty in the Vardar
valley as a child when the Huns who had followed Attila
had returned to burn the farms and cut down the humans
they did not drive away.

The shrine of the metalworkers was small and dark. Yet it
had the finest lamps of fretted silver, gifts of the smiths. They
bent reverently before the icon screen because within it stood
the painted likeness of the Mother of God they called "The
Guide to the Way." St. Luke had painted it, they said, in far-
off Jerusalem. This icon protected the city in utmost need.
What else could keep Constantinople safe?

Nothing in Constantinople was far from the water. The
great suburbs covered the hills across the Horn, where merchants dwelt by the quays of Sycae (modern Galata) or the
green height of Chrysopolis (Uskudar) of the farming folk
across the Bosporus. Where the Bosporus joined the sunlit
Marmora stood the churches and parks of Chalcedon (Kadi

Keui), whither came vessels from the great bay of Nicomedia (Izmit). The islands on the horizon of the sea were very much alike; all had fishing fleets on the beaches and new monasteries crowning their hilltops.

Because no tides troubled these waters, they served as an easy thoroughfare for the innumerable skiffs and caïques, the oared barges and sailing craft that plied steadily between the suburbs and the city on the promontory. Currents and shifting breezes kept the waters in constant motion, and at times a north wind stopped all ferrying within the metropolis.

Where Petrus had his quarters on the hillside overlooking the Golden Horn, he discovered that the city did unexpected things for its people. His district had one of the Steps leading to an arcade where, by presenting a wooden token with a number, he might obtain wine and bread and oil sufficient for a day; by waiting in its forum he might consult its public physician in case of illness. The night patrol served also to fight fires.

Down by the waterfront there was an odd hospital dedicated to Cosmas and Damian, the two saintly physicians. It resembled a courtyard shrine more than anything else. A sick person would be brought by barge to the garden to rest and bidden to sleep the night by the altar. Then in the morning the attendants would come to him with fruit and wine, asking him to relate what dreams or thoughts had passed through him during the darkness. Patiently they listened to the telling of the dreams, and explained how a cure might follow upon them. Usually the patients went away hopeful that the saintly physicians had healed them. At least their minds would be relieved. And Petrus sometimes wondered if this hospital of Cosmas and Damian did not follow out, in Christian guise, the method of the ancient Hippocrates.

Petrus soon discovered that each district had a population peculiar to itself. Because the university occupied the summit of his hill, his neighbors were Greeks, for the most part students and prostitutes. For the great Nymphaeum festival hall stood close to the auditoriums of learning, and girls who chattered together in the shadow of the arcades wore strips of scarlet cloth, as the law required, across their breasts. Their mantles hid the telltale scarlet until a likely man passed by and they slipped the mantles from slim shoulders to catch his eye. On the other hand, the rhetors, the learned lecturers, garbed themselves in gray and black—"they walk like storks," said the girls of the arcades.

Even the quacks who haunted the forum of the university lisped in Greek, the tongue of saintly Chrysostom. Some of the quacks made themselves out to be doctors of learning—to escape taxation—always from some far place like Ephesus, where ancient mysteries still prevailed. "Better than Physica," they assured their following, "is Mystica." And they hinted at familiar daimons to be summoned forth from the spirit world of angels, daimons, dominions, and heroes—at a price. These knowing souls possessed yellowed scrolls that revealed the secrets of Alchymy, which they claimed to be more rewarding than the books of Chymistry. Or they brought messages from the seances of the Apollo of Sarpedon. Their best customers were the prostitutes, who usually had money.

Even the teachers of law seemed to come from the mysterious East, from the school of Berytus beneath the mountains of Lebanon. Petrus, who had a keen understanding of law, found that the ancient *res Romana* had suffered change to new ideas which were very mixed. Apparently what *had been* was no longer so important as what *should be*. A young doctor from Delos laughed at that, crying that they all sought what is to be and found it not. Whereupon the youth ran to the forum fountain, washed his hands, and flung his arms wide, shouting above the street bustle: *"Glo-ria . . . in excelsis!"*

Petrus remembered this young Greek, Theophilos, who turned away from the riddle of the law to song.

He remembered how the wind brought the good smell of

warm bread from the Street of the Bakers below, and how, in the noon heat, the pigeons swarmed around the feet of the students who munched pieces of the bread they carried home. But most of all he remembered the hour of street lamp lighting, before the coming of darkness when the night patrols paraded forth from the Praetorium on the Middle Way.

With the persistence of a peasant in the fields, the Macedonian kept at his work after the reading lamps were lighted in the library near the Praetorium. At the coming of dusk, however, he took a half hour's rest, carrying his bread and olives to an observation spot deserted at that time. By climbing the circular stair inside the column of Theodosius he could reach the railed summit beneath the bronze statue of the enlightened Emperor who had built most of the university. From this aerie he could look over the forum and most of the city where the streets were winking into light. The palace itself became bright on its height against the glimmer of the waters where the Bosporus merged with the spreading Marmora.

It seemed to Petrus then as if the city became an island of light in the darkness of the outer world. Beyond his sight lay the far continents peopled by human beings who were in some manner different.

Without doubt as the years went by he came to love the city, its sore spots as well as its beauty.

✿ AN EMPEROR FACES DANGER

During ten years of obscurity the son of Sabbatius had become attuned to the moods and thoughts of the city of Constantine. In doing so, he had gained a useful habit of wearing his village clothing and speaking like a blunt barbarian, while his acute mind took in more than the listeners realized.

He understood to the full how the Sacred Palace kept almost invisible control over the workaday life of the varied people of the districts—how inspectors visited the money merchants behind closed doors, how secret agents percolated through the throngs attending the court hearings and the grain trading in the great basilica that had been the temple of Fortune. Remote from the teeming Middle Way, the treasury controlled the exchange of gold and held monopoly of precious goods—"gold goods"—like silk, and purple dye from the sea. Only the government could manufacture or store arms in the Arsenal.

Then, too, the almost invisible Emperor had his servants at work for him—the silentiaries, dedicated men who attended his person and reported only to him. For there was much to watch in the city, and Petrus had observed it all. Leaders of the demes—the people's parties—held their councils in the courtyards of their favored churches, where they might not easily be interfered with. Secretive yet arrogant, the knife-men of the parties, called Partisans, ranged the streets in their bands, daggers lashed out of sight against their hips. They were the descendants of the Blue and Green political factions that had come over from the older Rome, bringing their feuds with them. Apart from them ranged the gangs of the lawless youth, often boys of rich families capable of holding their fathers to ransom, or young bravoes, letting their beards grow, shaving their foreheads and tying up their long hair, striding in trousers like barbaric Huns. They showed their spirit by violating women dragged into corners, and proved their skill by killing passers-by with one blow of a knife.

Yes, the city had its sores and what appeared to be mysteries until one understood the human instincts at work. Often strange monks would parade the darkness, chanting their hatred of the prevailing sins. Then, too, the streets had their own sources of information quite apart from the palace. Smugglers landing at the Hebdomon brought tales of happenings as well as untaxed wines from the island of Delos; the girls of the arcades knew why magistrates had been stoned in Antioch or how the synagogues of Alexandria had withstood the Greek mobs. And in the taverns soldiers from the frontier regiments told the girls that the old Roman army was no more; the very names of legion and century had just been abolished. Imagine —no more tribunes or centurions! On their part the girls confided that the last gladiators had been banished from the swept earth of the hippodrome. Only the hunting of beasts remained to be seen.

Petrus' ears had become tuned to the muted warnings and exhortations of these plebeian folk. Because he shared their homes, he came to know their thoughts. When a marble-cutter stepped into the living room after his day's work, the man did not sit at the table board where his wife and children hurried to place the bowl of barley soup by the bread and herbs. He washed his arms and head in the trickle from the trough, and folded up his mantle to step to the icon corner where the lamp burned under a saint's picture. Sometimes they had an ornament in the one room, a marble hand from a broken statue, or a carved bit of amber.

As he ate, the cutter pushed the rest of the food over to his children carelessly, but he told painstakingly what news he had picked up at the Arsenal or along the Mesé. He fed their minds. The carpet of the sleeping alcove for the women had a woven design of horses drawing a chariot. The charcoal of the brazier that warmed the chamber might be gray and smoking, but the family group hung upon a tale of splendor, of a thousand candles carried in procession, or of the four marble lions brought to stand before the portal of the Holy Apostles. They met with others in a multitude only during the parades and festivals of the Church, or clustering around the gates of the hippodrome when the chariots ran. They could hear the shouting then. This listening and gazing at splendor made their days endurable. In the same way the broken marble hand held a fraction of beauty, of something that one day

might belong to the family. Petrus studied these people patiently, and a question formed in his mind and stayed there a
long time. These people of Constantinople did not belong to
a single race, as did his folk of Bederiana in the Vardar valley;
they held to no tradition, as had the citizens of ancient Rome;
and certainly they had no one religion. What, then, held them
together—and what would ever impel them forward?

Petrus had a way of chewing over a puzzle until he made
some sense out of it. Because he felt an odd envy of Theodosius the Emperor, who had built the great walls, he often
stopped to study the emblematic figures over the portal of the
Porta Aurea. Surely, in spite of the proud legend beneath
them, this Theodosius had brought no age of gold to his city.
(And his portrait statue badly needed cleaning.) The eagle, of
course, was the traditional bird of the Caesars, yet it had two
heads, as if looking two ways. Why? And above all, what did
the winged woman represent? When Petrus asked others in
the hurrying throng, they glanced up indifferently and answered Victory, or an angel, of course, or only God knows.
No one noticed the slender half circle of tarnished silver, like
a crescent moon, on her forehead.

That moon belonged to the ancient Byzantium, and the
mysterious woman might be the genius of the ancient city.

Legend told how the new moon, emerging from the clouds,
had revealed the phalanx men of Philip of Macedon stealing
up to the old acropolis. In that dim time the people of Byzantium had saved their city by tearing out the gravestones to
mend breaches in the wall; they had ripped the planking from
their homes to build new ships. Like vanished Carthage, theirs
had been a metropolis apart from others, a free city beyond the
rule of empire. Vespasian in anger had stripped it of privileges
—calling it an oligarchy—and Severus had crushed it, de-
molishing its defenses. Yet some power had intervened to
preserve the ruined abode on the Bosporus, and grim Severus
had been moved to rebuild its height, even adding a circus.

Like the acropolis itself at the mouth of the Golden Horn, the people had not changed in one respect from the inhabitants of legend. They held to the almost forgotten Greek right to overthrow rulers for misrule.

Byzantium had never sought to become the center of the world-state. Constantine had made it that. And in Constantinople the old custom of revolt still survived. Not by the patrician order alone, or the privileged senators, and certainly not by the intelligentsia of the schools, but by priests and demes and the working guilds—on those rare occasions when the city made up its collective mind to rebel.

This will of the aroused people was the one motive force of the community. It waited like a specter at a feast, to intervene in affairs. Petrus came to know that.

One evening the forum of Theodosius changed before his eyes. An army without weapons moved in from the streets and settled itself there over campfires, shadowy figures waiting. Across the way, the church was draped in black cloths of mourning. Over the distant waters, barges and fishing boats pulled in toward the docks and seamen thronged up from the waterfront to join the argument around the fires.

Word had gone through the streets that the people must have another emperor.

Rumors reached the students gathered to watch from the porticoes of the auditoriums. The orthodox Patriarch had been deposed by order of the palace. It was all the doing of the palace, and it stank of heresy—trying to change the Trisagion, the greeting to God. "That old goat Anastasius, trying to put new words into the Trisagion. Now we understand that his father was an Arian and his uncle a Manichaean!"

Anastasius, an old man, had been popular enough as emperor. But he had ventured to interfere in a religious matter, no less than the voicing of the creed of the people—at least of the majority now assembling in the streets. There was more to the grievance than that, but the mass of the marchers throught only of the loss of their patriarch and the changing of their hymn. "Holy, Mighty, Immortal Lord," they shouted in unison the old familiar words. Singing, they forced their way into the great church by the palace. They fought the armed guards who came to drive them out. This great church of Hagia Sophia—of the Divine Wisdom—belonged to them, not to the individual who happened to wear the imperial purple. And Anastasius himself had been no more than a silentiary of the Sacred Palace when the widowed Empress Ariadne had selected him for a consort.

So the rumors ran through the streets, until the populace found a voice. *"Give another emperor to the Romans!"*

On the Middle Way they started to pull down the statue of Anastasius. They fired the house of the Praetorian Prefect. Two military commanders without escort came to the crowd around the statue—Celer, a general from the eastern frontier, and Patricius, Master of the Guards. A volley of stones forced them to go back. After that, public criers appeared in the districts to report to the people that Anastasius would address them in the hippodrome on the morrow.

Accordingly, and without further disturbance, all the factions of the city assembled on the benches of the circus stands to hear their emperor. For the hippodrome, which adjoined the palace itself, was the assembly place of the people. The crowds that met together otherwise only in festivals or riots occupied their allotted tiers, each with its demarch (leader of deme or party) ready to rise and argue its particular grievance. In so much the hippodrome of Constantinople resembled the areopagus of Athens.

At such a time the beaten earth of the racecourse stretched empty; no officials took post on the central spine where the obelisk of forgotten Pharaohs of Egypt towered by the twisted bronze serpents of Delphi. At the starting end of the spine stood the portrait statue of Anastasius, only slightly above the memorial figure of the driver Porphyrius, who had won nine out of ten of his races.

That particular morning forty thousand pairs of eyes kept watch on the drawn curtains of the Kathisma, the imperial gallery above the starting end of the track. The armored guards waited there with standards lowered. At any moment the Emperor himself might appear between the curtains to defend himself before the citizens who were also his judges. Anastasius had promised to do that.

To farmers from the Asia shore, this was a spectacle of vast power at stake. To men—no woman might appear in the circus—of the government bureaus it meant no more than an election gamble; no matter who sat on the throne, the government bureaus would administer the country as before. A chief secretary, John of Lydia, who wore his toga in the old Roman manner, gave his verdict. "Anastasius was the mildest of men, yet he burned the documents of the income tax, thereby abolishing the tax." Lydus was employed in the Bureau of Memorials.

Another John, a hulking Cappadocian, gave a snort and a shout. "Then give me a soldier who will burn all the documents." He kept accounts in the War Office, after a fashion of his own.

From the north stand came the refrain, *"Give another emperor to the Romans."* The south stand answered *"Throw the Praetorian Prefect to the wild beasts."*

It may be that the aged man in the palace had allowed the multitude time to voice its feelings and thereby to become somewhat satisfied. For abruptly the impassive guards swung up their standards, cymbals chimed sharply, and trumpets sounded. The curtains swung back. A white-haired man stepped quietly forward. All the stands became silent. For Anastasius wore no imperial diadem, no belt or scarlet boots. He stooped a little under the mantle of a common citizen.

Before the throng recovered from its astonishment or a

demarch lifted his voice in challenge, the official announcer stepped to Anastasius' side. His trained voice flung out words distinctly. "The Emperor, Ever August . . . feels no guilt in his heart. . . . Yet since his people hold him guilty . . . he resigns his rank. Who, then, will you have . . . for emperor?"

Astonishment deepened at this. The factions had come prepared to challenge their emperor, not to name his successor. A quick tumult of voices followed, and then a single hearty laugh. John of Cappadocia, who had no right to speak, jumped up with a roar: "You win, Anastasius!"

This familiar cry acted like a keynote on the gathering. After a moment the crowd broke into cadenced acclamation. "Worthy! You are worthy, Anastasius! Ever August—reign as you have lived!"

The citizens remembered that in spite of his eccentric religion, their elderly monarch was in fact a religious man. They all went back to their homes, and the city became quiet. As for the Trisagion, the people chanted it defiantly in the old words, and Anastasius wisely bowed to their will in this matter.

In his earlier years Anastasius had dreamed of creating a stronger state and a nobler city; yet he had managed only to strengthen the provincial towns and to dredge some harbors and lay aside a reserve of gold; now he had aged too much to do more than show himself to the people as their Autocrat.

Soon after the Trisagion riot, danger appeared in another quarter, and this time Petrus Sabbatius was concerned in it.

That happened because of Justin, his uncle. Like most other Balkans, Justin had a strong feeling for his family; however, he had no children of his own. A generation earlier he had left his scanty farm at Bederiana, carrying a bag of toasted bread and a rain cloak, to walk to Constantinople and draw the "dust money" of a volunteer after his long walk. Being powerful in body and careful in carrying out orders, he gained a command on the troubled eastern front; having a knack of keeping his own counsel and of making influential friends, he was taken into the Guards of the palace itself. Handsome and taciturn, Justin claimed to be no more than a simple soldier, but he had a trick of making the dice fall his way when the stakes were high. After he won this honorable post and pay, he sent for his sister Praejecta from the Vardar valley, and she found a husband of good family, in fact a descendant of the famous Ancinii of the older Rome. They named their first born son Germanus, after an early soldier-Caesar, and gave him the hard education of a gentleman.

Lacking a son of his own, Justin sent to his other sister abiding at home, offering to educate and adopt her boy Petrus. By then Justin realized the handicap of his own poor schooling, and apparently hoped to make use of the brains of the well-read son of Sabbatius. The boy, he remembered, had been a devout churchgoer with an instinct for law. By keeping his enlightened nephew in the background, Justin could preserve his pose of a simple soldier. This agreement between them worked out well enough at first. Petrus had no interest in soldiering, but he haunted the auditoriums like a starving man admitted to feast tables. Yet after listening to praise of the ancient Divine Caesars, he read for himself Juvenal's satires on their human failings. Attracting no attention, he followed his own orbit through the city, amicable to everyone yet keeping the family reticence about his own thoughts. For one thing, he never mentioned his peasant father, Sabbatius. As the custom was, he took a name from his adopted father, the name being Justinian.

For a good reason he saw little of his young cousin Germanus. That boy went to the gymnasia where children of the affluent families learned to have sound, enduring bodies and dutiful minds. Otherwise they played at besieging forts and hunting down imaginary beasts in the brush-filled valley of the aqueduct below the university.

Schooling in Constantinople began within the family. A

girl as well as a boy learned to read at the age of five. Then a pedagogue arrived to begin grammar work with the children. This meant understanding as well as reading Homer and others. The teacher explained in the familiar Latin or Greek of street chatter what the poet had written in his ancient Greek. In their turn the children had to explain the virtues that made Hector a hero and the tribulations that made an end of Priam. At about the age of ten, girls left the grammar schooling to learn the skills and ways of the women's quarters.

At fourteen or fifteen a boy might leave the home to attend a hall of rhetoric—with the family pedagogue accompanying him. Now the rhetors of the halls, who were usually Greeks, taught much more than public speaking, although that was extremely important. The youths studied Demosthenes for his arguments against a tyranny; while they copied the style of Thucydides, they debated the ideals of his time. The rhetor in his gray and black mantle officiated like a priest; he quoted the sayings and proverbs of old time. Music and medicine were included in the sciences—but always by the writings of the ancients who had lived in a different thought-world, ruled by Plato. Lessons went on in the afternoons as well as the mornings. Often the boys would burst out in rebellious song or shout in unison a philippic against the tyranny of teaching. They sensed too well that the teaching within the halls had little to do with their life in the streets.

At that time there was no real aristocracy of Constantinople. Except for the new rich, who gained only oddments of learning from hired tutors, there were merely the families of the military commanders. The noble girls who drove to the shopping districts with veiled heads in carriages bearing silver crests, escorted by a chamberlain, were servants of the Empress. Women of unquestioned nobility kept themselves in seclusion, being wives of refugees or hostages from the outer barbarian kingdoms. Then, too, there were the picturesque visitors from the court of the Great King of Persia, or from

Arabia the Blessed. So it chanced that the young Germanus grew up in fellowship with lordly barbarians while Justinian made his friends in the depths of the city—a circumstance that had its effect on both of them.

When Vitalian's revolt threatened the city, Justinian held the rank only of a candidate, an apprentice guard of the palace. Obviously Justin had not troubled to gain a better post for him. Neither of them explained the matter, yet it appears that the stubborn nephew had no wish to play the part of secretary to the officer-uncle. And, as it happened, both of them narrowly escaped execution during the coming of Vitalian.

Ostensibly, this new crisis grew out of the religious disturbance that nearly cost Anastasius his throne. Actually, it was a swift move on the part of a frontier commander to seize, not the throne, but the power of the throne. Vitalian, Count of the Allies, a skilled soldier and ruthless gambler, led his troops in from the Danube on the plea of restoring the old religion. In doing so he brought along formidable contingents of barbarian allies, including some Bulgar-Huns on the promise of ransom to be gained from the city of the weak and aged Emperor. That kind of disaster had befallen western Rome many times, including the advent of Gaius Julius Caesar with his field army across the border river, Rubicon. In this case there were battles along the Danube and wary maneuvering all the way to Constantinople.

The true crisis came, as so often before, with a test of loyalties: who would keep his oath to serve the Emperor of the Romans, and who would cast his fortune with the fortunate Vitalian, a Goth by descent, but a military genius?

Vitalian collected his ransom, gave it in largesse to his army, and then broke his pledge of peace by moving suddenly down to the Bosporus to camp among the suburban villas and monasteries. Whereupon the citizenry gathered on the great wall to watch events—as couriers sped in through the military gates and agents of the palace posted up bronze plaques engraved with Anastasius' promise to remit taxes of the provinces where most of the soldiers had their homes. In the opinion of the streets, this was a matter to be settled among the officers of the armed forces. As to Vitalian, rumor pictured him as a gaunt, stammering bundle of energy, yet he was unquestionably a Roman officer and an orthodox believer, and he seemed to have the secret of victory. Leading commanders in the city pleaded friendship with Vitalian, and asked to be relieved from serving against him. They were relieved.

The mild but surprisingly determined Anastasius put his civilian minister in charge of defense and arrested all officers who had any connection with the defiant Count of the Allies. Among these, Justin of the Guard was taken into custody, and his sword and belt were removed. He was throwing dice, one hand against the other, under the interested eyes of his escort when other soldiers led in Justinian to join him.

By chance uncle and nephew had been confined in the quarters of a *magister militum*—one of the five masters of soldiers—nicknamed John the Hunchback. And by another chance John the Hunchback and Justin had helped each other out of trouble in the Persian wars. When the Magister discovered his guests at dice in his anteroom, he swore roundly that he had more need of a living officer than of a corpse hanging from a rope at the gate of the Praetorium.

Justin remarked that he agreed, but he was under arrest for the good of the Empire. The next day the worried Magister declared he had been given a portent; in fact he had dreamed that his two prisoners would one day become the salvation of the Empire. On the strength of this dream—which he liked to retell in later years—John the Hunchback secured the release of Justin and his nephew. He was justified of his friendship. In the decisive conflict that took place across the Golden Horn, Justin managed to drive off the dreaded Hunnish cavalry of Vitalian. At the same time a fleet gathered in the harbor and cleared the Bosporus of rebel vessels by use of a new weapon, a flaming liquid that burned on water. An unknown Greek had brought the secret of it to the Arsenal and had refused a talent of gold in reward—so that the flame weapon became known as the Greek's fire.

In due reward for their services, John the Hunchback became Master of the Guards at the palace, while the veteran Justin was named Count of the Excubitors ("The Watchers"), the three hundred picked bodyguards of the palace.

The resourceful Vitalian escaped with his horsemen to the frontier; other leaders of the revolt were promptly executed— a miscarriage of justice that Justinian did not fail to note.

To render thanks for his deliverance, the aged Anastasius went in the scarlet state barge up the Bosporus to the scene of Justin's victory, where he landed to make offering at the shrine of Michael Archangel, who had protected his city.

❁ THE ELECTION AT THE IVORY GATE

Three years later—it was the year 518 after Christ—on a hot midsummer night the old man died unexpectedly. With his life, the dynasty of Theodosius ended. Death at the age of eighty-eight not being entirely unlooked for, people were awake in the Sacred Palace prepared to carry out their duties.

White-robed silentiaries clad the body in the jeweled garment of audience; they placed candles at its head and feet so that it appeared to be sleeping under the mosaic ceiling that held the blue of the evening sky agleam with gold stars. After inspecting the chamber and finding it properly arranged, the silentiaries went out to the officer on duty in the corridor and repeated the words of tradition: "Our lord has ceased to exist as a man; now there must be deliberation guided by God, to elect an emperor."

The officer was Justin. As duty required, he summoned his

Excubitors to the gates to keep order, and alerted Celer, Master of Offices as well as a wartime friend. He also sent for the candidate Justinian, his nephew. Then while the chamberlains gathered together the belt, scarlet hose, and purple mantle to place upon the man who would be elected emperor, couriers raced through the night to warn the Patriarch, the other ministers, and leading senators. So much was written into the record of that night, which however, does not explain what followed except to mention that "much confusion ensued."

In this confusion Justinian took decisive action. The nephew of the Count of the Excubitors had little influence within the palace, but he had by now a profound knowledge of Roman tradition and an understanding of people. Moreover, he had allies in the three high officers, Celer and Justin and John the Hunchback. And during the first hours this triumvirate of the army held authority.

They never explained that they had agreed to act together, and Justinian as usual made no comment. But their actions brought about a result "beyond belief," according to the chronicler.

By sunrise the leading prelates and statesmen were hurrying into the Bronze Gate wearing the black garments of mourning. They were ushered into the secluded banqueting hall, where Celer greeted them. "We must decide on a name quickly," he warned them. "If we do that, the others will follow our lead without thinking. But if we don't act quickly, we'll have to follow them."

The others were the ordinary citizens, now beginning to trickle into the stands of the adjoining hippodrome. Custom required that a new emperor be named by the combined ministers and senators, with the approval of the Patriarch. The name, furthermore, must be accepted by the army, and the candidate then brought before the assembled citizenry for approval. At this last moment the city might reject the choice of the palace, with disastrous consequences.

As the morning wore on, the hippodrome filled up. As Celer had foreseen, the people's factions gave tongue when the curtains remained drawn across the Kathisma. "Long live the senate! Roman senate, do something! Where is our emperor, given by God, for the army, for the people?"

In the Triclinium hall of the Excubitors the statesmen— who had been roused from sleep to meet an emergency— found it difficult to make a choice. One of them must be named Autocrat and ruler of millions of souls. The dominant Empress, Ariadne, who could have made the decision for them, had lain in her porphyry tomb many years. The mild Anastasius had not presumed to suggest a successor. He had no sons, and the worthiest of his three nephews, Hypatius by name, had been captured in the early strife by Vitalian and held for a ransom of 90,000 pieces of gold—which hardly qualified him to rule. Celer had no name to suggest. The Patriarch waited silently in his chair to hear the decision of the statesmen. In a far corner Justin also waited, having no voice in the debate, being simply at his post of duty.

Over the anxious debaters lay the shadow of the Trisagion rioting. The new ruler must be no schismatic like Anastasius, but an orthodox believer. Over them also lay the memory of the recent civil conflict. A man must be found to deal with the Vitalians of the frontiers.

Echoes reached them from the vociferous hippodrome. Shouts came from the distant Ivory Gate where the chamberlains with the regalia of empire waited. Outside that gate the army was making its presence felt. Justinian had taken his place there with the soldiers.

These were the troops *in praesentis*—the household forces consisting of the numerous parade-ground Guards, and the few fighting Excubitors. (The lowly candidates had no voice in such a matter.) There between the palace and the crowds, the soldiers were naming choices of their own. Oddly enough, some Excubitors raised John the Hunchback to their shoulders

and shouted for him until a volley of stones from the Blue
faction on the benches assailed him, and Justinian intervened
to take his name to the Ivory Gate.

Whereupon the Guards gathered together to raise a master
of soldiers to a table, only to be attacked by Excubitors with
drawn swords. These armed men debated with their weapons.
Justinian drew the Magister away to safety, calling out his
name. At this the Excubitors caught Justinian, to raise him up
as their choice, but he broke away from them. Then the soldiers pounded on the gate, demanding that the robe and
crown be brought out to them. The experienced chamberlains
in turn demanded the names chosen by the people. At each
name, they shouted a refusal.

This unusual byplay at the gate increased the anxiety of the
senators, as it may have been intended to do. It seemed to be
urgent to name someone satisfactory to the army outside. At
the moment only the politic Grand Chamberlain, Amantius,
pressed for a candidate little known to the others, but undoubtedly an adherent of Amantius. He said that safety lay in
proposing a moderate man as the senate's choice. To reinforce
his argument the intent Amantius had brought a sack of
jewels of price, preparing to offer them around as the gift of
the Emperor-to-be.

At this point the impassive Justin, who had a quick eye for
the fall of dice, stepped forward to relieve the Grand Chamberlain of the sack and to offer the jewels wordlessly, while
Amantius followed him with whispered urgings. They must
waste not a moment more.

The troubled Patriarch rose to his feet. Before he could
speak, a parade-ground voice broke through the bustle. "Long
live Justin, our Emperor given by God."

Celer, watching the archpriest, cried it out. Certainly it
astonished the oblivious Amantius more than Justin. Senators
who were landowners and had suffered from the eccentricity
of Anastasius of glorious memory cried out in relief. For the

Count of the Excubitors was a sound old soldier who would not interfere with the economy. Not at the age of sixty-eight. Amantius shouted in fury that he was no more than a swine-herd. But the wearied Patriarch raised two fingers in blessing. Justin belonged to the Orthodox Church, and would at least be capable of keeping the peace.

Magister Celer waited for no more; he hurried Justin through the corridor with friendly senators escorting them, out through the Ivory Gate. In the throng outside someone struck Justin across the mouth, and he was bleeding as he entered the Kathisma.

When he stood before the curtains there was only the brief-est silence. The Excubitors roared at sight of their commander. The Blue faction rejoiced to see a man of their own conserva-tive order, while the mass of the people remembered him as the victor over the Hunnish horsemen. Although bleeding, he stood erect and handsome, crowned by white curls, a true sol-dier at attention.

"Justin, August, you will conquer!"

At this the watching guards raised the military standards. Others held their shields over Justin while a chain of gold was placed on his head and the imperial mantle fitted over his tunic. From the excited throngs came a chorus of greeting: "Reign as you have lived . . . be abundant, Imperator . . . worthy of the city, worthy of the world. . . . You are ortho-dox—an orthodox emperor reigns . . . restore the commun-ion and give us honest magistrates."

When he had been cleansed and robed, Justin made a brief answer to his people. He said that every soldier present would have five gold numeri and a pound of silver, and he hoped that everyone would have peace and prosperity.

So the official record of that day could say with much truth that Justin had been elected to lead the Empire "by favor of the Orthodox Church, by choice of the high ministers of the Sacred Palace and of the senate, and by the election of the army." Nothing was said about the verdict of the people or Justinian. He did not appear beside his uncle in the triumph at the Kathisma or the ensuing consecration at the great church.

Justinian had gained what the rebellious Vitalian had failed to win, a certain power behind the throne. This was not apparent to others as yet, and Justinian made no effort to assert it. It seems that he meant to make use of it in a way of his own.

❀ JOYOUS INTERLUDE

The heart of Constantinople beat strongly during the years that followed. That heart had not been planned by Constantine himself. It had grown of its own accord where the arterial streams of the population met in the space between the great Hagia Sophia, the senate house, and the palace itself. On the fourth side the wide Mesé, the Middle Way, descended into it and ended there.

This central space had been the market place of ancient Byzantium. It resembled in many ways St. Mark's square in still-to-be-built Venice. Although it had been named originally The Four Porticoes, people called it the Augusteum from the giant statue of Augustus Caesar standing over the Golden Milestone which marked the end of all the roads of the Empire—copied, like the statue, from the originals in the older Rome.

At least once every day most important people passed through the Augusteum square—officers on their way to the palace barracks, senators threading through the massed marble goddesses and chariot drivers that guarded their portico, ordinary citizens bearing petitions, inventions, or manuscripts to sell. These sought the benches on the shady north side to wait for possible admittance to the adjoining great Bronze Gate, where white-robed candidates sorted out the callers. Those admitted were taken to the Referendarius, who decided whether they might go farther. Naturally the Augusteum became the haunt of news-gatherers and wandering preachers. In fact news bulletins were often hung up by the Chalké (Bronze) Gate.

Like modern headlines they were meant to catch the eye. Some have survived:

Comet Seen: what Does It Portend? Masters of Science Unable to Decide. . . . Marvellous Italian Performing Dog: Points out Loose Women. . . . Monk of the Syrian Desert: Accuses Our City Clergy of Feasting while Lazarus Waits. . . . New Land Grant to Veterans. . . .

As the reign of the old soldier Justin began, these tidings were of peace, as he had promised on election, if not of prosperity. For little luxury was visible as yet within the city. In fact, men were distinguished more by the marking of their uniforms than by splendor in their attire. When the shadow of the gnomon left the great sun clock at evening, the Praetorian Prefect, or prime minister, emerged from the Chalké wearing a mantle of imperial purple which, however, reached only to his knees. Before him a single attendant carried the symbol of his office, a silver inkstand. He was the same shrewd Marinus, once a Syrian merchant, who had managed so well under Anastasius and had contrived to defend the city at the coming of Vitalian. As Marinus passed out to his lofty chariot waiting beyond the pillars of the Augusteum, all army officers saluted him. In doing so they obeyed the old law that civilian authority should be above the military. The busy Prefect of the City wore the ancient toga of a judge girdled by a plated military belt.

Among the officers who saluted were two young commanders from the frontiers. They were close friends although one was Mundus, the newly baptized son of a Herul chieftain, and the other a quiet, yellow-maned Dalmatian, a graduate of the military academy, named Belisarius. The two of them served Justinian as military advisers.

Like the Prefect, these men from the limes found that Justin kept order with an iron hand. The eunuch Amantius, who had schemed against his election, disappeared, having been put to death. If disorder broke out in the streets, leaders of all factions were jailed impartially. As for that prime mover of revolt, Count Vitalian, he was summoned to the palace and named Caesar—war lord—and consul. The eyes in the Augusteum took note that when the restless, overbearing Count Vitalian at last appeared through the Mesé columns, a band of barbarian swordsmen kept close to his back.

Men remembered that in the fighting of a few years before Vitalian had been careful to avoid being drawn into the city gates. A lone wolf is wary of traps. But Justin and Justinian and Marinus had pledged his safety as Caesar of the Empire. After all, he had taken up arms for the old religion, which Justin now upheld, having learned its prayers in the ranks of the army. As to Justinian, who kept so in the background, few people could say anything.

The unexpected thing happened during the quiet of an evening when the crowds had left the Augusteum. Swiftly as always, Count Vitalian rode up to the Chalké. He entered with only a secretary and a sword bearer following because he had been bidden to a light refreshment in the Delphax hall. He passed the quarters of the Guards, attracting no attention. Then shouting and the rasping of steel broke out in the corridor beyond.

Vitalian was found there dead. Attendants in the corridor said there had been a sudden brawl with armed Partisans of the Blues. There was no one to testify for the arrogant Vitalian because his two followers had been slain as well. But who had allowed Blue weapon-men to linger after dark in the palace itself?

The city considered the mystery and decided that the silent Marinus had disposed of his old enemy. It did not seem like Justin, who had willing Excubitors at his side, to call in henchmen from the streets. Years passed before his nephew was accused in whispers of this murder. By then in the eyes of observers Justinian had become a different person. As far as history goes, the riddle of Vitalian's end remains unsolved.

As a result, the aging Justin was rid of the one person who might have proved both strong and dangerous. Gradually it became clear that the new Emperor would not be a simple figurehead, as his friends the privileged senators had hoped. Illiterate he must be, because he signed his name by aid of a stencil wrought in gold; unthinking—except in army matters —he certainly was. Yet behind him there was some contrary impulsion, as if from another mind both decisive and determined. It could not be the mind of his wife because she had none, being a former camp-follower, Lupicina by name, and now as empress under the name of Euphemia—better sounding—interested only in churchgoing.

True, Justinian held no visible power. He held nobility only in name, and by rank he was no more than Count of Domestics—Celer commanded the palace troops. Uncle and nephew seemed to meet together only in the few hours when Justin was not on parade. However, an order given for the flogging of Blue leaders during Justinian's absence in illness was countermanded when he returned to his uncle. An invitation sent to the bishops in far-off St. Peter's in Justin's—stenciled— name brought these priests of the West to the Egnatian Way for the first time in long years of separation between the churches of East and West. It was Justinian who rode out to the ten-mile marker to greet them in the name of the Patriarch who had not summoned them.

Nor did this quiet man from the Balkan mountains have a patron among the magnates to back his career. Not unless it might be Tribonian, the eccentric master of laws who drew fees in five figures for taking a case, while arguing the folly of existing laws. At thirty-seven years of age, with gray showing in his unkempt hair, Justinian went his persuasive way, wearing a coarse woolen cloak in the winter cold. He gained more popularity in the shops of the Middle Way than in the palace itself. He kept asking why things were done. "A Diogenes without a lantern," witty Peter the Patrician called him.

In the office of the *Memoriae* inquisitive John of Lydia found no trace of Justinian's name in the decrees he filed away. Justin truly reigned. The wiseacres of the Augusteum who had prophesied that Justinian would be proclaimed Caesar after Vitalian's end were mistaken. In any case, John of Lydia assured himself that the great bureaus that he served carried on the work of Empire regardless of who signed the decrees. So-called emperors came and went—the bureaus endured unchanged. They alone preserved a remnant of "ancient grandeur." It did not occur to John that Justinian might have persuaded his uncle to change that state of affairs.

Observers in the Augusteum noticed that the Emperor's odd nephew seldom joined the throngs seeking the portal of Hagia Sophia at the Vespers hour when candles lighted up the dark nave of the church. More often, alone, he would be kneeling by the altar of the remote Studion where The Sleepless maintained their song of praise.

Because he made his way into the living rooms behind the workshops to watch the women and children, they came to call him *Akritas,* meaning, in the common speech, a protector. Not an armed guard, and not an overlord, but a protector in distress. Once when the wool-sellers were boarding up their shops at the hour of lamp lighting, he came upon a thin woman still working intently, her dark mane of hair bent over a loom. She was a woman still young, Theodora by name.

She had been an actress-prostitute—one thing meant the other—and by sitting at the loom she might have been posing to catch the attention of passing men. But she was poor enough, and she did not take her skilled fingers from the warp of the wool when she answered his questions.

Then one evening he led Theodora away with him, to his solitary rendezvous. They climbed the dark stair to the summit of the Emperor Theodosius' column to watch the lamps lighted in the pattern of the streets. The girl prostitute was much younger than he, and she kept silence in the dark aerie when he told her of his fancy—that the glow of the city lighted the darkness of all the outer lands.

Justinian often yielded to his imagination, as a young boy docs. Now he thought that the glow beneath them changed to a triumphal illumination, from lamps set in all the balconies, and that the great square was covered with carpets, over which he rode while streamers waved from the windows and acclamations greeted him, like a Caesar of old times: "Justinian, you have conquered!" Then the acclamation became the chant of The Sleepless: "*We poor and needy ones . . . praise thee, Our Lord.*"

This vision of the unreal satisfied the vanity of the indrawn man. It quickened his feeling of responsibility for the silent woman. Theodora told him she was afraid of falling without a railing to hold to.

Soon afterward Justinian took to working longer hours at night—although what tasks might make such demand upon a Count of the Domestics were not apparent. (Justinian must have felt the need of making up for Justin's lack of knowledge.) By the beacon of his reading lamp he pored over the decrees and reports written out for the Emperor during the day. What he read burned into his memory.

At the same time he changed his quarters to the House of Hormisdas between the palace and the sea. This new home he shared with Theodora.

The house itself had been built for a refugee prince of Persia, Hormisdas. Secluded from the streets it occupied the cypress-grown slope beneath the far end of the hippodrome and the residences of the palace. So it was, in a sense, a gate house. When the chariots raced, the roar of the crowd beat down on it: *"Nika, nika . . .* win, win, win!"

Although she had never been allowed in the stands, Theodora had heard this cry often in the years when she had been a hanger-on at the theater. Then at times she could hear the silver organ note and the fluting of a festival in the palace gardens. She could not enter the gardens, having been a prostitute, while Justinian might walk in his silent manner into the robing chamber of the Emperor. There were so many differences between them. Because she had suffered from the callousness of men, and because she had an inward fear of the tenacious man, her master, Theodora decided that she would never be subservient to him.

It must have seemed unreal to her, when she became Justinian's mistress, to preside over a house of her own. She kept carefully to its seclusion. Theodora had a craving to be close to the sea. Here, designed it is true for a homesick Persian grandee, were chambers of gleaming tiles and sea-green marbles opening upon a gallery that overlooked the masts and busy quays of the New Harbor. Sometimes when the north wind kept them from their proper anchorage, pleasure barges of the ladies of the *propoloma,* the diadem and veil, who waited upon the Empress, appeared beneath the gallery. Always the rising sun lighted it, tracing a dazzling path across the sea to her couch.

Theodora had an imagination, which she kept to herself. She had learned that illusions can be painful. Across the sea in Cyrenaica she had been driven from the house of another man of substance. She had walked into the desert, to leave a girl child during days of poverty with kindly people on the river Nile. The years had left her without moral sense, but she knew how to hold fast to those she cared for and to take savage retribution upon anyone who slighted her. She had, besides, a dread of poverty.

They say she had beauty. Her brows met over dark, questioning eyes; her slight body grew tense with feeling. She could mimic solemn people, and she had learned to smile when she was hurt. Justinian found her always gay, for she had learned very quickly how to please him. (His habits were as predictable as the dripping of the water clock that marked the hours.) It was more difficult to anticipate his thoughts, but Theodora managed to do that as well, having the gift of clairvoyance—a heritage from her ancestors, women of Asia.

Justinian must have been fourteen years older than the pantomimist of the theater. He felt an instinct of protection for a lovely child, and passion for this woman who could stir him to new desires. His passionate love endured as long as she lived, and Theodora had full realization of it. By a clumsy play upon her name, he called her his gift of God.

In the opinion of the Augusteum these two who mated were different in nature as quicksilver from iron ore. It was not at all apparent that both natures touched the absolute in determination—Theodora's in her resolve never again to feel the filth and starvation of the caravan tracks of Africa, Justinian's in his determination to tear down the structure of the Empire he served.

❋ "LONG LIFE TO OUR MOST PIOUS AUGUSTA!"

During the joyous interlude at the house of Hormisdas, Justinian blossomed before the eyes of the city. His tall striding figure became well groomed; he let his mustache grow. When his name appeared—as Flavius Petrus Sabbatius Justinianus—on the roll of the patricians, he discarded the gold neck ring of a Domestic for flowing white edged with scarlet. More than that, he put new life into public festivals, and so became the idol of the crowds.

He led the dominant Blue faction in parade to music on the birthday of the city. Named consul after the demise of Vitalian, he opened the hippodrome to games without heeding the cost. (By then the ancient rank of consul meant only the honor of a name inscribed on the ivory diptyches, and the expense of entertaining the common folk.) They thronged happily under the flying banners to watch massed athletes and listen critically to the choruses. Vicariously they felt the thrill of hunting down wild beasts. (The records say that Justinian provided twenty lions and forty leopards and held the games at a cost of 288,000 solidi. The clerks in the treasury noted that he drew upon the gold reserve, the 320,-000 pounds gathered painfully by Anastasius.)

When the chariots raced, cripples from the Samson hospital waited on benches through the night to be sure of their places; soothsayers edged through the crowd with portents to whisper and talismans to sell to predict the winners; country folk climbed to trees or roofs overlooking the arena where the chariots sped and clashed for the brief moments that freed the spectators from all other anxieties. During the week of racing, Justinian the Consul often appeared alone in the Kathisma above the motionless four bronze horses of Lysippus. The long hours of public display had begun to tire the aging Emperor.

Justinian by now could do the work of both without tiring. As years passed, the invisible balance of their uncle-nephew relationship shifted. Without a son of his own, Justin needed the aid of his adopted son. For this he paid in his blunt way by ceding to the younger man estates from the imperial treasury—lands that turned out to be near Theodora's ancestral home. But more than that his pride would not yield up.

One morning a group of senators waited upon the Emperor of the Romans at an early hour when he was being robed. They were friends of Justinian, and in this unguarded moment they ventured the suggestion that Justin might well name his adopted son Caesar of the Empire. The old man gave little heed until he realized the significance of their words. With the rank of Caesar went command of all armed forces. Then abruptly he gripped his belt, heavy with miniatures of protecting saints, and a fold of his purple mantle.

"Guard yourselves, my masters," he cried out, "against giving these to a younger man."

This display of anger ended the politic attempt to bring Justinian nearer the throne. Whatever he did had to be carried out by the signed order of the older man. With their loyalty to family, these two had all the stubbornness of their Balkan mountains. The veteran soldier would see only military necessity. To him it was unthinkable that a civilian who had never led the regiments toward battle could hold a post of command.

And then a law was changed. Until then women of the theater had not been allowed to marry men of noble rank. Now at Justinian's urging, the Emperor decreed that such a marriage might take place "if the woman has lived in purity for an interval." It fitted Theodora's case.

Justin felt only sympathy for the slight pale girl who knelt before him with such evident devotion. In his day he had had an eye for the best of them, while Theodora had real respect for the aged man who could bestow ten thousand gold numeri with a word. He declared her worthy to be enrolled among the patricians, the only women who could enter the palace. This triangular agreement was broken unexpectedly by objection from the secluded Empress. Euphemia, who had been Lupicinia of the camps, emerged from her pious occupation of building a church with her tomb attached. She made her one remark of public record. As empress she would never greet as wife of her adopted son this brat from the circus. Theodora understood why.

When the aged peasant woman had been laid in her porphyry tomb, only one obstacle remained. The Church must give consent to the marriage. And the imaginative Justinian feared for his mistress in such an ordeal.

Theodora surprised him by flinching not at all. There was a stillness in her at such a moment. Without pretense she responded in whispered Greek words to the questions of the Patriarch. She took his blessing upon her.

All this shadow play within the palace reached the outer city only in rumors. In reaction, Justinian had visitors who hinted that the way to highest rank would be opened to him if he took for his bride a chaste daughter of an ancient family. Cynics remarked that while empresses had been known to become prostitutes, no one had ever heard of a prostitute becoming an empress. Without heeding, Justinian quietly married the female pantomimist of the theater.

They say that before he did so he made a gift to her of the House of Hormisdas. For a reason of her own she asked for that.

Whereupon something happened outside the Chalké gate. It did not come into the records because it was a voiceless movement, a thing we call popular sentiment. Theodora broke her seclusion. Unveiled in simple dark robe and chlamys, she drove through the streets. Two white mules drew her carriage; a chamberlain with his staff stood beside her. Running slaves opened a way by calling her name. That name had been half forgotten. In this manner, a sight for staring eyes, she greeted the people of her streets, and they liked it. She had been one of them.

It was more than Theodora's doing, however. There was

need to think of the reign. Obviously the ailing Justin could name no one to succeed him, nor would it matter much if he did so. Apart from the palace, the crowds of the forums and church steps remembered how Justinian had come among them like an *Akritas* and how he had thrown out sackfuls of silver at the festival of his consulship. Without debate, he became the candidate of the popular parties eight years after the crowning of Justin.

At length Justin acted of his own accord. An old wound in his ankle had failed to heal, and now gangrene ate into his leg. He knew what that meant. Only weeks instead of years of life remained to him. There was one way to keep disturbance from the weak dominion after his death. Justinian explained how Diocletian, a soldier also, had tried it.

A few days before Easter of that year 527, Justin was helped to his throne seat in the bay of the Golden Triclinium. His favored Excubitors flanked him, impassive as the silvered double axes they held. Before him gathered the leaders of the senate who had supported him, with the Patriarch Epiphanius, named by him.

They knew beforehand the announcement he would make, but he used an odd phrase. "By *will of my people*, I appoint my nephew and adopted son Justinian to be emperor with me."

When the Patriarch added his prayer, the commanders of the army joined in the response: *Amen*. In the silence of agreement Justinian came to kneel in front of the old man to have the symbolic ring of gold placed on his head. Within a few minutes this small gathering dispersed. Justin had not been strong enough to appear in full audience in the Hagia Sophia.

So it happened that only after Justin's death that summer did Justinian enter the great church to be anointed Emperor of the Romans, Ever August.

Afterwards he did something unwonted. Wearing diadem

and cloth of gold, and on his shoulders the imperial purple embroidered with the emblem of sovereignty, he turned aside from the Augusteum to enter the Kathisma. There he gave greeting to the throng clustered in the hippodrome.

At his side Theodora appeared. For the first time she stood inside the arena of the people. The eyes of the multitude beheld her slight figure resplendent in violet-purple descending to folds of cloth of gold, her dark hair agleam with pearl strings.

Perhaps her beauty won the approval of the crowd. For she could play her new part well. There was enthusiasm in the ritual acclamation: "Worthy to reign! Long life to our Most Pious Augusta!"

In this way began the rule of the woman of the theater and the peasant from the mountains. It was August of 527, and the darkness of the western world was very near to the city of Constantinople.

III

A
NEW
WAY
OF
LIFE

STAGE OF THE PALACE

WHEN HE WAS proclaimed Justinian the First, Emperor of the Romans, he had his full strength at forty-five years of age. To his straightforward mind his coronation meant one thing: he must rule his people in the great tradition of the vanished Caesars or half-legendary Constantine. He never forgot that.

A mechanism for acting the part lay ready to his hand. For two centuries, since the dynamic Constantine had walked around the foundations of his new abode, the mechanism had been tested by emergencies until it did its work as steadily as the dripping water clock that marked the hours in Justinian's corridor. In fact he needed only to step into this machinery of government to help it carry out its task.

He woke in the morning within the glimmer of white marble walls, beneath the sky-blue of the mosaic ceiling— as if he occupied a niche alone under the canopy of the sky. Indeed, his sleeping chamber had a unique name, the Sacred Cubicle. When the fall of the bronze ball in the water clock chimed the first hour of light, Justinian had only to wait patiently for the human instruments of the palace to serve him. With a warning jangling of keys the Grand Janitor passed by to open all the doors. When a voiceless boy peered in and drew back the curtain, silentiaries in white robes appeared at the Emperor's side with a silver basin of water and fruit and cakes to stay his night hunger.

Before the second hour struck, vestiaries waited in the anteroom with his attire for the morning audience; chamberlains—veteran eunuchs for the most part—saluted him by whispering any tidings that might be worthy of his hearing. The Grand Chamberlain brought a carefully written agenda of names of those who would approach him that morning, an account of any gifts to be offered, and a list of the rewards he might make in return for the gifts. (Not that Justinian needed written memorandums.) He was sheathed in the stiff mantle of deep purple that no other might wear. Under his right arm stretched the golden panel embroidered with symbols of his rank; on his right shoulder gleamed the jeweled orb of the earth beneath a cross; from the diadem covering his head hung four great pearls.

When these servitors made way for him and he stepped out into the corridor, he no longer resembled the son of Sabbatius; he had become the Autocrat of tradition. He paused at the lighted shrine of Michael Archangel to offer a prayer. At the head of the stair Excubitors fell in before him, his palace attendants behind him. At the chiming of the half hour he stepped from a narrow corridor into the bay at the end of the audience hall, to the small throne that fairly shone among lamps of colored glass within walls plated

with gold and inlaid with mosaic marbles. Before him, separating him from the unseen audience, hung curtains of
luminous cloth of gold.

This was his stage. At a nod from him, chamberlains in
the wings drew back the curtains. He faced an assemblage
of senators, officers, visitors, and petitioners, who did reverence to the appearance of the purple. Swiftly the steward of
the palace itself and the counts of the two treasuries made
their daily reports—wasting no time on details already written
into the accounts—before the first person approached the
three porphyry steps leading up to the throne.

Justinian did not speak unless he was moved to do so. He
listened between the two bronze eagles that spread their wings
protectingly over his head. The Grand Chamberlain made
routine responses for him, until Justinian signed to him
and the curtains were drawn again. Then the Chamberlain
passed through the assemblage, murmuring "If you
please—" to show that the morning audience had ended.
All heads were bowed in the response: "Many years, many
years, servant of the Lord!"

Not until then might Justinian return up the stairs to
seek the women's quarters, where Theodora waited to share
the midday meal with him.

This was no idle display. It was carefully schemed to give
an impression of power that hardly existed. The eyes of
strangers beheld the man on the Triclinium throne as supra-
human, to be reverenced. It all formed part of the plan of
the Constantinopolitans for survival.

Especially when a barbarian chieftain desired a sight of
Justinian, as most of them did, the Sacred Palace put on its
best act of glamour.

Take the case of Grod. He is a newcomer, a Hun from the
Cimmerian steppes, with a horse's mane hanging between
the braids of hair on his back. This Grod has brought his

family and atabegs to behold the mystery and magic of the imperial city.

With trumpets sounding before him and icon-banners following, Grod is escorted down the thronged Mesé into the Augusteum. His escorts are the cataphracts, mailed riders with shining iron helmets and rigidly uplifted lances—the cavalry respected even by Huns of the East. In the applauding Augusteum, Grod's wives, children, and henchmen perceive the honor paid him as the Master of Offices takes his rein to greet him.

This minister with the gold-hilted sword and baton is Hermogenes by name, also a Hun by birth, but a baptized Christian, schooled in the city. He has seen the prairies and the folk of the north.

Hermogenes takes the silent, attentive Grod on a long ritual walk. Past the massed red plumes and mirrorlike shields of the motionless Guards, past the forest of axes of the giant Excubitors, they walk by the statue of the goddess Daphne into the immense colonnade, where servitors bow to them. They turn into the Triclinium, where the nobles make way for them.

Grod stands at last before the luminous curtain. Faintly he hears voices rising and falling in a hymn. Under his booted feet stretches a white carpet; an immense cross appears in the ceiling above him; around him hang tapestries revealing angels bearing up the symbol of Christ. The curtains part and he beholds the figure of ineffable splendor above him.

"But your emperor," Grod ejaculates afterwards, "he is a god."

This kindly god appears again at a feast in the Magnaura (The Great Hall), a pavilion of marble in a moonlit garden. Justinian presses upon the monarch of the steppes gifts of gleaming enamel and translucent alabaster, talismans of wrought gold, saddles silver trimmed. Apparently he has no end of treasures to give away.

After that it is not at all strange that the barbaric Grod
should wish to be baptized, like Hermogenes, especially when
Justinian consents to become his godfather. Grod's bleak
mind cannot grasp the meaning of *Christian*, but he is eager
to become the acknowledged son of such an unmistakably
powerful father.

(When Grod returned to his steppes as a Christian, he
wore about his neck a chain with a medallion of Justinian,
his new father. Thereupon he was killed by his people, who
held fast to their tribal gods.)

Now in the Grod affair Justinian had merely acted out a
scene played before him by Justin and Anastasius and other
wearers of the purple, as part of "the science of ruling the
barbarians."

But Justinian was not as old as the others, nor was he
either soldier or bureaucrat by nature. It became clear to his
matter-of-fact mind that the splendor of the Triclinium had
no meaning unless the Empire itself regained power. For the
last dozen years he had chewed away at the question—why
was the Empire, the *imperium*, weakening? He had observed
the working of the mechanism of the palace, and now he felt
an overmastering fear. The Roman Empire, like an aged man,
was sinking to its death.

In these first crowded months, Justinian did not explain
his fear. He kept it in the withdrawn part of his mind while
going through the daily ritual of a benevolent autocrat. In
that part of his mind he followed his imagination toward
mighty achievement. He could do that easily enough. But
he took action cautiously. It was never easy for him to reach
a decision.

He made his first attack on the apathy of those around
him.

Across the long colonnade of the Daphne palace—so called
from the statue at its entrance—there was a secluded chamber
that his elderly predecessors had used to take a nap. Justinian

stripped it of comforts, including its couch, and furnished it with a long wooden table and a few benches. Except for brightly burning oil lamps it now resembled a monk's cell. During the afternoon hours Justinian worked here at the table with a jar of drinking water by him.

A person entering found no one to speak to and nothing to do but step up to the table and explain his presence to the man carefully reading piled documents. Justinian would listen patiently, saying little. At times he would call in a young confidential secretary to make a note of his words with a stylus on a writing tablet.

It soon became evident that the odd Justinian was taking on his shoulders the labor of the great civil service which had been created to relieve the ruler of such cares. To do so it had its own staff of interpreters, and of shorthand writers. "If a problem appears to be insoluble, bring it to the Emperor," he said, and meant it. Listeners paid little heed at first because autocrats new to the throne had a way of making rash promises.

The Scrinia—the recording bureaus—continued to lay before him their findings beautifully written on clean parchment. Each one bore at an upper corner its colored filing emblem, miniature purses or swords or scrolls; reports from the provinces had the tiny mountains, streams, forests, or roads that identified their subjects; family records bore the crests of the families concerned. This careful tabulation pleased Justinian even while he questioned what he read. *Why* was this done?

Why was a murderer of his father condemned to die sewn up in a sack with a viper, a cock, a dog, and an ape? Such was the law of Pompey. It had been carried out for centuries of years. Justinian declared that henceforth a parricide need only be drowned in a sack, which would deprive him of burial in the earth he had dishonored.

That excellent inscriber of records, John of Lydia, mourned

when Justinian demanded swifter writing on cheap papyrus sheets instead of snowy parchment. "On leaves of *paper*, with cheap writing that smells of poverty!"

Then Justinian, after demanding speedier work, began to interfere with old customs. His earliest edicts (*Novellae*) freed slaves from prison. As to slaves outside the cells, he gave owners the right at all times to liberate them by a spoken word. He attacked the ancient Roman "power of the father" over the family, making children owners of one quarter of a family estate, and allowing bastards to inherit. Yet such ancient customs were the very foundation of Roman law, according to the proverb: *Moribus antiquis stat res Romana.*

"All children are born free," he reminded Tribonian, the most brilliant and unscrupulous of the jurisconsults. Genially Tribonian assented, realizing full well that Justinian headed a society made up of illustrious and noble men, free citizens, freedmen, serfs, and slaves. But in a naïve way, Justinian meant what he said.

Laws could be made to serve human beings, not the other way around.

Again Tribonian assented. The two of them had worked out a solution to that apparently insoluble problem. What passed for law in Constantinople was the mass of ancient legislation, mixed up with the decisions of generations of judges and filled up anew by the decrees of all the emperors. As the Roman state had spread over other nations, foreign customs had crept in, until finally the Christian Church appeared to question all the pagan past. Meanwhile the records themselves had been scattered in thousands of documents hoarded away where few could be found. The Code of Theodosius had attempted to rewrite this enormous mass of documents, but in doing so had merely added new laws to the old.

So it was a poor rhetor who could not unearth some law to justify his client. Tribonian himself baffled the magistrates by his brilliance in quoting forgotten laws. Perhaps he had suggested to Justinian how to legalize the marriage with Theodora.

Now he had a very simple solution of the endless puzzle of the laws. It was no use, Tribonian declared, to attempt to make a new code like the Codex Theodosianus. Not even the gods of old—and Tribonian sacrificed to them secretly—had been able to create a Cosmos out of such a Chaos. No. The only way was to choose the few laws you needed, like jackstraws out of the mass, and make use of them alone. Call them the *Corpus Juris*. Apply them to every Sicilian olive-grower as well as to the Roman state.

"Then we can keep decent order," Justinian meditated, "and by Roman law."

The new Body of Law, Tribonian agreed, could be completed with all interpretations in a score of years.

Justinian gave him one year in which to do it. And Tribonian hit on a way to accomplish that, as well. A working model could be made in a single year. Justinian gave him ten assistants, among them the honest young Greek, Theophilos. (And Theophilos did most of the work for which Tribonian got the credit.)

Feeling himself faced by the impossible, Tribonian accomplished it. At the end of a year Justinian had his skeleton of a *Corpus Juris* written out on a few pages of cheap paper. Whereupon the meditative Emperor made a brief announcement that attracted little attention at first. He stated that henceforth his interpretations of the new laws would override all older legislation of any kind.

What he did next caused stir enough. He closed the schools of philosophy in Athens which had been open to the cultured world since Plato's day. He closed all schools of law except the two in ancient Berytus and modern Constantinople. He closed all schismatic churches in the city itself, thus giving supremacy to the Patriarch of the Hagia Sophia.

This was obviously the beginning of something—but of what? From his workroom the intent Justinian spoke to all districts of the city through the voices of the criers. "Your emperor labors through the nights to devise, with the aid of God, what will be useful for his people."

In the palatial homes on the height by the mausoleum of Constantine it was said that their new Caesar had become an *imperator plebis*, an emperor of the populace.

At the same time Justinian rewarded Tribonian by giving him a greater responsibility.

✿ MEN OF THE SILENCE

Across the colonnaded way from Justinian's study there was a long chamber. A painted map decorated one of its walls. It opened into a gallery overlooking the seafront of the city and the distant dark hills of Asia. Within this space a dozen men met to administer as best they could, and safeguard, as they must, the dominion of Constantinople. Officially their gathering was a *Consistorium*, but because they kept their counsels pretty much to themselves it became known as a Silence. The Constantinopolitans disliked official names, perhaps because they usually disliked Latin.

A Silence was more than a cabinet meeting of our time. It tried vital cases, dealt with any treason, or strategy of war, and channeled funds into the operative departments. Its members enjoyed the highest privileges and wore the officer's belt as a reminder of Diocletian's notion that they served like soldiers.

In fact the magisters of distant armies often appeared—

after speeding in from the post roads—at a Silence; sometimes senatorial leaders were called in or the high clergy summoned. Naturally the Praetorian Prefect attended, being responsible, like a prime minister of today, for taxation and the upkeep of the army. The counts of the two treasuries had their duties, and the Master of Offices—in the guise of foreign minister—passed in and out. But the man with power was the quaestor. As chief magistrate of the realm, he might veto an undertaking; he ruled the ministers of the great Scrinia. Justinian named Tribonian quaestor.

So, after making a Hun diplomat-in-chief, Justinian raised a millionaire scoffer to the post that demanded integrity above everything. He seemed to reason that responsibility would bring out the genius of such eccentric men.

Traditionally, these prime movers of empire worried out their problems before reporting to the Emperor. Justinian, however, began to attend their meetings. Seemingly he liked to draw his ideas from the clashing of other minds.

Unmistakably, however, he drove the others to greater efforts. Just before his election, catastrophe had struck twice in the East—when an earthquake laid mighty Antioch in ruins, and when smoldering warfare flared on the Persian frontier. Justinian would not sanction the Council's plans to send only food and funds to the stricken city. Instead, they would rebuild it entire with great paved forums.

As for the incipient war, Justinian named young Belisarius to take charge of it as master of soldiers in the East. Older officers in the city—knowing that Justinian had no experience in managing armies—objected that Belisarius had merely taken chances and been lucky. In fact, Belisarius had last been reported seeking refuge with his small forces on islands in the river Euphrates. Justinian retorted that those islands were beyond the border, and however much Belisarius failed to do, he waged his war outside Roman soil.

To these youthful or questionable companions in work,

Justinian added a living paradox, John of Cappadocia. Pallid and hulking, unschooled—except by his own experience—this accountant of the War Office came from the mountains of Cappadocia, an area of rebellion. His unknown ancestors might have been Hittites. With the manners of a bear, he had all the tenacity of that animal in getting things done. He argued that to get honey you had to break open a hive. To build a new house, you had to pry granite from cliffs, hew down forests for timber, dig clay out of streams for bricks. You had to destroy in order to create.

Among the things John of Cappadocia wanted to destroy were the privileges of the favored Blue faction, the sinecures of the great bureaus, the immunity of the tax-free aristocracy.

The Praetorian Prefect at that time was a certain elderly Demosthenes, probably leader of the conservative senators who had helped elect Justinian and believed him to be their man. After watching both of them for a couple of years, Justinian retired the well-meaning senator and appointed the ruthless John as Praetorian Prefect. "He thus became," wrote the chief secretary, John of Lydia, "our Lord High Brigand."

The advent of the Cappadocian to power had many consequences, the first being the revolt of the following year. He also came into abrupt collision with Theodora.

❀ THEODORA THE LADY

At the far end of the Daphne, Theodora discovered that she was mistress of a court of her own. Secluded in the women's chambers on the upper terrace, guarded by silentiaries, the actress of the theater entered upon the duties of an Augusta of the Empire with surprising ease.

Once she had crossed the threshold, tradition laid its hold on her small body. Noble girls of the propoloma in white

peplums flecked with purple attended her rising; the aged
Mistress of the Chambers bowed before her and advised her in
whispers what she must do. Even the going to her morning
bath became a parade with slaves carrying salts, ointment, and
perfumes behind her. Caressing hands robed her in the proper
costume for each appearance—and the touch of the sprays of
jewels hanging from the diadem against her hair made her
catch her breath. Her chamberlain (selected with care by
Justinian himself) repeated over for her what she must say.
If she left her quarters, officers of the Guards and Excubitors
paced before her, and sometimes musicians followed.

When she heard the murmured acclamation "Glory of the
purple—joy of the world," her blood quickened. She knew very
well that the salutation was ritual and would be given to the
dumpiest female who happened to wear the diadem. Still,
Theodora fancied it was a little different in her case, and very
soon that proved to be true.

In those first years she found that she served only one purpose, to personify the splendor of the reign. She waited her
chance to do more than that.

Then she discovered that her chambers were haunted. The
ghosts of three other women lingered there in memories.
Deacons of the chapels still breathed their names in prayers
or curses: Pulcheria, Athenais, Ariadne. Theodora coaxed her
elder servants to tell her stories of the ghostly Theodosian
ladies, pretending to be amused while she took note of the
dangers revealed to her.

Pulcheria, more resolute than her weak-willed young brother
Theodosius, fought the moody fancies of the boy. She vowed
herself to virginity, to gain the loyalty of the ministers by her
devotion. Pulcheria forced herself to make decisions like a
man. Since the wayward Theodosius must marry, she chose for
him as bride a lovely Greek, Athenais, a dark-eyed, fearless
pagan (and did not the sister hope to contrast, Theodora
wondered, her own pious devotion with the skepticism of the

Athenian girl, who might be destined only to bear the children of her brother?).

Tragedy entered their lives. For Athenais, giving birth to a daughter, is hailed Augusta; she demands that the imperial chamberlain serving Pulcheria be bestowed on her court. An ambitious eunuch, Chrysaphius, feeds the anger between the Empress in reality and the Empress in name, until Pulcheria abandons the palace, sending her chamberlain to the Greek. And Athenais refuses to acknowledge the Church. Defiant in her paganism, she cries to an assemblage of Greeks, with a verse of Homer: "I *boast* that I am of your blood and race!" (Fearless, yet foolish, Theodora thought.)

Now Chrysaphius feeds the rumors of the corridors. Athenais has lovers among the silentiaries. (Did she, in truth? Theodora speculated, and doubted it.) Athenais braves the whispers of misconduct, yet makes one small mistake. An apple given carelessly to a handsome officer she vows she has eaten herself. A trifle, that preys on the brooding Theodosius.

Athenais is cast out, to journey to Jerusalem as pilgrim, to tramp in her light sandals among the shrines that she disowned and still respected—her last act of life, to send to Pulcheria that precious painted relic, the Madonna of the Way. (And what did Pulcheria feel, when it came to her?) The wayward Theodosius dying from a fall from his horse— Pulcheria coming from her retreat to wed in middle age the soldier Marcian, to preserve the dynasty, and to behold the bloody end of her husband. Then the girl Ariadne, wedded to a victorious Isaurian, carrying on the task that had been Pulcheria's—through the chaos of strife with the German soldiers. Until, a widow in old age, she stills the conflict in the city by going before the people to name the silentiary Anastasius as emperor and her husband.

Such were the memories of the three noble women who had preserved the Empire by their will. They had refused to give up the reign. Considering them, Theodora believed that she, at least, could act out a part. She had done that in the theater. And she made a saying for herself: *One of us who wears the purple must never take it off.*

Henceforth with all her intensity Theodora watched that no whisper of misconduct should compromise her. She sealed within herself the secret of the daughter she had left in Egypt.

When the people of the Daphne had a rare hour of amusement, and Paul the Silentiary repeated clever epigrams in the garden theater, Theodora smiled appreciation while she listened for any quip that might be aimed at her. Discreet glances sought her out, to judge what the onetime mimic of the theater thought of the performance. They beheld the regal consort of the restless Justinian—a man who relished neither acting nor poetry.

Someone coined a title for the pallid girl with the tense mouth. It was a Greek word, *Despoina,* their Lady. It meant more than the cold traditional Domina, and Theodora welcomed it when she heard it. Because she understood Greek as well as the dialects of the eastern provinces, she picked up information never meant for her ears, and she startled her servants by asking gaily for more. She did not bother to read books. Apparently from the first she tried to gain the friendship of the older servants of the court, she listened sympathetically to the brittle Narses, a chamberlain of Justinian's. Being a eunuch taken captive in Persian Armenia, Narses had no close companions; being both sensitive and vain, he was grateful for the courteous attention of the Despoina. While she discovered that the silent Narses longed to be free of the palace and to command troops, Theodora gleaned tidings from him of her own homeland in the East. Because she avoided other men, Narses became devoted to her. And Theodora gained a servant who could warn her of danger in the outer halls of the Daphne.

In a different way, quite undiscoverable, she won the friendship of the noble-born wearers of the propoloma. Perhaps she led them to confide their troubles to her. Women have a way of banding together when faced by men in authority.

For all the ceremony surrounding her, Theodora's own authority ended at the threshold of the women's chambers. When she was summoned forth, as at the New Year reception or the Easter festival, she became the voiceless consort of the Autocrat. (Had not Pulcheria labored apart with her brother Theodosius; had not the dominant Ariadne appealed to the factions of the city to allow her to decide for them?) It did not seem possible that Theodora could change this situation, nor did she attempt to do so at first. The crisis of the Nika gave her the first opportunity.

Yet she could influence Justinian, who called her his "gift of God," who thought in terms of laws and human rights. Theodora had no respect for legal righteousness; she set herself to gain an end regardless of the means. Traces of her persuasion appear in Justinian's earliest edicts. . . . that a daughter may have an equal right with a son to inherit. . . . that a wife's dowry becomes her property again after the death of a husband. . . . that the child of a woman slave need not be a slave. . . . that brothel-keepers may be outlawed from the city, "for it is known to us that some people go about the districts offering shoes and new clothes to poor young girls, and in this way carry them off to hidden dens in this fortunate city, where they are shut up and given little food and clothes, while putting their bodies at the service of visiting men. These brothel-keepers have the girls sign bonds that bind them to this, while the keepers pocket the fees they get. Some of these men are unholy enough to pollute girls less than ten years of age. . . . we were secretly informed of this, and it is our determination to free the city from such pollution."

The formal wording evidences Justinian's sense of law. True, the girls signed a bond. Yet even if they were of age to do so— that is, more than fourteen years—it was illegal for another person to pocket the money they earned. Moreover, Justinian provided funds for buying the release of the inmates—about four dollars for each.

What Theodora hated she fought without scruple.

In a very different way, her personality wrought a change in the architecture of the palace. By now her treasurer controlled the income of great estates in Anatolia, given by Justinian to his wife. But Theodora held fast to her private possession, the isolated House of Hormisdas. This was now connected to the garden of the Daphne and to the women's chambers. Oddly enough, the small adjoining church—where she and Justinian must have gone to prayer—was rebuilt entire. Its shrine of Sergius and Bacchus, the two martyrs under the pagan emperors, was transformed by an architect of genius. It became a miniature dome of light above a simple altar. Its octagonal sides gave the illusion of merging into the bright dome overhead, and on the capital of every column appeared the initials of Justinian and his wife. Later on, an invocation to the martyrs stood over the pillars—that they might have in their keeping "the reign of the vigilant monarch, and increase the power of Theodora, divinely crowned."

By unusual chance this first shrine of the husband and wife has survived with their inscription for more than fourteen centuries. It became known as the little Hagia Sophia.

❦ RISING OF THE STORM

It is clear that neither of the two perceived the signs of danger within the city. For one thing, with John of Cappadocia installed as Praetorian in the year 531, Justinian had become intent on a venture beyond the seas.

Restless even in his hours of leisure, the man from the Balkan hills had formed the habit of walking alone through the

palace grounds. Here clustered the oldest churches and the
varied work places of his administration, with the Samson
hospital, and the Arsenal, reached by an underground passage
from the sprawling Daphne. Beneath the Arsenal lay the
laboratory of war, with the maps and secret records, and the
chemists who sought to improve on "the Greek's fire." Beneath the vaulted foundation of the Daphne, great stables
cared for the imperial horses. There was even a small hippodrome to exercise the horses. At the bottom of the garden
slope stretched the low sea wall, with the miniature harbors
filled with the scarlet rowing barges and swift sailing yachts of
the Emperor.

Justinian wanted other vessels than those. At that time
Constantinople possessed few of the long dromonds—the
fighting galleys that guarded the merchant fleets on their
way into the Dardanelles. For, beyond the Greek isles, the
Mediterranean had been lost to the barbarians. Nearly a
century had passed since the Vandals of Gaiseric had swept
over St. Augustine's city of Hippo and Carthage itself on the
African coast—on into the Tiber to ravage Rome and carry
off with them as a final indignity the insignia of empire and
the imperial princesses. In those years, from 430 to 455, when
Attila's Huns scorched the earth of Europe, Roman power
had ceased to be. Now Vandalic fleets cruised along the coasts
ruled by Gothic kings.

When he inspected a palace harbor, Justinian usually found
refugees from the outer sea squatting over dice with the crews
of his barges. Feeling themselves safe in the city, they thought
only of the fall of the dice. (Already Justinian had struck at
the lethargy of the street idlers, bidding his prefect of the city
make an end of gambling in the streets and of all public
games.)

As he paced his grounds like a commander of some fortified
post, mute voices appealed to him. At the far end above the
Golden Horn a gray column rose among the trees. A monu-

ment, he had been told, to some emperor, victor over the Goths. But which Caesar? Valens had died under the swords of the Goths near Hadrian's City; the strange Julian had marched into oblivion in the deserts beyond the Euphrates; Valerian had died a captive of the Persians.

Then at the near end beneath Theodora's chambers stood the ancient *pharos*. This light tower had once been a beacon for ships coming in from the great Middle Sea. Now that so few came, it served as a signal tower to flash messages to the Asiatic shore, using mirrors by day and fire by night.

It is not strange that Justinian brooded over the lost sea of the West. Yet out of his brooding came the thought to return to it with a fleet bearing an army that might wrest back Africa from the barbarians. He told the Council of his plan, and his officers had no praise for it. Listening to them— as Augustine phrased it—"with the ears of his mind, not of his body," he knew they saw no hope in it. The last ships of Constantinople to be sent toward Africa had been trapped by the Vandals and burned by fire vessels.

Afterwards John of Cappadocia sought him out alone. "Thrice August," the big Praetorian grumbled, "you are willing to listen to us and at times you follow advice we give. When we speak against your mind, anger does not bite you. Now, may I tell in plain words what I think of this?"

John dismissed the expedition to Africa as an excellent plan, nothing more. They had not the means to carry it out. Their military forces were strained to hold the land frontiers, and new taxes were needed to pay the soldiers already under arms. The people's parties would not make such an effort. And if the city turned against Justinian, that would be the end of the new Imperator.

"And if I had the means?" asked Justinian.

The man of Cappadocia stretched forth grasping fingers. "Have you dragon's teeth to sow? Well, then, summon up

The Hagia Sophia, built during the reign of Justinian, as it appears today. The structures in the foreground were added after the Moslem conquest of Constantinople.

Interior of the Hagia Sophia, as it appears today.

twenty thousand swordsmen." One finger after another he held up. "Promise them loot, instead of pay. Put them on ships, if you can find ships. Can they win their way past Vandalic battle fleets? Let a miracle destroy the Vandals! What follows? Caesar, can your army master and hold a continent? Let Saint Michael aid the commanders to victory! How long will they be content to serve you for pittance pay, if they hold the African coast with the treasures of Rome and Jerusalem?"

Justinian admitted that his peasant-born Praetorian spoke the truth. No dream of victory could prevail over the hard realities of warfare.

Then the monks came in from the desert of Tripoli, having walked all the way to the Bosporus ferry. Hairy, sun-darkened skeletons, they refused to partake of food before they faced Justinian and Theodora in the gleaming Magnaura hall. Arrogantly they shouted at the Christian Emperor. Did he serve the earthly gods, instead of God? Did he take no thought for the Christians abandoned in Africa?

Justinian showed no anger at the clamor of the monks. Theodora—who had wandered within sight of the red waste of Libya—thanked them for coming. Their plea worked upon his indecision. Beyond the reasoning of policy, what was God's will in this matter?

Were there not orthodox Christian families surviving in Leptis Magna, the port of Tripolitana, and in Carthage itself? They waited in their darkness for some word from the Emperor secure in his city of Constantinople. Beyond the sandy waste of the Syrtes they waited, and surely they would aid a ship that found its way to them.

In that year the kaleidoscope of the land frontiers shifted into a brighter pattern. In the north, the army of the Danube under the barbarian-born Mundus forged its way westward, to sight the Adriatic. Eastward, couriers brought report of a

victory by the resourceful Belisarius, and a rumor that the
aged Persian Great King, Kavadh, was at last near death.
These tidings gave satisfaction to the War Office and relief to
the Council, but to Justinian they offered new hope for his
venture into the West.

At once he acted. He summoned both Belisarius and Mundus to Constantinople with their personal troops. He dispatched his most skilled negotiators, Hermogenes and
Rufinus, eastward across the Euxine by swift galley. There,
Tzitas, commanding in the Caucasus, was to take Belisarius'
place, and there Hermogenes was to contrive a lasting peace
at any price in gold with the failing Persian despot—who
would be inclined to peace in his last years.

What Justinian did was to call his most dependable armed
forces back to the city, while he trusted that peace would keep
the Persian frontier quiet. When he ordered the naval
arsenal reopened to build new transport vessels, the news went
through all the city. This could mean only one thing, war in
the West. And only one person, Justinian, demanded it.

The people of the sheltered city did not want it.

The rumors from the waterfront met with grievances elsewhere. In the Amastrian forum hung the bodies of criminals
who had been partisans of the Blue faction and the Green as
well; when the harvest festival brought crowds hopefully out
to the Hebdomon park, no free wine awaited them. By order
of Justinian. No silver coins were distributed from the Steps
on the eve of the Nativity. On the other hand, the Street of
the Bakers paid a new tax on bread. The ruthless Praetorian
Prefect taxed the bread in people's mouths!

Then came a riot that killed some harmless watchers. The
City Prefect arrested seven leaders of the tumult, and condemned them to be hanged. It was done under guard, but not
precisely as the Prefect planned. Two of the condemned broke
their ropes and fell to the ground. Aided by the spectators,

the pair escaped to sanctuary at the altar of St. Lawrence near
the gate of the Blachernae Virgin. Their preservation had
something miraculous about it; moreover, one proved to be a
Green partisan, the other a Blue.

So at the ides of January 532 the people thronged to the
hippodrome with grievances to relate. That year Justinian
had appointed no consul to entertain the city as custom
ordained. He acted as consul himself, and he announced that
the games would be no more than a week of racing.

✿ REVOLT IN THE CIRCUS

A north wind chilled the city Tuesday morning. The
crowds pressing down the Mesé toward the hippodrome wore
cloaks and carried their own refreshments. On this first day
of the races there would be a debate between the Emperor
and the democracies of the streets, the people of the demes.

Most of the groups gathered in the forum of Constantine,
a popular rendezvous. Delegations of farming folk from the
outlying towns followed their priests. The hard year had
brought disturbance as far distant as Tarsus and Antioch.
The priests acted as spokesmen for their congregations, as
rhetors acted for the city districts.

Down the Mesé on the left the Street of the Silversmiths
had its shutters up, its doors barred. The basilica of the
lawsuits was closed, and soldier-police stood around the
Praetorium, headquarters of the City Prefect. Distant from
the throngs, the wide Strategium—with its drill ground and
barracks of the army—was occupied by certain regiments which
had arrived a little while before from the frontiers. These
troops, being mostly of barbarian stock and poorly paid, had
no kindly feeling for the prospering citizens, and had been,

accordingly, confined to quarters by order of their commanders, Mundus and Belisarius. They were, however, to play an important part in the happenings of the next days.

At the end of the avenue on the right, the Baths of Zeuxippus stood open beneath the outer wall of the hippodrome. Here waited the demarchs of the two great democracies, the Blue and the Green. No one lingered in the steam rooms that morning; men clustered in portico and lounge, sipping wine and munching nuts while they debated quietly.

For the two parties were much more than racing factions. Originally they had been city militia. Each faction had its section of the mighty Theodosian wall to man at need; each must supply crews for emergency naval craft. There having been no such call upon their services for the last years, both factions had reverted to their civilian characteristics as militiamen have always done. Artisans and merchants filled the ranks of the Greens, while farmers and landowners wore the Blue color. So the first formed, as it were, the faction of the city, the second that of the outer country. As in our day, the politicians of the streets tended to be radicals, while those of the agricultural areas remained conservatives. All being deeply religious, the Blues on the whole supported the Orthodox Church while the Greens inclined toward evangelical or rebellious faiths. It is not true that one faction represented only the rich, the other the poor—the *potentiores* and *humiliores* of the older Rome.

Just then the Green democracy complained of poverty because, favored—they said—by Justinian, the Blue partisans had driven their wage-earners from the streets to take refuge in the countryside. Actually Justinian's iron hand had been laid on the leaders of both parties. But that morning all thoughts were on the two culprits, one Blue and one Green, penned in the sanctuary of the St. Lawrence Church by the spearmen of the City Prefect.

Among the faction leaders percolated many agents who

were strangers to the city. They served as the eyes and ears and sometimes the voices of the real *potentiores*, the magnates. Some of these had senatorial rank, but all, being possessors of wealth, ruled vast estates; they were miniature monarchs with armed retainers to enforce their orders and attentive judges to shape laws to their will. The magnates had been too powerful to tax, yet under the whip of John, the oaf of Cappadocia, they had been assessed and bidden to pay land-tax and person-tax. This, to their minds, was a change for the worse from the benevolent reign of Anastasius of glorious memory. Was it not needful, then, to restore those happier conditions? Three nephews survived Anastasius, and surely they had a stronger claim to the throne than the obdurate Macedonian, Justinian, who seemed to be intent on founding a Justinian dynasty, if not a dictatorship.

Through the portico of Zeuxippus wandered a silent figure from the palace. The eunuch Narses had little to say. With his Oriental sensitivity, he caught the mood of the throng now pushing into the marble tiers of the hippodrome.

Squarely across the circus arena ran the invisible line that separated the Autocrat of the palace from the people who had elected him. He had his own entrance. It led from the guarded Daphne through the small Ivory Gate, up a spiral stair into the chapel of St. Stephen and the retiring rooms of the Kathisma. A roof sheltered this gallery where Justinian took his seat on the throne-chair behind a low rail. His attendants occupied recesses on either side. Out from him and beneath him extended the Stama, the terrace where Excubitors kept their post. Beneath all this lay the stables and handling chambers of the racers, men and beasts. So the Kathisma almost filled the northeast end of the arena. It was isolated from the stands, behind guarded doors.

By tradition, the Blue party occupied the stand on Justinian's right. This was the favored, shady side. The Greens had their place on the left.

At Justinian's appearance the throngs greeted him with the usual acclamation: "Long life to the Thrice August!" Some voices added with enthusiasm: "Justinian—you will conquer."

He was still favored by the populace. At that moment the dislike of the spectators lay upon the City Prefect, Eudaemon.

When the chariots broke away from the starting point, the crowd strained to see the first turn of the Spina. The familiar intoxication of the race gripped it.

A mass of men packed the promenade that circled the stands above the last tier. They clutched their talismans and shouted their prayers as the distant chariots completed the laps and the gilt balls dropped on the indicators at the Spina ends. Immobile above this promenade, figures in brass and stone gazed over the city—a crouching Hercules, a fishlike monster devouring the seamen of Ulysses, a Sphynx from an eastern temple. These symbols of power, so unlike the ancient gods of the Tiber, had been brought hither by Constantine and the other emperors. Among them stood a memorial of the first Augustus: the statue of the peasant with his ass who had provided an omen before the battle of Actium. Questioned by Caesar's sentries, the peasant had answered that his name was Victor, and his ass was Victoria, and he wanted to go to Caesar.

When the last balls fell on the indicators, the winning chariot swerved and plunged to a halt. After the shout of triumph another call came from the crowd.

"Thrice August—may you reign forever! Release the two who were hanged!"

After each race the shout went up, more insistent. "Thrice August, set free the twain who were condemned by your prefect and yet spared by God!"

No answer came from the Kathisma. Justinian, unwilling to revoke the judgment of his prefect, gave no visible attention to the crowd.

After the last race there was no immediate stir of departure. Through the murmur of talk came a clear shout: "Long live the wretched Green-Blues!"

This meant that the factions were joining together. The multitude moved down into the streets, toward the Praetorium, demanding that the police cordon be taken from the sanctuary of St. Lawrence. Gaining no satisfaction, the crowd caught up firebrands and rushed the building, killing the soldiers who blocked their way.

There is a time when a marching crowd can be reasoned with. When that time passes, the crowd becomes a mob driven by its own impetus to destroy any obstacle in its way. By nightfall the mob held the half-burned Praetorium, snatching up weapons and releasing all the prisoners in the cells beneath the building. Pouring into the Augusteum, another crowd swung carts filled with blazing straw against the closed Chalké Gate. This caught fire.

The fitful wind whipped the fire to the portico of the Senate house, which blazed up in turn. Burning embers fell on the dry timber roof of the Hagia Sophia. Through the night the great church burned.

The next morning, Wednesday, Justinian ordered the races to go on. If he hoped to quiet the aroused multitude, he was mistaken. The crowd no longer desired to watch races. Instead, the demarchs of the parties demanded that he rid himself of the ministers who oppressed the people. By name they called for the dismissal of Eudaemon and John of Cappadocia, and of Tribonian, who had made the new laws.

Leaving the gallery, Justinian called leading senators into conference with his Council. Watchers on the Daphne roof reported that families were hurrying out of the city by the wooden bridge over the harbor entrance and by boat to the Asia shore. His advisers pressed him to appoint new ministers, popular patricians. By then most of the senate and high officials had left the streets for the protection of the palace grounds. After long hesitation, Justinian agreed with them.

"The government," an observer related, "acted like a tyranny, but not like a strong tyranny."

Headed by the military commander Mundus, envoys went out to announce the dismissal of the Prefect and the ministers. They found the demarchs holding a mass meeting up in the forum of Constantine. Here the assembled people heard that the Emperor had met their demands. The crowd chanted a hymn of thanksgiving on learning that Phocus, a patrician of integrity, was the new praetorian. (If Justinian had done as much at the hippodrome that afternoon, disaster might have been averted.) Having heard, the democracies of the streets delayed answering. Mundus and his companions went back to report only their misgivings.

Then Justinian made a second mistake. Announcers went forth to all the districts, crying that quiet would be maintained and the games resumed the next day. This might have calmed the multitude the day before. Now the agents of hostile senators were at work urging the factions to make a *tabula rasa* of the question. The real need of the city, the agents pointed out, was to have another ruler. Otherwise Justinian might change his mind—as he was wont to do—the next day. Having gone so far, was it safe for the populace to draw back now?

The pressure of the magnates who knew their own minds won over the popular groups. The delegations from the outer villages had no clear idea of what was happening. The crowds kept the streets, and messengers sped from one to the other giving commands—to search for weapons, to gather along the Mesé. The watchword of the night would be *Nika*—Victory.

Leaders made their way to the southern waterfront, seeking for Probus, a nephew of Anastasius. Probus, who had often opposed Justinian, would be a fitting candidate for the purple. They discovered that Probus—wisely—had departed from the city, and in unreasoning anger they burned his house. Then they stormed the arsenals that stored weapons for the defense of the city.

In his colonnade by the statue of Daphne, loyal silentiaries sought Justinian to whisper warnings. Within the outer barracks the Guards huddled about their officers, debating what they should do. Many of the senators, submissive to the Emperor's face, discussed their own profit behind his back. Narses, coming like a shadow out of a dark corridor, related that arms were appearing in the streets. Smoke from the ruins of the great church increased the obscurity of the night. The invisible line of demarcation between the palace and the city had become a battle front. The consequences were unpredictable.

While Justinian preserved his usual quiet, he was tormented by indecision. He had counted on keeping control of the people, and he was suffering now from his own faulty leadership. Justin would have used force before now, at no matter what cost in lives.

Reluctantly Justinian ordered the veteran *numeri* quartered in the Strategium to be marched into the palace grounds. At early dawn Mundus and Belisarius led in their regular troops, no more than 1,400 in number.

That day Theodora left her women's chambers to join her husband. Better than Justinian she realized that their throne was at stake.

❀ BELISARIUS OBEYS ORDERS

For the next three days the palace was besieged. Obscurity covered the forces of the democracies in the outer streets, while rumors added to the uncertainty of those within the palace. Only Belisarius, fresh from warfare in the eastern mountains, appeared undisturbed by the fighting and the conflagration outside. Always careful of his dress, the Dalmatian-born Master of Soldiers buckled a bright red cloak over his wide shoulders, over the green tunic embroidered with golden eagles. When he donned battle mail to lead his troops, the links had the gleam of silver.

His followers were no ordinary regiment; they were *bucellarii*—biscuit-eaters—hired to his personal service. Being Goths, they took their oath of loyalty to him seriously. They wore the full mail of cataphracts—having left their horses in the barracks perforce—and kept their small powerful bows. In the same way Mundus led a force of Heruls, bearing ax and sword, kinsmen of the Huns who had been their enemies.

When Justinian ordered Belisarius to drive back the armed crowds, a battle seems to have taken place in the Augusteum square. New fires started, spreading beyond the blackened skeleton of the Hagia Sophia, to the Samson hospital, where the mental patients raged like trapped beasts. It spread to the oldest of the churches, St. Eirene.

The veterans of the frontiers managed to clear the rebels from the scarred grounds of the palace. But they fared badly the next day when Justinian bade them bring the Middle Way under control. Streets were barricaded against them, houses were defended, and women hurled stone blocks from the roofs. Around a corner, the crowds rallied against them from the massive Octagon building. When the soldiers in their turn took to firebrands to burn down the buildings, the vicious wind carried the flames to the splendid House of Lamps. Across the avenue, the Baths of Zeuxippus burned, with the portico of the Augusteum itself. Heat from the con-flagration penetrated the great Daphne palace, where the Guards who would take no part in the civil conflict fought back the flames.

Worse befell when the priests of the ruined Hagia Sophia went out in procession, holding high their crosses and treasured icons. They chanted as they went out, hoping to make the fighters lay down their arms. By ill chance the priests came among ranks of the pagan Heruls, who fancied that a new kind of attack was being made on them by such bearded exorcists. The Heruls beat back the marchers. By the Vespers hour on Saturday, Belisarius and Mundus admitted failure and led back their contingents. Their strength was not enough to clear the swarming thousands from the streets.

Having used force and failed, Justinian took the responsibility upon himself. Little time remained to him. The supply of food in the palace could no longer serve the throng pent up in it. Saturday night Justinian sent out the coterie of senators and nobles whose loyalty he doubted. Most of them were glad to be dismissed, but two nephews of Anastasius begged to be allowed to stay with him. It was no longer possible for his tiring mind to decide if he could trust them.

Sunday morning he did as he had once seen Anastasius do. He sent messengers to the streets to announce the hour in which he would face his people in the hippodrome. When the time came, he picked up an illuminated manuscript of the Gospels and walked out the private way in full robes of audience.

The curtains were drawn back as he stepped to the Kathisma rail. From his guards he beckoned the mandator to repeat his words to the multitude, silent at sight of him. The announcer lifted his voice:

"Justinian, Imperator and Augustus . . . promises full mercy for all that has happened. No one . . . will be held guilty or harmed . . . for what he has done . . . these last days."

There was a murmur at that, of surprise or satisfaction. Raising the heavy book in his hands, Justinian cried out: "I alone am guilty. This I swear . . . upon these holy Evangels."

The murmur grew to a roar of argument. Rhetors and leaders exhorted the contingents around them. In the crowd,

however, waited agents of those who planned the downfall
of Justinian and Theodora; halfway measures did not suit
them. Some feared retribution for the bloodshed; others were
too angered to heed any words.

A single shrill voice cut through the uproar. "Ass! You are
lying!"

Agreement came in shouts. "How will you keep your word,
Justinian? Once you pledged peace to Vitalian. Where is
Vitalian now? So, then, you swore on the Evangels!"

The thousands were on their feet, roaring at him. Justinian
had lost his appeal to the people. Lowering the book, he left
the Kathisma. But the listeners sensed a turn in the conflict,
and word sped back to the forum of Constantine—"Victory."

To all appearances the rebel forces had won the city. Where
the leaders held council beneath the giant statue of Constantine,
they could see the burned area stretching to the palace
itself. To strengthen them, new contingents of armed retainers marched in from the estates of the magnates. To
counsel them a score of senators hostile to Justinian and
Theodora came forward, urging on the revolt. Some of these
had left the palace only a few hours before, and they knew
the weakness of Justinian's forces, the refusal of the Guards
to defend him. Most of the senators spoke for an immediate
attack on the Daphne. Only one, Origen, advised holding
their ground and waiting. He was sure that Justinian and
Theodora would try to escape by sea—and give up Constantinople without further fighting.

The crowd looked to its leaders for advice. The citizen
factions were awed by the blackened ruin of the main streets.
Several hundred of the Green party moved off to force their
way into the Daphne, while the senators and leaders sought
for a man to succeed Justinian. Their choice was Hypatius,
the eldest nephew of Anastasius, who had once been captive
to Vitalian. Hypatius, a middle-aged veteran of the Persian

war, was well-meaning and weak. On leaving the palace he had retired to his house.

"They declared Hypatius emperor," an observer explained, "and prepared to lead him to the market street [the Mesé] to bestow the power on him. But his wife, Mary, a knowing woman, caught hold of her husband and would not let him go. She cried aloud to her kinsmen that they were leading Hypatius to his death. But the people pulled her away from him. They bore him along against his will to the forum of Constantine. Because they had no diadem with which to crown him, they put a gold chain on his head and proclaimed him Emperor of the Romans."

Within an hour Hypatius stood in the Kathisma. Someone had found a purple mantle for him. Throngs poured into the hippodrome to shout his name and to hear his coronation speech. Behind him the guards of the Kathisma waited on events. Hypatius himself, impressed by sight of the power rallying to him, became excited. He seemed to feel that the conflict was over.

Then happened one of those odd chances that alter destiny. Hypatius called for a palace messenger, and to one named Ephraim he gave a message for Justinian. What he actually said remains unknown, but it might have been a warning. The important thing is what Ephraim did.

Running to the palace entrance, he collided with an imperial secretary hurrying out. The secretary exclaimed that Ephraim would not find Justinian, who had left the palace with Theodora to flee in a ship. Being human, Ephraim merely gave his message to the other, and hastened back to the Kathisma, eager to be the first to bring the new Emperor tidings of his victory. The rumor of Justinian's flight reached the multitude. Like a chant the cry of *Nika* rose in the arena.

Thomas, the secretary, may have snatched at the chance to betray his emperor, or he may have sighted the transport ship mooring at the Daphne harbor and the chests being carried out of the private treasury. Most of the corridors were deserted.

In the Delphax hall Narses stuck to Justinian like his shadow. Few others held to their loyalty—unless they knew their lives to be forfeit. John of Cappadocia said he would prefer to sail from the Bosporus than be thrown into it. Who first urged the flight to Heraclea with the gold treasure is not clear, but Belisarius spoke for it. His troops could cover the embarkation. He was weary, smoke grimed, restless in this strange warfare of the corridors and streets. More than weary, Justinian sat in silence, unable to decide. Into their hall came the echo from the hippodrome: *Nika.*

Then against all tradition Theodora spoke in the council of the men. She stood to face Justinian.

"Caesar, you can leave without any trouble. The sea is there. The ships are ready, and you have money enough. But if you leave, will you never ask yourself in exile: 'What if I had stayed?' I shall stay. I believe that those who put on the imperial purple must never put it off. The day that they cease to call me Augusta I hope I shall not be living."

Their heads turned toward the slight woman, and they listened. Theodora smiled at them with an odd gaiety: "I like the old saying that purple makes the finest shroud."

No one tried to make Theodora change her mind. The fact that she would stay brought the need to defend her. Of them all, probably only the woman felt hatred of the clamoring populace and the nobles who had deserted them.

If they were not to take to the ships, not a moment could be wasted. Swiftly Justinian agreed with his two commanders that Mundus and the Heruls would defend the Augusteum gate while Belisarius brought his cataphracts into the Daphne, leading them through the corridors to force a way into the Kathisma to seize the leaders of the revolt.

It was not to Belisarius' liking, this crowding between narrow walls. With Narses guiding him, he led his following out to the Ivory Gate and found it closed and barred. The Guards on his side remained motionless at their posts. On the far side no one answered his shouted commands. Bedeviled by this silent barrier, the big Dalmatian forced a passage back through his men to tell Justinian the attack could not be made.

"If you can't get through," Justinian ordered, "go around." He never forgot or forgave the silent resistance of the palace Guards at his door.

❀ THE IRON CAVALRY ENTERS THE CIRCUS

Perhaps it was Theodora who sent the anxious Narses to prepare the way for Belisarius, but Justinian must have given him the gold. With a small treasure in his girdle, Narses slipped out to the blackened halls of the baths, to the leaders of the Blue faction. Adding prophecies and warnings to his gifts of gold, the eunuch asked each man what he would gain from the rule of the rabble in the streets. Those who heard him began to ponder the question.

Following swiftly, Belisarius led his cataphracts around through the burned Augusteum and the baths. He had to lead them, because the bodies that glistened in iron, moving shoulder to shoulder behind him, belonged to Goths accustomed to obey no one except their chieftain in battle. With sheathed weapons they crossed the burned area and entered the hippodrome by the portico of the Blues. Because Narses had been there, no one opposed them. But when Belisarius climbed the stair to the north entrance of the Kathisma he found this door, also, closed to him. The Excubitors posted here and in the Stama were not inclined to yield up Hypatius and the leaders of the revolt. Belisarius failed for the second time to seize the Kathisma.

Then chance intervened. The crowd beneath sighted the soldiers pressing into the stands. Poorly armed but wildly excited masses surged up against the gray ranks of the "iron cavalry." Caught between the Kathisma guards and the thousands below, Belisarius acted instinctively, calling for weapons to be drawn and the ranks to face the assailants in their rear. Outnumbered and scarred by the street fighting of the last days, the soldiers drove back the human packs savagely. Partisans and armed retainers could not face methodical flights of arrows and flashing javelins.

Hearing the uproar within the stands, Mundus and the Heruls forced their way in through the gate on the far side. This was the *Nekra*, the Gate of Death, by which the bodies of gladiators had been dragged out in earlier years. Wielding short hacking swords, the powerful Heruls swept into the arena. Narses appeared with the small contingent of *Spatharii*, the picked swordsmen of the palace.

There was no one to take command against them. The multitude of thousands fell into wild disorder before the advance of the trained soldiers.

By the end of that Sunday afternoon, the revolt was over. The Excubitors, seeing where victory lay, opened the doors of the Kathisma. A master of offices—taking the place of Hermogenes absent in Persia—came in to arrest the stunned Hypatius and his brother Pompey. The streets emptied as word of the slaughter in the hippodrome spread through the districts. Rumor related that thirty thousand had died there; in truth, some thousands had been killed.

Someone heard the prisoner Hypatius say to his brother: "Do not weep for them—they deserved what befell them."

Taken before Justinian, Hypatius argued that he had kept the mob in the hippodrome from attacking the palace. Justinian replied: "You did not hold them back from burning the city." The eldest nephew of Anastasius still wore the gold chain, forgotten, on his head, the purple chlamys on his shoulders. Many persons heard Justinian order the two brothers to be imprisoned beneath the palace that night. Some maintain that the Emperor would have spared them, but that Theodora demanded their death. Others believe that soldiers entered the prison the next day and put them to death. Certainly, the body of Hypatius floated ashore, to be gathered up and sent to his grieving wife.

As with Vitalian, Justinian must have held the lives of Hypatius and Pompey to be forfeit. Yet he did not reach that decision too easily. Soon afterwards evidence against the third brother, Phobus, was laid before him. After reading it through Justinian tore up the papyri sheets and exclaimed: "I find no guilt in him. Let him pray God that he is guiltless."

A Diocletian or a Theodosius would not have let the third brother live. A Constantine would have carried out a blood purge of all leaders of the rebellion. Justinian did condemn the secretary Thomas who had spread the false rumor of his flight from the palace. With Thomas died the instigators who had roused the factions to arms.

The survivors waited in their houses for the proclamation of city-wide arrest. It did not come. Troops from Thrace and Asia entered the gates, led by loyal officers, among them the youthful Germanus. They were set to work to clear the debris from the streets and to set up field hospitals in the forums, while fresh food was furnished at the Steps. After a few days, fugitive families returned to the crippled city.

Something unexpected had come into the mind of the wearied Emperor. Each day he walked through the burned area that had been the heart of Constantinople, while the bodies of the slain were carried from the familiar gates of the hippodrome. The vagaries of the north wind had carried the fire from the Octagon quarter down the winding, porticoed streets of the merchants to the harbor. The black scar of it stretched from Justinian's living quarters to the docks, where only the water craft survived.

In Justinian's mind he himself had been the cause of the disaster. He had been the *Imperator plebis* and he had failed his people in this first crisis of his reign. "The guilt is mine alone," he had told the democracies gathered in the hippodrome. Now thousands of those who had listened to him had been slain at his order by the weapons of hired Heruls and Goths. So, when he had the power to order general punishment, he carried out instead the promise he had made from the Kathisma. He granted a general amnesty to the rebellious factions. He never put to death another political offender.

"He restored to the children of Hypatius and Pompey all the titles held by their fathers, and much of their confiscated property," testified a witness who hated him.

More than that, Justinian soon revoked his own sentence against the senators who had joined the revolt. Eighteen of them who had been exiled were allowed to return to their homes near the Church of the Apostles. The senate itself, however, suffered a change. After the blood and fire of the Nika week, it never regained its age-old prestige. The ancient letters S.P.Q.R.—*Senatus populusque Romani*—ceased to have meaning. The Macedonian who had been obliged by tradition to consult with it now went his way alone.

That way led him back to the people. He had realized that the core of his dominion lay in them—the unthinking masses avid of holidays, games, and food. Yet to meet their desires, to favor them as a benevolent despot, would breed sickness in them. Only as a judge could Justinian reveal the pity he felt.

After that terrible Sunday, he ordered the nepenthe of the races to be done away with for an indefinite time. The hippodrome itself was closed to the popular meetings. Probably Justinian had no realization that in acting so he was putting an end to two great institutions of the earlier city-state—the Roman senate and the Greek areopagus. Yet very quickly the hostile witness saw the significance of his actions. "He kept tearing down existing institutions," Procopius observed, "as if he meant to change all things into another form."

In fact Justinian was becoming a solitary ruler, an autocrat, facing a single people. He felt his immense responsibility to them, but how would he conduct himself toward them?

Very soon he attempted to give the populace officials of its own. "Defenders of the City" were to decide all small lawsuits of the neighborhood variety involving less than 300 numismata. And the bishops of the congregations could intervene for their folk. (Thus the smaller personal claims were taken out of the hands of bribable judges and persons of influence.) A praetor of the demes would watch the streets for thieves, extortioners, and traders in the occult.

At one stroke Justinian did away with spies. There would be no more pay for the army of *agentes in rebus* which had served the emperors since Diocletian's day.

Then there was the influx of throngs from the country seeking food or wealth within the charmed gates of Constantinople. The authority of the new Praetor would turn away all migrants who did not have a family to visit, work to do, or business to transact within the walls. Those who did have such cause for entering would be aided in carrying it out, and returned quickly to their homes.

Within the city itself, Justinian would have no more marching of militia to music, no more beggars or drifters among the charities. A man on the streets must have work to do— and there would be work aplenty in rebuilding the city.

For in his imagination Justinian beheld his city arising in new splendor from the ruins. It would be more than a refuge or a market place; it would be in every aspect the ruling center of the world.

IV
VOYAGE INTO THE WEST

THEODORA GOES TO BITHYNIA

A T DAWN of Good Friday in the next year, A.D. 533, criers went through the districts shouting: "Old derelicts—go back to your home. Go flying!" They shouted in the Greek *koiné*, the popular dialect the derelicts would understand.

Close to what was left of the Samson hospital stood the scorched brick walls of a hostel for the aged homeless. Custom ordained that in the morning of Good Friday, before the hours of the Passion, the ruler of Constantinople would walk like any ordinary citizen to this hostel and there make his gifts to the inmates. Since their hostel had burned down, the old people, who had holed up elsewhere, could not decide whether the Emperor would appear to make his gifts. After the criers summoned them, they scurried and helped each other back through the streets. Plenty of beggars from the Amastris joined them.

They sighted the gleam of the Excubitors' silvered axes, and, standing in the empty archway of their hostel, the tall shimmering figure that could only be Caesar himself. And, surely curators of the Private Purse waited behind him with heavy sacks in their hands. Silent cubiculars had brought an ivory chair for him, but he stood on his feet patiently waiting.

Each of the aged homeless came forward to kneel and adore the enameled images of saints on his broad girdle. To each he gave a small handful of silver coins. Nodding his grizzled head he said: "I leave my gift—even if there is no altar."

The words were vaguely familiar. Naturally enough, after counting their coins, most of the aged folk perched on the brick piles to rest themselves and enjoy the spectacle. Toward the hour of noon the Emperor prepared to leave because the ruins of the great church had been torn down, and he had to walk to the Church of the Apostles, by the mausoleum of the blessed Constantine. Before he did so he spoke to a chamberlain, who said: "This hostel will be rebuilt by the day of All the Saints."

As he passed through them, the Emperor himself said in labored Greek: "It will have larger rooms. The sun will shine in them. That is the wish of the Most Pious Augusta."

Justinian understood how to start the street-dwellers talking of better things to come.

These were hard months in the city. The rigor of his rule and the catastrophe of the Nika had done away with the popular concept of Justinian as the Caesar from the streets. In much the same way Theodora had lost the glamour of the theater girl turned princess. She acquired a very different personality.

That last Sunday of the Nika she had risked everything, including her life, for empire. In so doing she had probably

saved Justinian's throne for him. Seemingly he could erase
the thought of his enemies from his mind, but Theodora did
nothing of the kind. Henceforth she *would* be the wearer of
the purple; ever after, she distrusted the throngs of their city.
Against any whisper of conspiracy she mobilized the forces of
her defense, and they were becoming formidable.

For one thing she found spies to serve her throughout the
quarters of the city. Where her attendant women and eunuchs went out to the markets, they picked up messages
left for the Despoina by visitors, merchants, and especially by
pilgrims from the East. After the Nika revolt she made a gift
of her House of Hormisdas to shelterless monks; it became
known as the House of the Monks. There they could attend
the offices at the small Sergius and Bacchus Church, but they
could also visit the women's chambers, which Theodora was
turning into a veritable court of her own. Many wanderers
brought tidings from Antioch, beloved by Theodora. In exchange for their news, they could count on aid from the
Despoina. One arrived, unnoticed, in a patchwork robe that
won him the name of Jacob Old Clothes. He had in him
a power not revealed as yet.

Rumor had it that the slim Augusta could influence Justinian to her will, and she made no denial of it. Because of that,
envoys from foreign parts took care to offer a gift to the
chamberlain of Theodora's hall as well as to the Referendarius
of the Daphne. Theodora had a way of keeping visitors waiting—if they happened to be men—until she could discover
what they wanted of her.

They said she pampered herself, lying late in bed (while
Justinian would be reading his reports at sunup). Over bath
and toilet she would spend more hours while she listened to
the gossip of her women. There was a new, hard brilliance in
her. To the public gaze she appeared always graceful, in pastel
shades of blue merging with the imperial purple. On her head
the light of sapphires matched the shimmer of pearl chains.

For Theodora knew very well how to hold the center of a stage. Now her servants bade visitors prostrate themselves to kiss her slipper, rather than kneel to adore the purple.

To such submission Theodora had no shadow of right. She was no more than Caesar's wife. The constitution gave her no share in the throne; her name never appeared on the coinage as co-ruler. This parvenu Despoina possessed authority only over her own estates, known as the House of the Augusta. From these estates her curator gleaned a yearly income of some 50 pounds of gold—more than enough for her needs, less than her desires. Otherwise, she had to influence her husband to do things for her. Theodora had learned by experience how far she could go with him. On his part, the silent Macedonian probably understood the vagaries of his prostitute-bride more than other people realized.

After the Nika, Theodora made a remarkable excursion through the Asiatic shore land.

This lovely bank of the Bosporus had appealed to the city folk ever since the first Byzantium. No factories scarred this shore of fishing villages and palatial homes. Across from the entrance to the Golden Horn sprawled tranquil Chrysopolis, the City of Gold. Justinian seldom ventured across the water to this garden suburb. Confining himself to the palace by inclination as well as tradition, he was intent on rebuilding Constantinople itself. In fact, he tried to give the population a seaside retreat close to the Porta Aurea.

"As you sail in from the Propontis [the Marmora]," said Procopius, "there is a public bathing place on the left. There the Emperor made a park always open to those who wish to rest, or those who anchor as they sail by. Sunrise floods it with light, and evening fills it with pleasant shade. The sea flows quietly around this court, like a river. The park itself gleams with white marble colonnades. There also stands the Empress Theodora, upon a column. This statue is beautiful indeed, but still inferior to her loveliness. It is made of pur-

ple stone. Even when seen from far off, it manifests that this
is an empress."

Having closed the hippodrome and gaming places, Justinian offered his people a place of rest in their new hard labor.
Theodora, however, turned to the Asiatic shore, apart from
the city. There she purchased a run-down summer palace and
made it over as a refuge for the prostitutes who earned three
obols a night by haunting the arcades of the Nymphaeum.
Within this House of Repentance food was offered, and the
girls could earn their obols at drawlooms or embroidery. Often
by devious means of her own, the Despoina sent them would-
be husbands. Still, some Constantinopolitans dubbed the
women's estate the Prison of Repentance.

So she traveled over familiar ground when she entered the
Bithynian shore in splendor while the wounds of the Nika
were still raw. Deliberately she made a spectacle of her guards
and curators, her cortege of noblewomen, and herself in a
shining carriage shaded by billowing silk. With her came
physicians to attend the wounded, and that great preacher
John of Tella to proclaim that she would give aid to shrines
and monasteries.

Knowing her country people—from the boys spreading
fresh fish over ferns in the stalls to the aproned blacksmiths
who filled their doors to goggle at her—Theodora made quite
a scene of her passing. She bathed in the warm sulphur
springs and climbed to the snow summit of hoary Mount
Olympus, named by forgotten Greeks after their own Olympus. She left behind her an impression of the power of the
throne that had been threatened so recently. And she prepared the way for a flight, in her own time and manner, to
the Bithynian shore.

For Theodora no longer trusted the city upon which
Justinian centered all his labor. Against its patricians—those
who had sought their own fortunes in the revolt—she leveled
her spite. Those who opposed her were treated with impish

mockery. One named Timothaeus made the mistake of seeking justice from her. He did so because he could not collect some money owed him under bond by several of her followers. Timothaeus was not only an elderly patrician, but also an official of long service, quite sure of his legal rights, but unacquainted with Theodora.

After discovering the truth of his affair from her servants, but before admitting him, the robed Despoina summons her women and eunuchs to give them her cues and their responses. Admitted to her presence, Timothaeus has to go through the prostration and slipper-kissing while the attendants form a half circle around him. Under these circumstances, Timothaeus voices his argument, which is that, being a patrician, he leads a hard life; because of his nobility, he may not ask mercy from the creditors who dog his steps, nor may he ask payment from those who owe *him* money.

Theodora speaks her cue: "Poor Patrician Timothaeus!"

The ring around him intones the response: "What a big hernia you have."

Timothaeus tries to appeal to the Most Clement Augusta, and hears again the response chanted as if in church, whereupon he flees from the audience chamber.

Another man of substance, as righteously indignant, experienced more public mockery. He had wed one of Theodora's girls, who had been a dancer. After the marriage night he told in the streets that she "had been tampered with." Very quickly the gossiping husband met with a band of the Despoina's attendants, who used their staffs on his back. When he roared in protest, they tore off his mantle to throw him upon it and toss him into the air like a child in a blanket. "For wagging your tongue," they explained to him. After that the husband said no more about his bride.

The magnates of the city began to fear the Despoina. They heard that even when she supped alone on her terrace, she kept regal state, served with the white wine of Gaza and red wine of Cyprus in vessels of gold-glass by attendants who wrapped their hands in linen. Her servants, in or out of the palace, remained silent about her doings. If questioned, they merely explained that they served the Augusta. Apparently she had no favorites.

Justinian on the other hand made little of a meal, eating a piece of bread, with green herbs soaked in vinegar or oil. Drinking barley water, not wine, he left the table before his hunger was satisfied. He grudged the few hours that he slept, with writing tablets laid out in readiness for his waking. It was becoming clear that he depended on his chosen group to aid his thoughts as well as to carry them out. He rewarded Narses by making him master of the swordsmen—an odd appointment for an Asian eunuch. Quietly dismissing the popular patrician Phocus, he recalled the unruly John of Cappadocia to be Praetorian Prefect, and summoned back Tribonian, who labored at the full *Corpus Juris* in its fifty volumes. With the return of Hermogenes, Justinian thus reassembled his old companions of the Council. Only one of them had been born in Constantinople.

None of them could restrain their Autocrat from his mad venture of that year.

❊ THE DOME OF LIGHT

The great church of the city had been destroyed in the conflagration. The people naturally expected Justinian to rebuild their Hagia Sophia, but they thought he must be insane to tear down the ruins—as he did within forty days—of the old basilica in order to build anew from the ground something vaster, never beheld before by the eyes of men in the West.

Justinian, however, set about doing it. He could be very persuasive in arguing away the difficulties of such a project of his imagination. More ground was needed for the fantastic new edifice. One elderly woman refused to sell her adjoining property at the assessed price until the Emperor himself called at her house, whereupon she agreed to do it for him. Another owner of ground, they say, was an addict of the races, and starved for lack of his sport. Justinian ordered one day of racing to be held in honor of this devotee; but he would not give the signal for the start of the first race, when the chariots were at the post, until the man had signed a deed of sale for his ground.

For the plans of the greater Hagia Sophia, Justinian—who knew something of hydraulic engineering but nothing of building—called upon a man of genius, Anthemius of Tralles, among other architects. Anthemius had designed the small Church of Sergius and Bacchus, and he possessed vision. The records yield no clue as to what passed between the Emperor and his designers. Clearly they would use no wood, which had caused the loss by fire of so many structures. They would build only with stone, masonry, and marble, and on a plan never attempted before. Their edifice would hold as many people as the great temples of the Pharaohs, but without the elephantine columns and flat roof of the Egyptians. In the Christian East, architecture had served religion; the structures had grown outward from the altar itself—taking the form of a cross or a hexagon. Thus the outside had been sacrificed for the splendor of the central altar beneath a small dome. In the West, Roman architecture had served the Caesars with triumphal arches and vaulted baths. There the early churches had taken the form of the existing basilicas, the halls of lawsuits and banking. Thus the altars had been placed at the end of a long nave with rows of columns, the whole admitting very little light.

Anthemius and his fellows rejected all these models. Their great church would be flooded with sunlight reflected back from many-hued marbles of the walls. In shape it would be neither a narrow oblong nor a square. It would rise in the center to a vast "suspended dome," one hundred and sixty feet above the flooring, mightier than that of Agrippa's Pantheon. In reality the dome would rest upon four arches rising from four central piers—with two of the arches concealed, thus creating the illusion of a suspended dome.

A dome of that size had never been constructed upon a quadrilateral base. Perhaps the master-builder, Isidore of Miletus, who had experimented with the calculations of Archimedes, worked out a method to do that. They were dealing with weights of masses and thrusts unfamiliar to them—with stonework that could not be held fast by ordinary cement. Justinian observed that it was foolish to limit a building by the qualities of its materials. The chemists went to work on a stronger cement, fused in heat.

One riddle in the construction of the Hagia Sophia has never been solved. How did Anthemius and his fellows complete the plans for a structure like that in the two months it took to clear the ground? Had Anthemius or Isidore sketched the design before then? Or did they work at a speed incredible today?

Clearly Justinian pressed them to make haste. Skilled workmen were drafted from the eastern cities, and it is said that very soon two hundred foremen—competing against each other in four teams—drove nearly ten thousand workers at the great task. After a little, a contagion of eagerness seized the builders. Each evening at the sundial clock, each mason and stonecutter was paid a silver coin into his hand. While estimating the cost, John the Praetorian objected that 2,000 pounds of silver would not plate the sanctuary walls. Justinian said it would take 40,000 pounds, and John would find the money. They were building a church to excel Solomon's Temple of Jerusalem.

The new Hagia Sophia, in Justinian's mind, would be the

religious dedication of his new city and of the effort to create a world-state around it.

Engineers of the Arsenal warned him that Anthemius' dome would fall of its own weight. Its fate would be certain as that of the Tower of Babel, raised against the will of God.

Contractors warned him that it would take them five years to cut and polish and ship to Constantinople the marble from Thessaly, with onyx and jasper from the islands and the porphyry from Egypt.

Justinian told them that in five years the Hagia Sophia itself would be a finished building. The transport by sea would not be as difficult as they thought, he said, because within a year Africa would be conquered and the sea lanes opened.

It seemed to many observers that he was stricken with madness.

❀ MESSAGE FROM CARTHAGE

Justinian rewarded Count Belisarius for his service in the Nika revolt by giving him a more impossible task.

One morning in June 533, when the stone piers of the Hagia Sophia were rising within their scaffolding, the Patriarch and the Emperor went in procession down to the shore at the tip of the palace point. Icons were carried behind them above waving myrtle branches. Marching choirs joined their voices in the refrain, the octoechos.

"*Rex gloriae, Domine virtutum* . . . King of glory, Lord of armed hosts. . . ."

Then the robed Patriarch Epiphanius gave his blessing to the war galley moored close inshore. When the men on the galley shouted response and ran up the square sail, the upper part of the sail was seen to be painted scarlet. Atop the short mast a great lantern was secured. This vessel, carrying Count

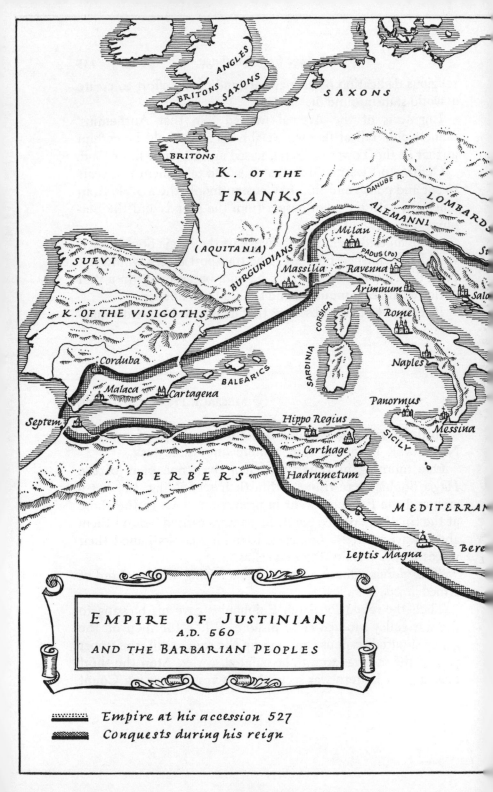

EMPIRE OF JUSTINIAN
A.D. 560
AND THE BARBARIAN PEOPLES

░░░░░░ Empire at his accession 527
▓▓▓▓▓ Conquests during his reign

Belisarius and his staff and navigators, would guide the convoy of ships to Africa. The scarlet-tipped sail would mark it in daylight, the masthead light in darkness.

The long oars swung out and struck their red blades into the water. The fresh breeze from the Bosporus bellied out the sail, and the dromond sped past the point. From the harbor a host of vessels followed in its wake. They were mostly cargo craft or grain transports—chartered shipping that had no appearance of a battle fleet. As long as they passed by, the *Magnificat* hymn sped them on.

When the flotilla dwindled into the Marmora, Justinian walked back through the gardens to his work table, well aware of the weakness of the improvised fleet. It carried away some 10,000 troops of the regular *numerii*, who deeply resented being sent off to sea after long years on the eastern front. Although serving the Emperor for pay, they were still Armenians, Isaurians, or Thracians in their aspirations. With them went some hundreds of Huns and Heruls, serving only by treaty and in the prospect of loot. The transports carried about 5,000 horses.

The steadying force of this small army of 14,000 lay in the personal following of Belisarius, the "biscuit-eaters" who made up his *comitatus* or retinue. Some of them had followed him into the decisive struggle of the hippodrome. With his comitatus, Belisarius would need to maintain discipline over the rest of the army to have any chance of success.

That chance was very slight.

For one thing the Middle Sea could be crossed by such a convoy only during the summer calm, from May until November. The autumn storms would cut off an army.

Modern histories assure us that Justinian resolved then and there to reconquer the lost Roman empire in the West. That is not true. In June of that year Constantinople faced the stubborn fact that beyond the sands of the Syrtes and the moun-

Justinian's palace cistern today—the Yere Batan.
Interior of St. Vitalis, Ravenna, showing mosaics in background.

Theodora and her retinue, mosaic in St. Vitalis, Ravenna. The Empress was probably suffering from her last illness when this mosaic was composed. The ornament around her head is more splendid than that in Justinian's portrait (see frontispiece), undoubtedly by order of the Emperor. She is offering a chalice to the Church, and on her robe the Three Magi are represented.

tains of Greece the empire of the Caesars had passed to barbaric nations. The Vandals held Africa, the Ostrogoths ruled
Italy, the Visigoths had settled down in Spain. Uncouth
Franks swept through Gaul, submerging the sturdy Burgundians.

These barbarian nations understood how to glean crops
from the soil; they summoned up their feudal armed hosts
by a word of command. But Christian man—in Justinian's
thought—does not live by bread alone, nor does he survive
by taking to the sword. It seemed as if the barbarian kings and
chieftains had some awareness of that. At least many of them
made use of Roman bureaus and secretaries to manage their
affairs; often they showed a certain respect for the civilized
Autocrat in Constantinople by stamping his image on their
coins and making treaties with him as their overlord. But this
lip service would end in the hour when one of them became
strong enough to seize Constantinople.

Justinian, who had been a Balkan peasant, understood this
state of affairs very well. So had other soldier-emperors understood it, and failed to remedy it. Justinian believed, as few
others had believed, that the incoming tide of barbarians
would not ebb. Behind the half-Romanized Goths of Italy
pressed the tribal hordes both Germanic and Hunnic of Ale
manni, Lombards, and still-nomadic Heruls and Gepids. Beyond them, the wild Avars approached in the steppes. How
far off was the day when an Avar khagan would ride into the
Augusteum, and a son of Justinian would hold his rein?

It was to hold off that day that the stubborn Balkan sent his
ships out from the haven of the Golden Horn to the Mediterranean. The men of Constantinople no longer had illusions
about the grandeur of waging war.

They meant to find a way across the sea. The Asdic Vandals
—who had followed Gaiseric—reigned over the African lit-
toral. These Vandals possessed the only battle fleet of the sea.
Their galleys faced no greater task than hunting down the

pirates of the Dalmatian inlets. They had not the least expectation that a Roman fleet would reappear, after all these years. So there was a chance that Belisarius' motley flotilla could slip past the dreaded Vandal ships and land with complete surprise on the tranquil African coast. Then, if Belisarius could make himself master of the coast, the enemy fleet would be severed from its ports, left without a home. And the sea itself would be a barrier between the small Roman army and the overwhelming power of the other barbarian nations in Europe.

So Belisarius was sent that June, not to regain the lost Empire of the West but to make a landing in Africa.

Justinian trusted Belisarius to do it. They had nothing in common except this tremendous task. The Dalmatian commander was younger, schooled in warfare at the Strategium, and a favorite of the soldiers he led in person. He gave away spoils recklessly, and his men in the ranks believed that he had good luck. The elder magistri militum of the city distrusted him for the same reason, saying that he depended on luck to win a victory.

Before his departure, Justinian had made an extraordinary compact with Belisarius. He gave his soldier unlimited authority, with the title of Autocrator. "Your order will be as mine." In return, Count Belisarius took an oath that he would never lift his hand against the Emperor. Justinian relied on that pledge, but he gave Belisarius as *Domesticus*—chief of staff—a capable eunuch named Solomon from his own household, as faithful as Narses. Moreover, the commander of the regular cavalry was a certain John the Armenian, headstrong like all Armenians, intolerant of Belisarius' leadership.

The first news from the fleet at sea was discouraging. The Egyptian and Syrian shipmasters, accustomed to carrying freight, made a mess of the transport of troops; water turned foul in the casks, baked biscuits proved to be only half cooked, and turned sour. The ill-assorted vessels crowded into the first anchorage, piling up in a harbor until they had to be fended off with poles. Finding their way from island to island, they reached shelter at last in Sicily beneath the shadow of Mount Aetna. Sight of the smoking volcano seemed to the ship-weary men to be an evil omen.

They were venturing where no East Roman army had been seen for a century. More than the sea itself, they feared the sight of the Vandalic fleet, and they lay half-mutinous in their huts on the Sicilian shore among the deserted temples at Catana. Officers complained that the favored Belisarius had brought along his wife Antonina, who demanded luxuries as well as the devotion of Belisarius and was, besides, a whore. Only Solomon, who was not an officer, but an Oriental fatalist, had no misgivings. Justinian always read his reports with care.

At first Belisarius drove his people as he was accustomed to drive them. He bought grain from the countryside with his own money—he had wealth because loot often stuck to his fingers. When two dissatisfied atabegs of the Huns got drunk and killed a comrade, Belisarius had the two impaled on stakes within sight of the camp—a dangerous disciplining because the Huns might turn against him in the next battle. Then, as if to bear out the evil omen of Aetna, sickness swept the camp, and the commander of the Armenians died.

As the days passed, Belisarius fell into one of his rare black moods, exclaiming to Procopius, his writer and friend, that he could not know *where* the Vandal fleet was lurking nor *how* he could meet it with his land army. He had no information as to the Vandal method of fighting.

At that time Procopius of Caesarea in Palestine was Belisarius' devoted shadow. A small man, Procopius had failed as a lawyer, yet dreamed of writing history after the manner of Thucydides. Attached to the Magister as civilian adviser he had written with zest of their war in Persia. But now he suffered from the prevalent fear of the barbarian hordes until he dreamed that he beheld Belisarius the master of a fabulous city. Somewhat reassured by this omen, Procopius—who prayed inwardly to all-powerful Fate—was sent down the coast to pick up what news he could at Syracuse. He returned much excited with a slave who had left Carthage in Africa only three days before.

Questioned by Belisarius, this slave insisted that the Vandal rulers knew nothing at all of the Roman expedition, and were in fact roaming the interior, while most of the Vandal fleet had departed elsewhere.

This had not happened by chance. In Constantinople the war council had moved to aid Belisarius by diverting the attention of the African overlords to other points. The pilgrim monks had carried back to Tripoli word that a Roman ship would follow them. The ship arrived with a commando-like force of 120 picked men who aided the Roman faction to rise along the Libyan coast. A rumor, heard in the intelligence cells of Constantinople, related that the governor of distant Sardinia set himself against his Vandal overlords. Immediately Justinian dispatched an envoy to that island with authority to promise anything. And this envoy promised liberation of the Sardinians, with full protection from Constantinople. So it was fortunate, but not by simple chance, that the Vandal fleet sailed from Carthage with 5,000 soldiers to put down the insurrection on the island.

Other envoys visited the Gothic court in Italy and by devious means arranged for the sale of provisions to the hungry Roman army. Agents disguised as traders found their way to Carthage itself to hint to the native population that Roman power was on the way to release them.

As pledge of that, Justinian had given Belisarius a letter signed in purple ink. It was addressed to the principal men of Carthage. "It is not our purpose to make war on the Vandals. Nor are we breaking our treaty with Gaiseric. We seek only to overthrow your dictator, who keeps your rightful king in prison. . . . Help us, therefore, to free yourselves from tyranny, so that you may have peace with liberty. We pledge you in God's name that we will aid you to gain these blessings."

There was truth in this propaganda. In wealthy Africa, Gelimer, a headstrong usurper, had wrested the throne from the Vandal ruler, a descendant of Gaiseric the conqueror and a kidnapped princess of Rome. Justinian counted on religious feeling to win over the descendants of Romans. Belisarius carried a banner with the monogram of Jesus—a visible sign that the faith of St. Augustine would be restored to the lost churches of Africa.

So in Constantinople civilized brains had labored to deceive and weaken inwardly the superior power of a barbaric nation. In truth, they had less wish to make war on the Vandals than to steal a victory. Beyond this point everything depended on Belisarius.

He did not lose a day in acting. The good news brought by Procopius put an end to the three-month inertia of the convoy. At the summons of the massed trumpets, the ships sallied from Catana. A fresh east wind brought them to the African coast the next day. Even in that brief crossing, the ill-found fleet strayed off the course to Carthage, to land under barren waterless headlands five days' march from the city.

But once Belisarius had his people on solid earth, he kept them there. ("I for one have no wish to meet the Vandals on the sea," he assured the officers who urged him to sail along the coast.) He found them water by digging into the beach—a miracle in the estimation of the superstitious Procopius. He drove them inland, buying fresh horses from villages on the way, allowing no plundering of the natives. ("Do you want to face *two* enemies, the Vandals and these people?") With his cataphracts mounted again and watching the moody Huns, he raced the horsemen ahead of the plodding infantry across the rich red plain toward Carthage. Sympathizers in the towns gave his skeleton army one priceless bit of information. It seemed that the Vandals, taking their ease in their new kingdom, had pulled down the defense walls of all the towns except Carthage itself. They did so with the idea that they could make themselves secure in their capital whereas an invader coming to the coast would find no other fortifications to serve him.

It occurred at once to Belisarius to throw his expedition into the Carthage citadel before the enemy could muster their forces against him. His anxious followers needed no urging toward such security and wealth, and his blundering ships could anchor at last safely in the port of Carthage.

Soon the hurrying marchers found the paving of a Roman road under their feet; they made a camp in the fruit plantation of a Vandal prince. A day came when the weary mercenaries, racing against peril, wound around a stagnant lake. On the other side gleamed the salt of a dry lake. Where the road twisted through a labyrinth of bare hills, the first riders sighted a milestone. It told them they were no more than ten miles from Carthage. And here thousands of Vandal horsemen swept in on the marching column from all sides.

There ensued the battle called the Ten Mile Post. It might well have ended the march, and the army, of Belisarius in Africa if it had not been for several peculiar circumstances, including the action of Belisarius himself.

In that network of hills no one could see very well what was happening elsewhere. Riding as usual off by themselves, the brooding Huns took note of the gold and rich arms of the Vandals attacking them and became intent on looting such wealth; loosing devastating flights of arrows, they pursued their foes across the dry lake. Elsewhere dour John the Armenian gained a hilltop with his contingent and proceeded to defend himself there, regardless of the fate of his commander.

All the Roman regular cavalry broke and fled before the

charge of Gelimer, the king, and the main Vandal array. So
Belisarius heard the conflict in the hills before he saw anything of it. He was riding with an escort of one hundred
swordsmen. His single dependable force, the veteran comitatus, was screening the plodding infantry and wagons far back
on the road. On him and his band burst the tumult of fugi-
tives, crying as frightened men will, that the Vandals were at
their heels.

Rallying a few of them, the Magister went to see for himself. He found the wide valley at the ten-mile post filled with
thousands of the enemy, dismounted. Believing the fighting
at an end, the Vandals were inspecting the battlefield while
Gelimer arranged funeral rites for a slain kinsman. After
studying the tableau in the valley, Belisarius led his small following in attack down the slope. Surprised in their turn, convinced that a great force must be descending on them in the
drifting dust, the Vandal array made haste to escape.

From that moment Belisarius took control of the battle
and the war. He had taken the measure of the barbarians.

Weeks later a fast-sailing dromond rounded the palace
point of Constantinople with streamers flying. A courier
came up the gardens with a message for the Thrice August
Emperor:

"Carthage is Roman."

❀ TO THE GATES OF THE SEA

The much-feared Vandals had been crushed not so much by
the Roman expedition as by themselves. They were no longer
the desperate tribal fighters of Gaiseric's day. For eighty years
they had enjoyed the luxury of the African province, with all
the amenities of Roman life, without the necessity of defending it except against the Berber inhabitants of the inland des-

erts. When at last they roused all their man power, they could not break into the walls of their great city in the hands of veteran soldiers under the eye of a Belisarius. When they retreated to the encampment at Tricamaron to wait out the winter, they brought in their wives and slaves for comfort and their treasures as well. Before the winter fairly set in, Belisarius disturbed this comfortable arrangement by attacking them— this time leading his mailed cataphracts. Gelimer ended the struggle by fleeing to the Berbers in the hills.

Besides, there had been a prophecy in the land that the Vandals would rule it until an army marched in from the sea. That did not seem likely to happen, until Belisarius did it.

All this delighted Procopius, who had seen the realization of his dream. "For these Vandals," he wrote, "became accustomed to taking to the baths every day. They came to enjoy the best sea and land food on their tables. Covering their bodies with gold ornaments and Persian silk, they went to theaters and hippodromes, and most of all to hunts. Giving banquets in their private parks, they amused themselves with dancers and mimics, and gave themselves up to every kind of sexual excitement."

It almost seemed as if Fate had taken a hand: the Vandal fleet sailed back, unaware, from Sardinia to find its home port in the possession of Romans who had apparently sprung from the sea. After that Belisarius did not lack for serviceable shipping. A treasure vessel that Gelimer's family had loaded and dispatched toward safety on the Spanish coast ran into a storm and turned back to an African haven, to fall intact into the hands of the Roman soldiers. All in all, the value of the Vandalic treasure turned out to be beyond expectations. Belisarius became the master of the spoils of Gaiseric's conquest, which included the imperial regalia of Rome of the Caesars.

The anxious councilors of the Daphne must have felt something like awe of the impassive Emperor who had cast their bread upon the waters. A single Roman army had humbled a

nation of barbaric conquerors. John the Praetorian knew that
the treasury had been drained by the rebuilding of Antioch,
the restoration of the burned heart of Constantinople, the
"Perpetual Peace" with Persia—which Hermogenes had
bought with 14,000 pieces of gold—and the cost of launching
the expedition itself. Now Africa would repay them in gold.

Justinian now called for the immediate recapture of the islands of the sea.

It was swiftly done. Sardinia and Tripoli already awaited
the Roman eagles. Craggy Corsica yielded its fastness. With
the coming of sailing weather, Belisarius dispatched squad-
rons of his captured ships—with Vandals on the rowing
benches—westward to the Balearics, where remnants of people still remembered the lost rule of Rome. An amphibious
expedition pushed west along the coast to the twin heights
known as the Pillars of Hercules (Gibraltar and Jebal Muza).
Beyond lay the open ocean.

In those weeks of swift victories the Middle Sea became
Roman again. How many thousand stadia stretched from the
Gates to the Caucasus over which rose the sun? There must
have been much conning of neglected manuscripts of Strabo
and of Eratosthenes, who pointed out that one great parallel
of latitude ran from the Gates through the strait of Sicily and
Athens of the philosophers. The map on the wall of The Silence must have been painted in new colors.

Justinian, for one, realized the opportunity offered by the
new sea routes. Whereas the barbarians held the land roads of
Europe, an East Roman army could now move freely by sea.
And he began to ponder the position of Sicily, accessible by
water, yet almost touching the toe of Italy.

He also pondered the unbelievable success of Belisarius
with men at war.

Even while the Council marked the map of Africa with the
ancient provinces of Tripolitana, Byzacium, Africa, Numidia,
and Mauretania, disturbing warnings came from Carthage.

Officers either zealous or envious, wrote under seal that the Autocrator was conducting himself like a reigning monarch in his conquest. He took up his quarters in the palace of Gelimer and gave feasts prepared by its servants. To Berber chieftains who rode in to greet—and appraise—the Roman conqueror, he gave silver staffs and gilded boots and caps that looked like crowns. He protected Vandal nobles who sought sanctuary in the churches. More than that, he kept all the captured bullion guarded in his coffers. All these signs indicated that the supreme Magister Belisarius planned to make himself master of Africa in defiance of Constantinople.

Was Belisarius merely building up Roman prestige? ("The task of a commander is simpler if he can create a legend of victory.") Or was he taking the profitable way to treachery? Constantinople could not mobilize another army to challenge a Belisarius entrenched in Africa. Theodoric the Goth had entered Italy as a field commander of Constantinople and had remained to rule in Ravenna. Justinian, who held the record of the past in his memory, could single out a month in 456 when the two halves of the Roman world had been divided among barbarian war lords: between Gaiseric at Carthage, Theodoric the Visigoth at Toulouse, Ricimer at Ravenna, and Aspar the Alan at Constantinople itself.

Isolated in the Daphne, a thousand miles from the palace of Carthage, how could Justinian decide what to do? In such a case Diocletian had traced a bitter memorandum: "Four or five people join together to deceive the Emperor. They set a decision before him. Shut up in his chambers, he cannot know the true situation. He can only know what they tell him."

Even the resourceful Theodora would not make this decision. She merely pointed out that Belisarius cared too much for his wife Antonina, who was eight years older, and ambitious like most older wives.

At last Justinian sent a message to his general. The Emperor would like Belisarius to return in person with Gelimer and the captive lords of Africa and the treasure. But Belisarius must decide himself whether he should leave the African coast.

Belisarius sailed home.

❀ THE FESTIVAL OF VICTORY

From his throne-seat, the strategist of empire gave only cold, courteous thanks to his soldier—"our devoted benefactor." He named Belisarius consul for the year and did not question the large share of spoils he claimed. He seized the opportunity to give the people of his city a vicarious taste of victory. The doors of the hippodrome were opened in March 534 to a pageant of triumph in the old fashion of the Caesars.

"Aided by God," Justinian made announcement, "the Roman people will triumph over their enemies."

The performance itself would have struck Trajan or Hadrian as very odd. The scars of the conflagration were hidden along the Mesé by painted hangings, myrtle branches waved from the balconies, and silk billowed from the church portals. At the head of the procession robed priests swung incense, and a choir of monks chanted *Te Deum laudamus.* (There could be no triumph unless by the providence of the Lord of Hosts.) After them rode the great servants of the Empire, from Praetorian to City Prefect. (Their labors had sent the expedition on its way.)

From the multitude on the tiers of the hippodrome a roar went up at the entrance of the comitatus of the conqueror. Their iron gray figures rode in perfect ranks around the long Spina, and after them followed the strange Huns. (Belisarius had won their loyalty by promising to return them to their home steppes, and he kept his promise.) The multitude rose with a beating of hands as Belisarius appeared, not mounted, but afoot in his battle dress, with no laurel wreath upon his half helmet. From that moment he became the city's hero.

For after him marched the captive Gelimer and the Vandal princes wearing chains for the occasion. (Belisarius had promised them comfortable estates with servants on the shore of Asia.) After them carts dragged the captured treasure, with gleaming gold displayed. The crowd took instant notice of a wagon led by barefoot monks. It bore the hallowed treasure of Jerusalem—the seven-branched candlesticks, the shewbread table, and the Seat of Mercy that had been the splendor of the temple of Solomon the King.

Rhetors among the crowd remembered that these relics of the ancient temple had been carried off from Jerusalem by Titus; they had been wrested from Rome by Gaiseric's Vandals. Now they had been brought back from Carthage to Constantinople. Surely this was an omen of God's favor. Yet soothsayers whispered that wherever they had rested, the loss of a kingdom had followed. Would Justinian dare house them within the Hagia Sophia?

From the draped Kathisma, where the recaptured standards of the legions stood, Justinian announced that by these tokens the Romans would rule again in the West. "We hope that God will grant us to regain the other lands that the ancient Romans possessed, as far as the two oceans." From his side the lovely Despoina watched the triumph of Belisarius inscrutably. Obviously, the victor at Carthage would be a power in Constantinople henceforth. After the triumph Justinian felt a growing jealousy of the younger man who could prevail in battle and win the devotion of a crowd so easily.

As for Gelimer, who did not need to die to make a spectacle for these unpredictable Romans, they say that when he was escorted to the garden of the villa where he would spend his years as a pensioned enemy, he cried out: "Vanity of vanities! All is vanity."

No, this triumph of Belisarius did not re-enact the triumph of an ancient Roman conqueror. It was the pageant of a new force within Constantinople moving toward its destiny.

❀ THE DIVIDING FORCES

When Belisarius marched on foot in that big parade, the people of Constantinople beheld in him something more splendid than a magister of soldiers. In their eyes he became a second St. Michael whose flaming sword could drive away dark angels. He had triumphed against the enemies of their faith. Probably Belisarius would have been completely surprised if anyone had said that to him, but Justinian comprehended it very well.

The inhabitants of the Guarded City had become incurably mystical; they held fast to relics like the Madonna of the Way, and they looked for miracles to aid them. In particular and above all, they—or most of them—held to a belief in the Trinity of the Father and Son and Holy Spirit. Any baker or mule-driver would put aside his work to argue that the Trinity offered the only way to a soul's salvation. Had not Constantine of glorious memory, held to this same creed of the Nicaean Council, the veritable truth? Accordingly they looked upon the vanquished Vandals as Arians and heretics—enemies of the truth. Had not Theodosius the Great declared that unbelievers were heretics and foes?

Surely the Apostles testified that Christ was divine, being the Son of God. Yet since Paul the Apostle had preached to the congregations against pagan idols, the Christian churches had divided like the waters of a great river separating into streams. Arius preached that Jesus was no more than a human being of such rare virtue that he had been drawn into Heaven itself. But could a common man, a carpenter's son, open salvation to the human race? If Mary had given birth to a common child, could she be—as she indubitably was—the Mother of God, and their Madonna of the Way?

These people, we understand today, turned away from a realistic doctrine to a mystical one. They sought the blessings of anchorites from the desert who seemed to them to be, as in the days of the apostles, the "champions of Christ"; they reverenced a St. Jerome who shared his cave with a desert lion, and they gathered up the dust dropped down on them by pillar-sitting ascetics. They cast their anger against Nestorius, who had been patriarch of their city, who preached that both divine and human natures were in the one man, Christ. That was the belief of the more eastern folk. The city knew it as the Monophysite doctrine of the One Being. It was in fact the most ancient belief of the eastern people, that there could be no god but God.

Christianity itself had arisen in the eastern lands. The churches of ancient Alexandria and Antioch claimed primacy over Constantine's city. They held tenaciously to the Monophysite doctrine. The growing religious controversy often caused resistance to the authority of the new city of the Emperor.

During the fifth century the conflict within the churches tended to break out of control by the state. Mobs attacked dissenting monasteries; patriarchs anathematized opponents and were exiled in their turn. At the Council of Ephesus (431) Nestorius was exiled with his followers, who deserted their shrines at Edessa to migrate into Persia and on through Asia. To calm the strife of the churches, the devout Pulcheria and the anxious Marcian summoned the Council of Chalcedon, near their city. At Chalcedon (451) the leaders of the churches gave voice to the doctrine of the mystics, of the Trinity and the divinity of Christ. This conformed to the doctrine of the uncompromising Leo, Pope of Rome. But it antagonized the older churches of the East. The rulers of

Constantinople were caught between the tides of religious feeling in the East and the West. This conflict was not doctrinal alone, because the patriarchs of the East felt their traditions to be involved; Antioch and Alexandria denied the authority of the priests who tended the tomb of the Apostle Peter. Historically, the schism between East and West took place in 481, but the cleavage had been there for a long time.

Then, too, the eastern clergy at that time beheld only enemies in the West. Arians. That happened by one of the chances that affect destiny. A bishop of Constantinople, an Arian, had once become a missionary to the armed forces and then to the barbarians the armies fought. St. Ulfilas (Little Wolf, 310–383) had translated most of the Scriptures into Gothic. He had given songs to the marching barbarians, and beyond them to the newly converted peoples. After St. Ulfilas, the Ostrogoths and Visigoths and Vandals and others as well became Arians. So as these barbarian nations completed their conquests, the orthodox churches—with the faith of the Father and Son, in the Trinity—were closed except for a few in Gaul and those of St. Peter's in Italy. When Belisarius regained the African coast, the old churches were opened again and the Arian clergy expelled. Before then—as soon as Justin had come to the throne in 518—Justinian had ended the schism between the clergy of the East and the West by summoning bishops of Rome to Constantinople. He had seen the inability of the elderly Anastasius—a Monophysite believer—to hold the churches united. Vitalian's revolt had not been the only one under Anastasius.

When he passed up the Mesé in processions, Justinian always saw the statue of Constantine on its high porphyry column. On the base of the column an inscription had been carved, probably by order of Constantine himself: "*O Christ, master and ruler of the earth, to Thee have I consecrated this obedient city, and this scepter and the power of Rome. Guard Thou it and deliver it from every harm.*"

The words held a warning. The self-proclaimed divinity of pagan Caesars such as Caligula had been eclipsed by the downfall of the pagan city. Yet an almost insuperable responsibility had come to the Christian emperors of Constantinople since Theodosius' day. Because the scepter and all power rested in their hands, they had the task of ruling according to the will of God. The people looked upon them as entirely human, yet as vice-gerents of Christ. This duty lay upon them; the power they must find.

Justinian accepted the responsibility in a way of his own. Quite simply he tried to get the most necessary things done. Being the one emperor of the western world, he proceeded to draw up one law, in the *Corpus Juris*. He sent his army to drive out the Arian clergy as much as to regain territory. It seemed to his uncompromising mind that nothing would avail very much unless the conflict of the religions could be ended by the establishment of a single Church. He declared the "primacy in honor" of the western popes, while he persecuted the leaders of the eastern Monophysites. He kept authority in his own hands.

And he hastened the building of the new Hagia Sophia that would be quite different from the old basilica of Constantinople. It would be a church for all congregations of the Christians.

❈ CRACKS IN THE PIERS

The four incredible piers of the great church were rising higher than the summit of the hippodrome. They could be seen by sailors far out at sea. Under awnings in the rain and beneath flares at night, shifts of stonemasons raised massive square blocks into place as if laying bricks. And daily the anxiety of the master builders Anthemius and Isidore increased.

They were dealing with weights and pressures never before invoked in the West. Isidore said the trouble came from the perversity of materials. To allow for the great weight to come upon the piers they had poured molten lead into the interstices. This would take the increasing pressure of the rigid blocks. Yet vertical cracks appeared in two of the piers. Skeptics, watching the building, swore that the giant piers would collapse, bringing death to the workmen raising the summit arch between them.

Anthemius and Isidore suspended work on the arch. Its haunches projected toward each other, 120 feet in the air. When Justinian was called in, he asked if they were certain the columns would take the weight of the finished arch. They said that they were certain. "Then carry the arch across," he bade them, "and see what happens."

When the lofty arch was joined and the scaffolding taken down, the piers stood firm in spite of the cracks. (After more than fourteen centuries, they stand as they were built.)

Then, as work began on the overhanging dome, another danger appeared. The marble facing of the upper walls began to flake off. The strain was telling on the more brittle marbles like the green Carystian. "Take off the facing there," Justinian ordered, "and put it back when the strain of settling is ended."

Nor would he allow them to delay the work. Because they began to fear the weight of the dome itself, they made it of light, porous stone. Because the older type of capitals rested heavily on the smaller pillars, a new type was evolved, lightened by carving. Except for those capitals, no stone-carving showed in the interior of the great church. The varied marbles of pillars and walls gave it color without touch of paint. The open galleries and colonnaded aisles gave it depth to the eye.

"One marvels," Procopius related, "at the purple here, the green hue there, and again at the flame of crimson or the glint of white."

These artists of Constantinople were devising a canon of their own. In the reigning city gathered those who had come out of the East—from the schools of Alexandria or the deserts of Palmyra. Many of them had wondered at the vastness of space, the superhuman coloring of sunsets on the desert. The plain interior of the Hagia Sophia gave a sense of infinite space. Its coloring, darker along the ground level, lighter and brilliant in its summit, induced a mood. Justinian did not understand the technique of the artists. He relied on the best of them, and they found at his court the chance to do the work of their imagination.

Already under the impulse of their minds, the ancient canon of art was changing. A new style rallied the latent powers of the ancient art. Statues disappeared. Perhaps the conflagration of the Nika did away with many of them. Certainly the main endeavor of western Roman art, the portrait statues of dead generals and fathers of families, was abandoned. The pastoral scenes and intimate visiting angels of the earlier Alexandrian school changed into barely suggested vistas and angels who haunt the heights.

The portrait statue of Daphne still stood in the great hall of the palace—a young woman in flight with her upflung arms turning into the branches of a tree. It told the mythical story of the virgin Daphne with exact detail. But this was the work of an artist of several centuries before, imported by Constantine. It was no more than a human being acting out a myth. Out in the seaside park a younger artist erected the small figure of Theodora. Although a portrait, this modern work *suggested* majesty. The observant Procopius remarked that "from afar it reveals an empress."

There survives today a broken head that may have been this of Theodora. It is simply crowned, lovely in modeling, yet not entirely human. Like the head of a rider of the dynamic frieze of the Parthenon, it has been touched by imagination. In fact, Procopius mentions Pheidias in describing it.

These unknown artists of Constantinople no longer copied models of the past. They resembled the earliest Greeks in seeking to create something with new meaning. They were closing the circle of nearly one thousand years, from Pheidias through the Hellenistic mastery of skills—the intimate delightful virtuosity of Pompeii—to the tired replicas of the last Romans, the clumsy human effigies that act out scenes on the triumphal arch of Constantine. Already the Hagia Sophia resembled the Parthenon in its irregularity of measurements and its return to simplicity of form. It does not derive from that domed exhibition hall, Agrippa's Pantheon.

As in the creative arts, so in the city of Constantinople, a new characteristic appeared. *Roman tradition was failing, the Latin speech was dying out; Hellenistic culture still prevailed, while eastern methods of government were invoked. No longer a* Nea Roma, *the city was becoming a new Constantinople. To what end?*

❈ "WE HAVE LEARNED HOW ENORMOUS INJUSTICES . . ."

With his hands free of senatorial restraint in 534–5 Justinian made his great effort to reform his government.

Already he had taken measures to give magistrates to the city dwellers and to stem the tide of immigration that was depopulating the countryside and crowding the streets. There remained the economy of the whole. This was in bad shape—despite the gold reserve gathered by Anastasius—as Justinian had observed before his inauguration.

For one thing, it being a money economy, officials usually felt they had the right to make money for themselves. Usually, too, after buying their offices by the traditional *suffragia*, they tried to repay themselves from public funds. Judges as well as governors could be bought. Revenues stuck to too

many fingers before reaching the imperial treasury. Anastasius
had set up his own inspectors to remedy this, but after a while
the inspectors had joined the governmental hierarchy in taking payment for favors. Police officials took time-honored toll
from towns.

Probably in tearing down his machinery of government,
Justinian followed the ideas of his Praetorian, John of Cappadocia. John had prophesied grimly that soon the cost of
collecting taxes would consume two thirds of the yearly reve-
nue. And John devised means to get more of the tax revenues
safely within the Brazen Gate. But Justinian realized that
taxes could not be increased without increasing the ability of
the ordinary worker in shop or field to pay them. He set about
this task in his own way. As for Theodora, her hand was evident in abolishing more of the ancient *potestas patris*, in giving new rights to women and children of the family, and in
scaling down interest on borrowings as well as the right of
moneylenders to seize property pledged for loans.

Justinian's first blow against his officialdom came with
Novella VIII:

> That magistrates shall not buy their posts. The Emperor
> Justinian, August, to John, Praetorian Prefect, twice Con-
> sul, and Patrician.

In its *praefatio* Justinian confided in his people at large as if
he was speaking at their firesides:

> We spend all our days and nights thinking out what
> will be useful, if pleasing to God, to all of our people.
> Our watches are not in vain; they will deliver our subjects
> from anxiety. With care we seek the means to release our
> people from all charges—those heavy exactions—except
> the public tax. We have learned how, at times, enormous
> injustices have been done . . . impoverishing our subjects
> until they could hardly pay the lawful tax . . . how em-

perors sought to profit from magistrates by selling them their posts, and how these in turn reimbursed themselves from the people. For everyone knows how officials have not only paid, but also have pledged more to those who put the posts in their way. One who has borrowed to do this seeks to pay interest as well as the loan, and to earn a profit for himself on retiring from the post . . . he exacts triple charges from our subjects. . . . To tell the plain truth, the treasury itself suffers from this. Prefects and owners and farmers desert the provinces, pressing into Constantinople to complain rightly of the thefts against them. Brigands operate with the knowledge of governors because a weight of gold buys them immunity . . . we cannot say how widely the thefts of these governors extend; hardly a person dares bring evidence against them.

In his appeal to the populace Justinian rang many changes on his thought: "If the officials work with clean hands, the government and the citizens alike will prosper." His first moves against profiteering officials were drastic.

No one henceforth might pay for a post. (Salaries were increased, to compensate for keeping "clean hands.")

Every governor must visit the towns of his territory in person, and not send vicars in his stead. (To prevent off-record dealings by agents.)

After giving up a post, an official must remain in his district for fifty days. (To allow his accounts to be examined and complaints against him to be heard.)

Bishops and local councils would have charge of public works funds. . . .

Having attacked abuses, Justinian and John struck at the heart of the civil service, cutting down the swollen personnel, abolishing the sacred rule of seniority which raised to the most responsible posts only the oldest inhabitants of the payroll.

They challenged the growing numbers of "adjusters" and the younger "assistants" employed to aid the aged seniors to do their work. Ruthlessly Justinian cut in half the pensions paid by the central bureaus—pensions that had grown to ten thousand pounds of gold yearly. This earned him the cordial hatred of retired officialdom.

In the bureau of *Memoriae*, the secretary John of Lydia kept a diary in the ancient Roman manner, and in it he recorded his comforts until this great upheaval. "To encourage my activity the Prefect pointed out certain paths to gain. He kept office not quite a year, yet in that time I gained not less than 1,000 pieces of gold by my prudent activity. Naturally grateful, I composed a short eulogy of him. He was very pleased, and bade me take from the bank account a gold piece for every line."

When his protectors disappeared from the bureau, the placid Lydian—who always wore his uniform—believed that they had lost the favor of Fortune. When the popular colloquial Greek took the place of Latin in the records, John Lydus remembered a prophetic oracle: "Fortune will desert the Romans when they forget their native speech."

Many others in the civil service agreed with worthy John Lydus that a change in the ancient ways would bring disaster to Constantinople. The rites of their ancestors blended in their minds with their own cherished seniority and prosperity. Why should a man spend himself in labor if age did not bring promotion, with a title of some kind—John himself retired as a count of the second rank—and a pension to follow?

The strength of inertia resisted Justinian's attempt to drive his administrators to new achievement. This time he was blamed more than John of Cappadocia. Procopius echoed the anger of officialdom: "He kept tearing down existing institutions as if he should change all things into another form. He did this simply so that everything might be new and might bear the impress of his name."

Had he not given his name to the new laws? Did he not write out himself the rescripts of the Quaestor's office?

As he had appealed to the public in the first of the reform *Novellae,* the silent Emperor unexpectedly tried to explain himself in following edicts (536): "To make a law to adjust an evil is like giving medicine. You can't tell what effect it will have. . . . We have decided that it is necessary to change not only the edicts of previous emperors, but even our own. . . . Because nature is constantly changing—a fact we will repeat as long as nature goes her way—it leads us to make new enactments."

Despite the resistance of the civil service, the new dynamic administration began to take shape. But Justinian had been forced to assume personal responsibility for it. That brought an increasing torrent of appeals to Caesar from outlying towns with grievances. Their delegations waited in the Augusteum, refusing to meet with the Referendarius. They wanted to speak to Justinian. "For no one stands in the presence of the Augustus to speak for us."

Soon Justinian appointed special courts to hear appeals from the provinces, to travel through the villages and pass on the cases swiftly—within fifty days. From all magistrates he demanded an oath with teeth in it:

> I hereby swear by all-powerful God . . . and the blessed archangels Michael and Gabriel, on these four Evangels that I hold in my hands, that I will faithfully serve our masters Justinian and Theodora, his wife. I swear that I have given nothing and will give nothing to any person in obtaining my charge, or to protect it. I swear to accept only my salary . . . and to seek no other profit from my post . . . and to defend the rights of all

> *subjects of our pious masters. If I fail to do this, I will take upon myself the terrible judgment of our Saviour, Jesus Christ, the doom of Judas, the leprosy of Giezi, and the fear of Cain.*

The oath of the magistrates included the words *communicator sum sanctissimae Dei catholicae et apostolicae ecclesiae.* These officials who were to administer one law in the service of one Emperor must also belong to the one Universal Apostolic Church. Resistance to the oath of Justinian began almost at once.

The records show that Justinian judged one matter himself. Some of the Vandal treasure had been taken into the palace; the gold goblets and plate of ancient Rome added magnificence to the festival table of the Daphne. Some of the jewels were taken by Theodora. But the question remained of where to place the candelabra and the treasure of the temple of Jerusalem.

An elderly Jew who had seen them approached the advisers of the Emperor. Those treasures, he urged, should not be taken into the palace. After their seizure by Titus, misfortune had followed them in Rome, and in Carthage as well; they must be returned to the place where they had been in the time of Solomon, King of Israel.

Before that year ended, legates of the Emperor transported the sacred treasure back to the shrines of Jerusalem.

❀ MASTHEADS OVER PANORMUS

When Belisarius set sail for Sicily at the end of the summer of 535, the men of The Silence threw a screen of deception over his voyage. To all appearances the victor over the Vandals was on his way back to Africa. Only The Silence—and Justinian—knew that he had been ordered to steal the island of Sicily from the Goths.

That island loomed larger on their map now that they had regained control of the sea. It offered a way station on the long voyage from Constantinople to the Gates of the ocean, and a steppingstone from the point of Carthage to the toe of Italy.

This time The Silence outfitted Belisarius with care. His fleet was seaworthy, his officers were handpicked for loyalty and skill. His small army of 8,000 consisted of his own reliable comitatus, of regular cavalry, and of tough Isaurian mountain-bred infantry, with only small contingents of Huns and Moors. Best of all, everyone was in high spirits, going with the lucky Belisarius on such a pleasant voyage toward the plantations, the buxom women, and the innumerable slaves of Africa—as they thought.

Again Belisarius had been given overriding authority as Autocrator. And the councilors had weighed the risks with him. "Land where you landed before," they told him, "as if some accident made you put in to Sicily. There the Goths will suspect nothing. Occupy the island if you can do so without trouble. If you run into trouble, forget it, and go on to Africa." Once the Constantinopolitans held the island, the formidable Goths could do nothing but stare ruefully across the strait of Messina from the legendary Scylla to Charybdis. These land-bound Goths had no shipping to cross the strait. So said the councilors.

Belisarius carried out his part perfectly. Landing again at Catana, he sent detachments of his soldiers sight-seeing, and in doing so they seized the weapons of the scattered Gothic outposts. He took over Syracuse from its surprised commander. Trouble arose only in Panormus (Palermo), the walled port of the island. There the garrison manned the wall to resist him. Avoiding the land side, the conqueror-in-disguise sailed some of his dromonds in to investigate the harbor. Discovering that his mastheads overtopped the low harbor parapet, Belisarius

ordered archers into the small boats carried on the sterns of
the galleys, and hoisted these boats to the tops of the masts.
These bowmen drove the Gothic warriors from the defense
wall, and very soon Panormus surrendered to him.

With zest the diligent Procopius relates how Belisarius
paraded into Syracuse on the last day of his year as Consul.
He rode in with a silver organ sounding, tossing gold coins to
the inhabitants. It was a bloodless and resounding victory. Yet
the superstitious man of Caesarea notes that he heard a prophecy rumored around. No one knew from what oracle it came:
"When Africa is conquered, the world will be lost."

Procopius and the army had reason to remember that prophecy during the following years. They did not suspect as yet
that they were bound for Italy.

Italy, heart of the ancestral Empire, was firmly held by the
power of the Ostrogoths, a feudal nation in arms. As late as
the year 487 these Gothic warriors had forced their way into
the suburbs of Constantinople. Perhaps the intrigues of
women—Ariadne was in the Daphne palace then—impelled
them to turn away, to march west and take instead the lands
of Italy (489) from the barbaric Odovacer. Theodoric the
Amal, their king, was more astute than Attila. He held
the rank of magister militum of Constantinople, and he ruled
the conquered Italy as a tolerant war lord. He claimed only the
German title of king and he rendered lip service to the eastern
emperors while he settled in Ravenna to build a palace of his
own and found a dynasty. The mild Anastasius had conciliated
Theodoric, having no force capable of interfering with 40,000
German swordsmen.

In Italy itself the surviving inhabitants led the shadowy
existence of the half free. The senate still met unhindered to
debate laws, but Theodoric gave the judgments. Families of
senatorial rank still kept up their summer resorts in the cool
hills of Praeneste or by the baths of Baiae. Young Flavius

Cassiodorus, who wrote witty letters while serving Theodoric as mouthpiece, maintained the fiction that "it is a glorious thing to serve the city of Rome." Cassiodorus could write out a Formula for the Prefect of the Watch of the City of Rome, explaining: "Your office under the eyes of patricians and consuls will surely bring you fame. . . . You have full power to catch thieves, although the law gives their punishment to another official because even these wretched plunderers are still citizens of Rome." This secretary of a barbarian king still spoke of fame in the time-honored fashion, but he seldom used the word city—*civitas*—as of old. Instead he employed a new word, *civilitas*—the city culture. Roman culture, at least, survived and by it they might transform their barbaric masters. Cassiodorus dispatched a lute-player to the uncouth Franks with a whisper to Boethius the philosopher that the lutist might, like Orpheus, charm the brutes.

Boethius did not share that hope, and the anger of Theodoric cast him into prison, where he wrote the immortal *Consolation of Philosophy*. Whereupon the senate hastened to absolve itself by a decree denying all association with the stubborn Boethius. One man, Symmachus, great-grandson of the Quintus Aurelius Symmachus who had defended the ancient temples, spoke against the decree, and Theodoric had him put to death with Boethius (525). These two were the great names that ended a noble tradition. The politic Cassiodorus accepted the office of magister officiorum vacated by Boethius. In the next year, 526, Theodoric the Amal died.

He had been an Arian, king of an Arian nation. It seems that Justinian had roused him to fury in the last years by ending the schism with the orthodox Church of Rome, and—under Justin—closing the Arian churches in Constantinople. The death of the strong Gothic leader opened the possibility, in Justinian's mind, of freeing the clergy of St. Peter's from their Arian overlords. He summoned a fearless pope, Agapidus, to journey by sea to Constantinople and plan for his liberation.

There was no visible way of attacking the military power of the Gothic nation. But if the Goths could not be defeated in war, they might be overcome by diplomacy.

❄ THE DISASTROUS VICTORY OF MUNDUS

It took men of great skill to attempt to win back Italy without a battle. Justinian relied on a chosen few. Along the frontier of the Danube the devoted Germanus kept his barbarian neighbors quiet while his few regiments were withdrawn to serve against Italy. Some of them went to Mundus, the old companion of Belisarius. While Belisarius was occupying Sicily, Mundus moved west through the mountains quietly taking possession of the Dalmatian coast. Finding few Goths in his way, he entered Salona near Diocletian's palace, by then half ruined.

Meanwhile an envoy made his way through the enemies to the Frankish chieftains, masters of Gaul beyond the Alps. Illiterate—riding about in ceremonial oxcarts—these Frankish kings were still converts to orthodox Christianity, and Justinian's message reminded them of that. "This is your war as well as ours, because you are joined to us by the orthodox faith, which rejects the Arian heresy. We are joined together, as well, by the enmity we share toward the Goths." Justinian claimed Italy as a province of the Roman Empire; more realistically, his envoy made a gift of gold to the Franks—if they would drive the Goths from the Province (Provence) and the barrier Alps.

So at the end of 535 the leaders of the Goths became aware of forces aligned against them along the Alps, on the Dalmatian coast, and in Sicily.

By no chance whatever, a most skilled agent of Justinian was at work in Italy itself. Peter the Patrician—as he came to be called—had been a rhetor of Thessalonica. Peter was, besides, an amiable man of the world, unbribable, and full of guile. He had iron nerve and he needed it because his task was to work on the mind of the King of the Goths by threatening a war that his master the Emperor wished to avoid.

That would have been madness in dealing with Theodoric the Great. But Theodoric's death had left only a daughter to succeed the Gothic conqueror. Amalasuntha had had her father's spirit, but the Germanic warriors submitted only uneasily to the rule of a woman. In her distress Amalasuntha had taken a husband of the Amal blood, yet a man more given to books than to warfare. This Theodahad, called the Philosopher, had made the mistake of having his courageous wife slain as if by accident while bathing in a lake. Now Theodahad reigned alone in the Ravenna palace, yet fearful of the vengeance of the Gothic nobles who had been attached to their queen. Would they dare slay the last man of the Amal line? Tribal tradition still kept them loyal to the family of Theodoric.

Upon the uneasiness of Theodahad Peter played with faint mockery. His emperor, he reminded the Goth, had taken the unfortunate Amalasuntha under his protection.

Theodahad the Philosopher offered to give up Sicily to imperial rule; Peter the Patrician reminded him that Sicily already was held by an imperial army. Whereupon, at a secret meeting Theodahad demanded to know what would happen if his terms failed to please Justinian.

"It will happen, Most Noble Lord, that then you will need to wage a war."

"Eh? Is that just, Ambassador?"

"Why isn't it entirely just? Justinian means to be a worthy emperor of the Romans. Is it not right for him to seek to regain a land which belonged to the Empire of old? It is wrong for you, a philosopher, to think of waging a war."

Peter's guile played upon the twofold fears of the monarch of Ravenna. Across the Adriatic waited the armed host of

Mundus, its destination unknown. Theodahad yielded to his dread of the invisible, and pledged himself secretly to surrender his rule to Justinian, with payment of tribute and the service of 3,000 Gothic warriors.

At this point the machinations of The Silence seemed to have won a hold upon Italy. Cassiodorus, that perpetual secretary of the Amal royal family, wrote out a beseeching letter to the distant Emperor for Theodahad. "We give thanks to the Divine Being . . . that you do not seek to pick idle quarrels . . . you do not delight in unjust gains. . . . Glorious Masters [Justinian and Theodora] beloved in your own land, how much will you be revered in Italy if you preserve your disposition to peace."

This appeal was sent by the hand of "the most eloquent and worthy Peter, your ambassador." It delighted Justinian, who immediately accepted the terms.

Then early next year the whole picture changed around Italy. The forthright Agapidus died. In Dalmatia an armed host of Goths appeared. Mundus had all the fighting instinct of his Herul ancestors, and he led forth his army to attack his racial enemies. Even then the conflict might have been slight. But in it Mundus' son was slain; the Herul Master of Soldiers drove headlong into the Goths, dying under their swords. Although the Roman regiments won the field, few of their leaders survived, and they withdrew from the coast.

Learning of this disaster, The Silence called upon a reliable officer, Constantinian, Count of the Stables, to hasten by sea with fresh troops from the city to restore the situation in Dalmatia.

But while Constantinian was at sea, devastating news reached the generalissimo Belisarius in Sicily. Africa was in revolt, the Roman army of occupation disintegrated, Carthage besieged. The eunuch Solomon, who had been chief of staff and then military governor of the African conquest, brought the news to Syracuse. Solomon had escaped with his life from an attempt to assassinate him—fleeing with Procopius in a fast sailing vessel to appeal to Belisarius for help.

What could the commander do?

🏵 FAILURE OF A STRATEGY

Belisarius could not embark his small army for Africa without abandoning Sicily to the aroused Goths. There was no time to send to Justinian for orders. Belisarius acted immediately. He started down to a ship with no more than a hundred of his biscuit-eaters; he gave out word that he was going on a coastal inspection trip, and sailed instead in a fast dromond for Carthage. He took his standard and trumpeters, and during the short passage south he learned the particulars of the upheaval in Africa.

He should never have left that coast. Without a firm hand to direct it, the conquest had simply dissolved into the human elements that made it up. The garrison troops had become too conscious of the wealth and isolation of their coast, while their pay failed to arrive from Constantinople. Most of the soldiers had taken up with Vandal women, and most of these women had owned homes, if not farming land. Such property the Roman mercenaries looked upon as their own, whereas the officials in Constantinople claimed it as state land—or as estates of almost forgotten Roman *potentiores*. Moreover, the orthodox priests had closed the churches to all Arians, depriving the Vandal women of communion.

Solomon himself understood only how to enforce orders, and the orders from distant Constantinople could not easily be enforced with the soldiers mutinous. They had chosen leaders of their own, setting up a Soldiers' Republic, as they called it. Naturally, many of the Vandal warriors who had enlisted to escape slavery deserted to the Republic. Some others who had departed as slaves on the rowing benches of ships seized the vessels and rowed back to their homeland. These Vandals had been deeply attached to their homes and families. Naturally also, the original inhabitants, the Berbers of the hinterland, took to arms and raided the disordered towns. The situation was about as bad as it could be.

Belisarius landed in Carthage, where a remnant of loyal troops held out. The experienced Magister made certain that word of his coming sped through the countryside. Wearing his familiar scarlet cloak, he paraded the streets of Carthage with his escort of cataphracts. His trumpeters sounded the assembly, collecting men to his standard. Among them were many Vandals, recently his foemen, who seized the chance to better their desperate fortunes. As soon as he had the skeleton of a command, Belisarius led it out to attack the mutinous army of the Soldiers' Republic besieging the city.

It was his old trick of attacking with whatever he had around him before his antagonists could prepare to meet him. As usual, it worked. The rebel forces retreated toward Numidia, and Belisarius followed on their tracks. On the way his strength increased while the rebel army diminished. It had many leaders who desired many things, but none of them wanted to stand up against Belisarius. When they reached a river, the forces of the Republic did make a stand. But Belisarius led a charge into them, and the regulars who had served under him simply dropped their weapons to the ground. The others broke and ran.

Afterward, Belisarius summoned the mutinous captains to his tent. He held out a coin in his hand, an aureus with Justinian's head on it and the letters D.O.M., which stood for Master. The soldiers had turned, he said, against the master who paid them and trusted them. The captains retorted that he had not paid them.

Thus Belisarius relieved Carthage and formed an army of sorts again. He faced the task of bringing order to the coast

A capital in St. Vitalis, Ravenna. It shows the new Byzantine form, constructed to bear weight without strain. The interlace design is surmounted by affronted beasts and birds of Christian symbolism. The Justinian mosaic reproduced in the frontispiece of this book is seen in the background.

Nave of St. Apollinaris, Ravenna, after A.D. 525. The mosaic procession of women martyrs leads toward the Three Magi, represented in far background (CENTER).

St. Agnes and St. Apollinaris, from a mosaic in Ravenna. Women of the Christian tradition appeared early in the imagery of Constantinople, much earlier than in that of Western Europe.

under the new government—a more difficult matter for a man who had spent his life in army camps. Nor could he win back authority for Solomon. On the other hand, Stotzas, the prime mover of the rebellion, was at large on the coast where the tribal folk waited to rush to the aid of the victor.

Before Belisarius could accomplish anything more, an order from Justinian reached him. When he broke the seal he must have stared long at the words on the folded papyrus sheet. The order was to cross into Italy with his small army, to recapture Rome.

At once he obeyed, starting back to Sicily, leaving officers in charge of Africa. They could not suppress the revolt in the interior. Justinian then called in a man of authority to aid them. He took the risk of bringing his cousin Germanus from the watch on the Danube. Germanus had the prestige of blood relationship to the Emperor, the rank of master of soldiers, and the knack of winning over barbarians. Arriving at bedeviled Carthage he made proclamation that he had not come to inflict punishments, but to hear grievances—and that all soldiers would have their back pay, even for the time of their mutiny. So many of them had grievances, and Germanus was so indulgent in hearing them, that he collected real armed strength and began to bring order into the chaos of liberated Africa.

In his monastic workroom, Justinian had learned of the failure of his strategy. The Goths in Italy had been encouraged by the Roman misfortunes in Dalmatia and Africa. Their unworthy king, Theodahad, promptly forgot his secret pledge of submission and locked the resourceful Peter into a cell at Ravenna where he could reveal nothing of Theodahad's treachery. On their part the Gothic nobles were calling their henchmen to arms for the war that Justinian had sought above all things to avoid.

Apparently he had only the island of Sicily left out of the

wreckage of the plans of his strategists. Justinian was not at all
ready to admit that. There was much more on the map he
had burned into his memory. The Goths had settled upon the
fertile valley of the Po. There in the north they might serve a
useful purpose. Beyond them swarmed the uncontrollable
Franks, the wild Alemanni, and the dangerous Lombards. The
Goths—who had gained a rudimentary culture in the preced-
ing three generations from the dying cities—could be made to
serve as a barrier against the Franks and Lombards.

But it was necessary for his armies to win back Rome, at
the center of the Italian peninsula. Perhaps the astute Narses,
who waited at Justinian's elbow, pointed that out.

And in some way Peter, his ambassador, had got one important message through to him. *Strike while the Gothic
leadership is weak; whether this numskull Theodahad leads
them or is slain by them, he chains their strength.* (Peter lay
in his cell for three years; when he returned to Constantinople,
Justinian named him patrician and master of offices, and he
served in that post all the years until Justinian's death.)

So, late in the summer of 536, Justinian called on Belisarius
to win a victory that seemed impossible to gain.

❀ ROAD TO ROME

Unknown to Belisarius, his wife Antonina had made his
task more difficult. During his brief absence she had amused
herself with a handsome youth, actually a godson of Belisarius.
Aware of this, officers like the hot-tempered Constantine resented Antonina's lording it over the camps. The officers did
not share the blond Dalmatian's worship of his wife, but they
could not tell him the reason for their hatred. A quarrel
smoldered between the Magister and his generals that would
flare up afterward.

Oblivious, Belisarius made the best of his small means—loading grain from the harvest on his fleet, detaching only minimum garrisons to hold Sicily. Navigating the treacherous currents of Messina strait—the legendary peril of Charybdis-Scylla—he landed safely on the toe of Italy, having first taken care to win over the coastal commander by offer of reward and patrician rank in Constantinople. Having no more than some 6,000 in the ranks behind him, he marched to music as if supremely confident, with the impressive fleet accompanying him along the coast. Being without Mundus and the army of Dalmatia he had not strength enough to meet the massed host of the Goths in battle.

At Naples (Neapolis—"New City") misfortune delayed him. This was indeed a new city, huddled on its height behind a wall, lacking the splendor of buried Pompeii. Free traders, largely Syrians and Jews, inhabited it, and the inhabitants, like the Berbers of Africa, could not decide whether their safety lay with the garrison of Goths or with the imperial expedition. Naples, in fact, was an embryo of the free cities like Florence and Venice which would rise to power in Italy thereafter. After taking count of the few regiments that followed the imposing Belisarius, the Neapolitans chose to defend their wall against him.

Belisarius lacked the skill of a Germanus or Narses in winning over people; needing the harbor for his fleet, he attempted reluctantly to carry Naples by attack. A month of siege failed to gain entrance for the Romans into the city, while every day added to the anxiety of Belisarius. His officers worked without spirit, his cavalrymen shirked siege work, and all of them knew that any day 50,000 Gothic horsemen might sweep upon their encampment to drive them back into the sea.

Then befell one of the lucky accidents that served Belisarius so well. An Isaurian infantryman bethought him to investigate the aqueduct that the Romans had broken through in the vain hope of cutting off the city water supply. Crawling into the dry water channel, the Isaurian discovered that he had entered the city. Belisarius at once realized that he needed no Trojan horse to put a few score men within the wall by night to open the nearest gate. He made his plans accordingly while he gave the inhabitants a last chance to surrender. So it happened that his mailed riders rode headlong into sleeping Naples, and out of his control. The Huns and Heruls in particular cut a bloody path to spoil, and their commander had trouble saving the Goths of the garrison who surrendered. It was an ominous beginning of the invasion of Italy. Belisarius left a garrison in Naples and hurried his column north on the paving of the Via Latina.

In the first of the winter rains they passed Cumae, home of the ancient Sibyl. They sighted the Mount of Casinum where Benedict of Nursia gathered monks and peasants about him. They passed deserted villas guarded by dark statues of forgotten men. In the cluttered village streets small bands of people shouted in amazement at the apparition of a Roman army marching. For three generations no such army had been seen. And to the marching men, these bearded, muddied peasants resembled the animals they tended more than any citizens of Rome. Apparently wealth remained only in the seaports like Naples.

Then the Via Latina wound out of the dark hills and entered the plain of the Campagna. Mist hid the buildings that crowded the roadway. Smoke rose from sheds clustered like birds' nests against stone ruins. There was a magical moment when a great brown wall appeared across the plain by the glint of a river.

On the ninth of December in the ninth year of Justinian's reign, these East Roman soldiers marched into the city of the Caesars. On the steps of St. John Lateran priests gathered to watch them. Men calling themselves prefects and senators waited in ceremonial togas to greet them. Cattle grazed in the overgrown garden parks. Down across the river, beyond the fortresslike tomb of Hadrian, rose the stone steps of the rain-darkened basilica of St. Peter.

The soldiers from Constantinople did not know the names of the places. They said they entered by the Gate of the Donkey-drivers. They heard that all the Goths had left the city that day by the Salarian gate. Where was that? Over on the north side. The Goths had taken the road to the north—all except their commander, a certain Leuderic, who had been moved by some impulse to stay at his post.

Belisarius had Leuderic brought to him—a large man, silent, with a gold chain heavy about his throat. Why had his war host departed without striking a blow? Leuderic did not explain.

Belisarius took up his quarters in the palace of the Pincians, on the height above the northern gate, and he lost no time in riding the circuit of Rome. It was clear at once why the Goths had not stayed to defend it. The great Aurelian wall stood high enough, yet it had crumbled away in spots; the parapet had broken down, and the fourteen celebrated gates were makeshift wooden affairs. This wall measured twelve miles around, and as many thousands of men could barely hold it. Moreover it fronted on level ground patched with vegetable gardens and farms. To Belisarius, who had been bred in impregnable Constantinople, the defenses of Rome seemed to be a plaything of giants who had gone off and forgotten it. Immediately he started to remedy what he could, digging a ditch outside the wall and setting fresh stonework on the parapet. He sent his light horsemen under Constantine and Bessas—a Goth by birth—to explore the country to the north.

If Belisarius was disappointed in what he found in Rome, the citizens were disillusioned at beholding the army of the distant Emperor. Instead of bringing protection to Rome, the army seemed to be taking refuge in it. When the grain ships of Belisarius arrived up the Tiber, he stored the grain under

guard and ordered the Romans to bring all foodstuffs from
their farms into the walls. Clearly he was making ready to
stand a siege, and the oldest of the Romans had no memory
of a war being waged.

To Justinian, Belisarius dispatched the keys of a gate, and
Leuderic, the Goth who had surrendered Rome. He had carried out his orders.

※ "LET THE ANGELS COME, AMAZED. . . ."

On Christmas Eve the silentiaries set the diadem with care
on Justinian's gray head. It was the end of the tenth year of
his reign, the end of the year 6028 of the Greek record of the
world. The Hagia Sophia was finished. That evening he
would dedicate it.

The solitary monk who attended his robing chose to repeat
some words from the Mount. "Leave thy gift before the altar.
Make peace with thine adversary."

On the way from his chamber to Theodora, Justinian bowed
his head where the candles lighted the icon of St. Michael.

Like Michael, the all-powerful servant, he, the Emperor,
had conquered. He had made peace with his adversaries in
the East; he had set free the church of the apostle, St. Peter.
By the wisdom of Germanus, the African coast, beloved of
St. Augustine, had been brought to Christian peace. Surely
mighty forces, invisible, had aided him, the unworthy Justinian.

At the head of the steps waited Theodora, resplendent.
Behind his slender wife ranged a veritable court, the bare-
headed bishop of The Apostles, her chamberlain, the silent
Narses, and the women of splendor. In her salutation, however, Theodora murmured the ritual "Ever August . . ."; she

did not whisper her personal word of praise: "Justinian, you have conquered."

Yet the feeling as they left the long colonnade, where the grandees of the Empire fell in behind, was of victory won.

The Brazen Gate stood sheathed in gold plate. Beyond it all trace of the great fire had vanished. Massed nobility and clergy filled the Augusteum under the glow of sunset. Justinian wished it had been sunrise.

Was not the beginning of this Christmas Eve the beginning of a new day for troubled Constantinople? Tribonian, the aging Quaestor, had delivered all the fifty books of the full *Corpus Juris*, to set in motion the modern laws; the City Prefect had brought order into the rebuilt streets; the Partisans were gone; the workers labored with fresh eagerness; seamen explored unknown waters in the vessels thronging out to the Middle Sea and to the ports of the Holy Land; the homeless were sheltered in their new abode; the sick in mind had work for their hands in the new hospital.

More than the laws that drove his people toward achievement had been the summons to every group to accomplish something for the others. Surely they were doing that. How many had helped raise the piers of the great church? Sight of Anthemius and Isidore reminded Justinian of that. Age stamped the faces of his architect and builder. They had accomplished a task of fifty years in five. Had they been driven beyond their strength to accomplish this? Would the mighty dome of Hagia Sophia stand after their death? The work was done.

Justinian rode from the square on a charger borrowed from the Strategium stables, as if he had been the commander in a war. (Belisarius was fighting with all his skill to preserve the Rome of the Caesars.) From his saddle he could see, above the festive crowds, the statue of white stone he had ordered made to face the great church. It was a fancy of his,

to have Solomon the King there, fittingly on a throne, contemplating the courtyard of the Hagia Sophia. For the new
church would be in every way what that early temple of
Jerusalem had been. Secretly Justinian thought it would be
more.

They passed the statue, and Justinian dismounted—helped
by the silentiaries because he could no longer lower his weight
easily from the saddle cloth—at the steps of the palace of the
Patriarch, Menas. The tall, bearded Menas raised two fingers
in blessing. At the entrance of the church Justinian lowered
the crown from his head. Another voice cried out in praise.
Paul the Silentiary, that maker of witty epigrams, let out his
voice in a cadence of wonder at sight of the Hagia Sophia.
"Green of spring in the Carystian stones—crocus blooming in
light of gold—blue cornflowers in white of snow."

What was Paul invoking, more than the simple colors of
every day? The lilies of the fields? Paul's arms rose from the
hanging sleeves and his head lifted. "The wonder of the
lamps—the flames of the lamps are dancing beneath the dome
—suspended in the sky."

When Justinian lowered himself heavily into the throne
seat across from Menas within the great church, the flames of
the lamps were dancing overhead. It was late in the evening,
and the last sun glow had vanished. Hanging in their silver
boats and bowls the colored lamps illumined the heads of
thousands of human beings, pressed together beneath the
dome. They flickered on the silver imagery of the iconostasis, on the sheer golden figures of the cloth covering the
holy table. Cleverly concealed lights shone upward against
the Virgin in her night-blue above the altar. Dimly above
her the features of a head showed, Christ the Pantocrator—
the consummation of the will of the invisible God.

Justinian's eyes traced out, from force of habit, the crossed
wings of the cherubim in the highest angles. Yes, the wing

tips touched against the opposing walls. *"And they stretched forth the wings of the cherubims, so that the wing of one touched the one wall, and the wing of the other cherub touched the other wall."* Such exact detail satisfied Justinian's mind; if this great church was to resemble that ancient temple of Solomon, the wings of the cherubim should be as they had been before. And touched in the same way with gold.

Another voice rose and fell in praise. It summoned the listeners to look up to the waiting mother where the star gleamed. Why was she waiting there? A deep-throated chorus answered. She waited there for the three Kings riding; she waited there for the shepherds to behold.

The choir from The Apostles was joined to the chanters of Hagia Sophia on this Christmas Eve, the first in the great church. The one voice told the story and the choirs gave the responses of the shepherds and the angels.

Justinian could barely see, below the dance of the lights, the tense body of Romanos, who had brought this new song, this *kontakion*, to the choirs.

Romanos, that odd, intolerant dreamer, had been drawn to the city from the synagogues of the East. He had the secret of the oldest Christian liturgy. There was no sound of instruments, but the magic of echoing sound wherein voices mingled and separated.

The one voice cried out to listen. The three Kings were riding from the East. They were seeing the star. Beneath the gleam of the star lay a path, and they followed it. Listen to them exclaiming!

Romanos held up one hand, his fingers opening and closing. Like all the thousands, he heard that joyful music of voices, yet for the silent Romanos it was not here in the great church, not in the echoing gallery where Theodora the Empress waited intent. Romanos saw nothing of that be-

cause his mind was intent on the place far away in that other
time.

"Let the kings ride up in wonder, let the angels come,
amazed. Let them behold the mother with her child."

❀ THE TESTAMENT OF JUSTINIAN,
FATHER OF HIS COUNTRY

After dedicating the Hagia Sophia, the son of Sabbatius
felt tired. He counted his years, fifty-five; he counted the
years of his attempt to rule in one way or another, eighteen
of them. When he opened the alabaster pane of his window
on a hot night the breeze from the north swayed the flames
of his reading lamps, and that made his eyes ache. More
frequently now he took a sip from the bowl of barley water
and got up to look out this window of his cell. By craning
his head a little he could see, above the arches of the Augusteum, the mass of the Hagia Sophia. It rose above the city
like a watchtower, without buttresses or flanking wings to
sustain it. It stood there like a natural thing, like a tree,
rising sheer from the earth.

Atop the dome shone a crescent moon of gold. This was
the symbol of ancient Byzantium, now vanished into the earth
beneath Justinian's palace.

No matter what the hour of the night might be, somewhere another watcher of The Sleepless would be awake,
chanting a psalm. Justinian could follow such a voice with
understanding; on the other hand the strange harmony of
Romanos baffled him.

Whenever he turned back from the window, the son of
Sabbatius glanced at the youthful silentiary waiting at the
door to take a message. The boy might not have been alive
when Justinian had watched his uncle, Justin, accept the

purple robe contrived for him. Sometimes he felt like breaking the silence between them, to ask the youth whether he
missed the races or wished to go to the war in Italy. But
now his weariness lay between them; because he was tired,
Justinian seldom broke the thread of his own thought to enter
that of another. Yet he relied more than ever on the quick
wit and heedless energy of the young. He had a way of turning
more to Theodora for decision.

Why had his wife failed to share in his awareness of
victory over so many obstacles? Surely no one had gained so
much as she. Justinian understood quite well that the Despoina had withheld from him some part of her plans; she
merely explained that her quarters had become overcrowded,
and that she disliked the clamor and bustle of the thronged
Daphne. She pointed out that with all his building, Justinian
had added nothing to the old palace itself except the imposing entrance, which was really intended to impress visitors.
Spies served her in secrecy, and Theodora had the knack of
winnowing the truth out of their tales. She could tell where
a jeweler of Silversmith Street had found his amethysts; she
could hear a message in the song of passing fishermen. . . .

Justinian put little trust in spies; his *agentes in rebus* had
tried to impress him by warnings of fancied danger; he had
got rid of them. He had come to disregard whispers of conspiracy against him. The reign of Tiberius Caesar had paid
a bloody toll to informers. For the five years since the Nika,
Justinian had refused to inflict a death penalty.

He disregarded as well the warnings of blunt John, his
Praetorian, that he was draining all money from the treasury for his expeditions and rebuilding. Truly the receipts
from all taxes—including the new emergency levy—seemed
to flow outward at once. But was there danger in taking the
hoarded money of individuals to create something that would
serve the whole people? Officials had a way of thinking only
about difficulties. They could be eloquent in arguing that a

water system or even a church could never be built. As long
as a man felt comfortable, he would not strain himself to be
otherwise. Faced by hardship, he would exert himself.

Yet there seemed to be no way to keep men of ability
from gathering private fortunes for themselves—if they so
desired. Justinian had been warned that his ablest secretary,
Priscus, passed out trade secrets to a ring of sea merchants
over in Chrysopolis. The merchants gave him, under another
name, a share in their profits. Within the gate of his new estate above the Valens Aqueduct, John the Cappadocian collected royal tapestries and gold tableware, and the bevy of
imported serving-girls had less to do with John's table than
with his pleasure after wine-drinking at night. Justinian depended on Priscus to keep a daily summary of accounts, and
on John to have any accounts at all.

Theodora had assured him of that, and where women were
concerned, she got at the truth. Sometimes when he drowsed
under the touch of the night breeze, Justinian fancied that
he labored like Sisyphus, son of Aeolus, in pushing a huge
stone block up a height, only to have it slip from his grasp
and roll down the hill again. Narses hovered over him like
a hornet, urgent with the need to find somewhere a force to
relieve Belisarius in Rome, to extract Peter the Patrician
from his chains in Ravenna, to pay the soldiery of Germanus,
to send a trusted Magister to hold back the Slavs on the
Danube.

To ease his own mind, Justinian wrote out a remarkable
prooemium to the *Institutes*—the explanation of the new law.

This should have been done, of course, by Tribonian. But
the Emperor took care to write with his own hand any
message for the people at large. And this was addressed to
"the youth desirous of studying the law." It gave them the gist
of the thing, so they might master in one short book what
had taken students before them four years to read up. In
it Justinian appeals to young minds to make speed. And he

portrays himself not as a supreme magistrate of ancient times, or a "Divine Caesar" of the earlier Empire, but as a benevolent helper inspired by God to carry out a difficult task. His vanity creeps in:

> *In the name of Our Lord, Jesus Christ.*
>
> *The Emperor Caesar Flavius Justinian, conqueror of the Vandals, the Africans, the Goths, Alemanni and Franks, and the Germans as well as the Antes and Alans— pious and prosperous, renowned, victorious and triumphant, Ever August,*
>
> *To the youth desirous of studying the law. . . .*

To the ritual titles Justinian adds farfetched honors and some plain lies. Who are the Africans and Germans? He has not so much as encountered the Franks as yet. He reaches out for what *might be. . . .*

> *The imperial majesty should arm itself with laws as well as armies . . . that the ruler of Rome may prove to be mindful of justice as well as triumphant over conquered foes. The barbarian nations know our valor, being brought after so long again beneath the will of Rome. All these peoples are ruled by laws which we have now formed by the deepest application. . . . Like seamen crossing the mid-ocean, we have completed this work of which we once despaired . . . with that distinguished man Tribonian, magister and ex-quaestor, and the illustrious Theophilos and Dorotheus. By our authority and advice they composed this book of Institutes by which you may learn your first lessons in law no longer from ancient fables, but by the brilliant light of imperial learning. You can now begin the study of them without delay. These have been collected from the immense volumes of ancient jurisprudence . . . and after examining them, we have given them the fullest force of our constitutions.*

Receive, then, these laws with your best powers and eagerness for study . . . that you may gain ability to govern such portion of the state as may be entrusted to you.

Given at Constantinople in the third consulate of the Emperor Justinian, Ever August, Father of His Country.

Here Justinian did not sign as a Caesar or dominus; instead he invokes paternal authority over the country. And the *Institutes* seek to make sharply clear the meaning of the law to all the people. "For it is useless to know the law without knowing the persons for whose sake it was made."

What is justice? "Justice is the set and constant purpose that gives to every man his due."

What is freedom? "A man's natural power of doing what he pleases, so far as he is not prevented by force or law. Slavery is an institution of the law of nations, against nature, subjecting one man to the dominion of another."

What are the rights of children? "Our children are in our power. The power we have over our children is peculiar to Roman citizens, and is found in no other nation."

Have people natural rights? Yes, to the use of flowing rivers, to harbors and access to the coast of the sea—to the gleaning of food, fuel, and the means of living from the land itself. Then the law enters in, to define the rights of the state, for its preservation, against the individual.

In such a manner the meaning of the new *Institutes* is made clear to any person reading them and thinking about himself.

V

THE
SIEGE
OF
ANCESTRAL
ROME

BELISARIUS AND THE ROMANS

AN ODD RELATIONSHIP had grown up between Belisarius and the citizens of Rome. They were very few, but they still possessed slaves to do manual work; they enjoyed their leisure hours in the great baths—in the chambers that could still be heated—and they complained when he rationed their food, and cut short their afternoon sleep.

On his part he came to understand that getting food had become all-important to them; under their Gothic masters, small comforts had become their great desires. They had ceased to imagine any change in their rudimentary life. The widow of Boethius carried her small charities to the tenements, but few others read the books of Boethius. The only library was being gathered together by the clergy of St. Peter's across the Tiber. Technical skills had fallen away surprisingly;

no mills made use of the water power of the sluggish Tiber; the harbor at Ostia at the river's end had silted up. Belisarius' horses found good grazing along the grass-grown battlements.

The anxious conqueror of Africa appointed a new praetorian prefect for the city; engineers of Constantinople recruited craftsmen to build catapults and mechanical "wolves" (missile machines) to defend the walls; corn mills were set going again along the river, and a citizen militia was trained—and paid—to watch sections of the walls as in Constantinople. Because the drainage system of the outer plain had not been repaired, swamps had spread close to the walls, bringing with them miasmatic mists. And Belisarius' force—dwindled to 5,000 by now—could not maintain a twenty-four hour watch on the great circuit of the walls.

The citizens thought it rare good fortune that they had the whole of the first winter to prepare for their ordeal. But Belisarius knew that the scheming of Justinian had kept the armed host of the Goths occupied far in the north.

Drawn by the gold and the summons from Constantinople, the expanding Merovingian Franks had invaded the Gothic settlements beyond the Alps. Justinian had hoped for a collision there between these warlike nations. After some wary prowling in dog-meets-wolf fashion, however, the barbarian chieftains decided to settle the matter among themselves. The Ostrogoths, having more at stake, gave up their area of transalpine Gaul, with a payment to clinch the bargain. Peace was agreed among them by oath—a binding pledge to forthright German minds skeptical of written treaties. So, enriched by their Alpine journey, the red Merovingians settled back to await events in Italy.

Meanwhile the aroused Goths had disposed of their weak king Theodahad by killing him as he fled. They hailed as king one Vitigis, an experienced warrior. When Cassiodorus wrote out the letter of announcement "to all the Gothic race," he made the most of the hardihood of this successor to Theodoric. "Our blood-kin raised us on their shields in ancestral fashion, circled by lifted swords. In no corner of an audience hall but on the spreading field of battle have I been named king . . . by no more secret dealings shall the might of Gothic arms be broken down. I have witnessed your courage, and I need no other evidence of your worth."

Then, too, the experienced Cassiodorus pointed out that if Vitigis was not of the great Amal family, he would show himself to be worthy of Theodoric's lineage by his deeds. To link himself to the Amals, Vitigis took a bride by force—Matasuntha, the young daughter of Amalasuntha. This earned him the girl's hatred, and she waited like another Kriemhild for vengeance. Vitigis left her in Ravenna when he led the main host of the Goths south to Rome.

It was the end of the snows, the coming of the first grass and the war that Justinian had meant to avoid.

The onrush of the Goths nearly destroyed Belisarius at their first meeting. He had called in the Roman observation forces from Tuscany, and he was riding out with a regiment to inspect the guard towers he had built at a river barrier where the Anio flows into the Tiber. He found his outposts vanished, the towers taken by the Goths, who were crossing the fords of the flooded Anio in masses.

In the next hour Belisarius was fighting for his life, covered by the shields of his biscuit-eaters. This hand-to-hand combat delighted Procopius, who wrote afterward how deserters told the triumphant Goths to cut down the rider of the gray horse with the white nose—on which Belisarius rode—and how his hero beat them off with sword and shield. But it was no place for the commander of a forlorn hope. Late in the day his cataphracts broke out through the enemy ring. They raced their tired horses back to the Salarian Gate of the city, to find it closed against them.

In the fading light and drifting dust the excited militia and sentinels on the wall either failed to recognize their blood-stained general or feared to open the gate.

Caught between the onrushing Goths and the great wall, where a healthy panic arose, Belisarius played a desperate trick. He led his surviving cataphracts out in a charge, down the slope of the Salarian Way. Taking this to be a sally from the gate, the Gothic horsemen swerved away. Belisarius was able to enter his city again. But he had his work cut out to quiet the panic.

As darkness fell, the people of Rome watched the dreaded Goths thronging in from the north. Resistance in that hour seemed to be hopeless. Torches flickered from the Field of Nero—beyond the height of St. Peter's—to the Praeneste Gate. An officer ran to Belisarius shouting that the Goths had broken in and that he must escape while he could to the coast.

Instead of escaping, Belisarius mounted his horse again to investigate the rumor and found no sign of the enemy within the labyrinth of streets. He ordered all officers to keep their posts on the walls thenceforth, no matter what was heard or seen. He called on his musicians to parade around the battlements to hearten the citizen militia and keep it awake. To the anxious prefects, he made a promise: "I will drive your enemy away." Procopius relates that when Belisarius came into his quarters late that night, he sat down without touching food, being too weary to eat. He was persuaded to chew some bread and drink water. He had the peculiarity of never getting drunk.

To the Goths he showed the same impervious confidence. Their spokesmen shouted reproaches at the populace for submitting to "this band of Greeks—a people who have never entered Italy before except as hired actors or thieving sailors." More formally, they offered to Belisarius the pledge of Vitigis that he would be allowed to ride out, armed, with his command and embark unharmed on his fleet. "Be sure of this," he replied. "The time will come when you will look for a place to hide your heads and will find not a bush to hide in. Rome belongs to us of old. And Belisarius will not surrender it while he lives."

❊ THE VANISHING RIDERS

The populace believed that Belisarius was simply foolish to be so confident. When the Goths attacked all along the walls, he laughed at sight of their clumsy siege towers dragged forward by oxen. The mechanical power of his catapults cut down the oxen and mailed horsemen alike. At a stretch of broken ramparts called the Out-Garden, he allowed the enemy to break through until a counterattack of his cataphracts churned them into a disordered mass caught among the broken walls.

The worst befell at the Aelian bridge, which crossed the Tiber to the brown marble mass of the tomb of Hadrian (now the Castel Sant' Angelo). With scaling-ladders the Gothic warriors swarmed at the sides of the great tomb, defended by Isaurian infantry. Covering themselves with their shields, they beat their way in over mangled bodies. Here the physical force of the Gothic swordsmen prevailed. When the bridge seemed to be lost and a way to be opened into the city, an officer intervened. The headstrong Constantine, in command here, forced a passage across the bridge into the circuit of the tomb and stiffened its defense. Procopius relates how Constantine and his men, running out of missiles, broke up the ancient statues upon the parapet of the tomb. They cast down the blocks of marble on the swarming scaling-ladders until the Goths drew off, pulling away their wounded.

The first assault of the Goths was beaten off.

Will power had withstood man power; a few professional soldiers had won, in this first test, against massed courageous sword-fighters. By that much Belisarius had diminished the odds against him. The Goths, however, had the tenacity of men bred to war. They settled down in their camps to starve the defenders of the walls; they blocked the Tiber to ships by occupying Portus at its mouth; they broke down the aqueducts to cut off the flow of clean water into the city. By so doing they put an end to the public baths. (As it happened, the mighty aqueducts were not repaired for a thousand years, and the people of Rome never returned to the relaxation of their daily bathing.)

The civilians felt the ache of short rations; they watched the army surgeons operate on the wounded under tents in the forums; they carried water up from the Tiber's banks and complained bitterly to the inexorable Master of Soldiers, who did not seem to understand that by simple surrender to Vitigis, they might have fresh fruit and water again and enjoy all the other benefits of peace. They could return to the baths of Caracalla and Diocletian.

In response the adamant Belisarius ordered all noncombatants out of the city. Civilian families were to march out with personal belongings and slaves, to seek shelter in the hill towns or Naples. They could no longer be fed within the walls.

Oddly enough, the Goths did not interfere with the exodus of the helpless folk. The barbarians had their code, not of ethics, but of personal honor. They did not invade the rich and undefended cloisters of St. Peter's close to their encampment in the Field of Nero. And the implacable Belisarius revealed his anxiety for the people of Rome in a letter to Justinian which no one except the writer, Procopius, saw. In fact, the letter of that spring is a blend of the hard realism of the Magister and the fine phrasing of his secretary, who imitated Thucydides.

I have carried out my orders; you have the keys of the city and Leuderic. When the barbarians attacked with their whole army, they came within a little of capturing both the city and us. As to our prospects now, I could wish they were better. It is not possible for several times 10,000 men [Belisarius had 5,000 reduced by casualties] to safeguard these walls for long. This city covers too much ground, and is cut off from supplies by sea. . . . Although the Romans are well disposed to us as yet, hunger will change that. Their friendship will not bear evil fortune. . . . Do you, my Emperor, take thought of this: if the barbarians gain the victory over us, we will be thrown out of Italy and will lose the army. We shall be looked upon as having ruined Rome, as well as its citizens who have risked their safety in loyalty to you.

I shall not leave the city while I live. But I will not hold back from you what it is my duty to say. Send us supplies and armed men enough to engage the enemy on equal terms.

Already the civilian population was breaking up into factions, turning against the "imperialists." A strange rumor reached Belisarius. One night the doors of the temple of Janus had been forced open. In pagan times it had been the custom to set wide the portals of the two-faced god when a war was waged. Now the locked doors had been prized apart by unknown hands; there in the corner of the great Forum stood the tall bronze figure of Janus, facing toward the sunrise and toward the sunset as of old. After that, Belisarius had the keys of all the city gates brought to him; he ordered locksmiths to change the keys and recast the locks. The Numidians of his night patrols—they took leashed dogs with them on their rounds—were ordered to watch inside as well as outside the mammoth walls.

The Roman senate had become no more than a municipal

council, but the senators had not lost their habit of speaking for the *populi Romani*. Now they asked pertinent questions of Belisarius. If his eastern Emperor commanded such power, why had he sent only the fragment of an army to defend Rome? The Roman citizens had quarreled with no one. Why must they bear hardships and suffering to remain in their homes?

Belisarius asked them to wait, to see what would befall. The first change came with the arrival of the horsemen in the night. They numbered only 1,600, and their transports had been delayed in Greek harbors by the winter storms. But as it happened they were a treaty-contingent from the far Cimmerian Bosporus (the Crimea strait). These nomad riders found no difficulty in drifting between the drowsing camps of the Goths. Promptly Belisarius added them to the *numerii* of his cataphracts to carry out a new tactic of his devising.

This was to stir the Goths to attack, to their disadvantage. (And to keep them from assaulting walls he had no means of defending.) A cavalry column would ride out, to draw upon them a charge of the barbarian warriors—and to retreat swiftly under the missile machines that tore the ranks of the Goths apart. He drew an advantage from the size of the walled circuit which compelled the Goths to scatter their encampments around a wider perimeter. His experienced horsemen would make for one camp and break in before the Goths of other palisaded camps could aid in resisting them. Under cover of darkness his Moors stole out to knife the barbarians and ride away with horses; the gray riders filtered out with empty wagons to forage in the towns of the Campagna. By the next day, when the Goths discovered them, they had rounded up herds of precious cattle and filled their wagons. They then would form up on a hilltop as if to give battle. When the Goths mustered to attack them, they would whirl away after their wagons and herds, back to Rome. Or they would wheel out of sight behind strong infantry advancing from an open gate. Nor could the impetuous Goths come to hand grips, after their accustomed manner, with the riders who loosed deadly volleys of arrows from their saddles. The heavy farm horses of the Goths could not catch the swift steeds of the Numidians and Huns.

In this way Belisarius hoarded the lives of his men and wearied the enemy. The civilized thinker could keep one move ahead of the barbarian chieftain, who learned only by hard experience.

Belisarius also made use of the river. The Goths held the banks of the Tiber with the tow path, closing it to the barges and square sail luggers of Rome. Belisarius fitted sloops with the fore-and-aft rig of Constantinople, and they beat their way down the river in any wind. Wooden screens along the rails shielded these blockade runners from the arrows of the Gothic infantry. Then, too, the Goths could only cross the river by the slow process of ferrying themselves on barges—which Belisarius kept out of the city limits by massive chains stretched from shore to shore. The Roman cavalry crossed on the bridges concealed from enemy observation. Vitigis could not manage to guess where these dreaded gray horsemen would appear next, and finally, enraged, drew his encampments together on the hilly left bank, north of the city. This left the line of the river open to the south, where Belisarius watched with desperate anxiety for relief to come.

The summer ended, and no relief came.

❀ SONG OF THE STRICKEN STREETS

Something remarkable was happening to the citizens who kept watch on their walls. Accustomed by now to the hardships, they felt the excitement of conflict. They beheld victories gained over the dreaded Goths, and they longed to carry their spears into battle.

A new song was heard in the night watches. It echoed ancient poetry, especially Vergil's. *"Hail to Rome, mother and pride of the world."* Religious feeling found clumsy words. *"Hear us, Peter, bearer of the keys of Heaven . . . Paul, bearer of our sins . . . hallowed by martyr's blood."*

In their new martial eagerness they made much of the Master of Soldiers, who seemed to hold the secret of victory. They begged him, who had vanquished the Goths at every turn, to lead them against the host of the Goths to final victory. And Belisarius found new cause for anxiety in their eagerness. He tried to explain that he had no secret; he had merely followed out a certain tactic. "The Gothic warriors on foot have bows, so we keep away from them. The Gothic horsemen use swords and lances and have no bows; my archers engage them beyond reach of their swords and lances."

In spite of his protest, the senators and prefects begged him to end the struggle by one glorious battle. Balkan and Isaurian officers of his infantry had grown weary of inaction, and demanded to be led with the cavalry against the richly furnished camps of the Goths. But the Magister feared to risk his army entire against the northern warriors; a long battle would bring into play their stoic courage, their hand weapons, and their numbers.

When hunger increased in the city and no reinforcements appeared, Belisarius was forced to agree to give battle.

He did what he could under the circumstances. Dressing up the citizen volunteers and sailors with shields and standards, he sent them out with a regiment of Numidian horse on the almost deserted right bank of the Tiber. He ordered the commander of the cavalry under no circumstances to allow the militia to get near armed Goths. (But the Numidians charged an enemy camp, and the eager citizenry broke ranks to rush to share in the looting; the Goths in the Field of Nero gathered themselves together and slaughtered those of the make-believe army who could not escape to the shelter of the walls.)

As soon as the march-out of the militia had drawn attention to them, Belisarius launched his horsemen out the gates on the other side. His Isaurian infantry then followed in phalanx array to provide a rallying point at need.

The attack drove into the Gothic camps, and ended there against a shield-wall of warriors. Other masses of Goths closed in from the sides with the instinct of hardened fighters. They came on over their dead, locking an iron ring around the Romans, who could no longer maneuver. The sweep of their long swords broke down the lighter weapons of the Roman horsemen. Belisarius extracted the survivors and got them back to the safety of the walls. The Isaurians sacrificed themselves to hold back the surging mass of the Goths.

Procopius, who watched the defeat from the wall, could find no resounding phrases to tell of it. "The battle," he wrote bluntly, "which began at the enemy camps, ended at our walls."

There was little singing on the ramparts after that. There was the gnawing of hunger, the sickness that spread in the hot months from the swamps, fed by the waters running from the broken aqueducts. Belisarius reminded the despairing citizens that sickness had entered the enemy camps as well, and all the plain of Campagna hungered. (The farmer-warriors of the Goths had not been able to harvest their fields in the north, and no grain could come in over the seas.)

In this ordeal the tenacity of the barbarians matched the will power of the civilized defenders. No news came from Constantinople.

As the autumn ended, Belisarius sent messengers he could spare and trust, Procopius and his wife Antonina, under escort to Naples. He bade them collect any armed men they found and any food they could buy, to send up to Rome by the river. Then at last in the November frosts, news arrived. A fleet appeared at Naples with grain and 3,000 Isaurian infantry. "Bloody John," the general who heeded no orders, was leading 1,800 horse overland from the Adriatic, collecting wagons as he came.

It was little enough to aid Rome. But rumors of Imperial armies approaching reached the Gothic encampments, and Belisarius was quick to add warnings to the rumors. More than that, he sent his cavalry on a headlong raid down the Appian-Latina Way, clearing the Goths from the road up which Bloody John would come. The rumors took effect on the uneasy mind of Vitigis. The wearied Goths despaired of taking Rome with fresh Imperial armies coming upon their backs, and sent their spokesmen to discuss a truce with the implacable Roman commander.

Belisarius awaited them as usual on a stage set for splendor. Seated before a crumbling arch of triumph in his cloak of the golden eagles and his plumed half helmet—with officers in court array behind him—he waited as if to hear their pleas. (The smallness of the reinforcements convinced him that Justinian had no greater strength to send, but Justinian had promised to raise another army, and Belisarius gambled on that promise.)

In silence he heard the preliminary orations of the tall German warriors—an Italian interpreting for them—that the war was bringing misfortunes to both alike. They wished to talk, not of personal repute (vital to German warriors), but of safety for all.

Belisarius had no objection to such talk.

The Goths explained that they had respected the Emperor and his laws. They had maintained Roman law in their land, and had never opposed him. Let Belisarius explain this to his emperor. Let him depart from the land, taking (as a concession) whatever plunder he had gained.

Belisarius: "You are speaking of Italy, the land of my master, and of property that is his."

The Goths: "We will surrender Sicily, valuable to you, who hold Africa."

Belisarius (amused): "I thank you. And I on my part will give up the whole island of Britain [unseen by Roman eyes for generations], which is much larger than Sicily. You see, I cannot accept such a favor without returning it."

Uneasily the Goths offered more—Naples, Campania, a yearly tribute.

Belisarius had no power to dispose, in this manner, of his emperor's territory.

Then the Goths would send an embassy to Justinian, to negotiate a peace with him. And to do so (the real point of their mission) they wished to make a truce with Belisarius.

Belisarius: "I agree to that. I have never refused to make a peaceful settlement."

❀ THE RIDE OF BLOODY JOHN

So a truce of three months was sworn to, in that December of 537. Vitigis sent his envoys to seek Justinian in Constantinople, but Belisarius snatched advantage from the truce without scruple. It cleared the way into Rome for the reinforcements—the Isaurian regiments and the grain ships sailing unmolested up the Tiber, Bloody John bringing his column of horsemen unhindered through the Goths up the Via Latina—and the astute Master of Soldiers allowed his enemy no time to realize how small the relief forces actually were. As the Goths vacated their posts along the river, he occupied them, and the hill forts around Rome as well. He gave no answer to Vitigis' protest that the Romans were breaking the sworn truce.

With food and fresh regiments within the walls, Belisarius went to work anew on the mind of Vitigis to drive the Goths away from Rome.

Hungering for grain, wasted by the fever of the swamps, the Gothic warriors watched the Romans moving out into their forts as if to surround them, while they listened to rumors of other mighty armies coming in from the sea to destroy them. The best of their heroes had died under the walls. They shouted their anger at Vitigis, who tried to imitate Belisarius' treachery by sending his swordsmen to steal into Rome by one of the broken aqueducts. The warriors got in, but found themselves wandering through the labyrinth of waterways and drains. They lighted torches to find their way, and heard the mocking laughter of the Roman soldiery over their heads. Their anger grew against Vitigis.

Belisarius put his hope in two messages. One from the girl Matasuntha in Ravenna offered to open that city to the enemies of her hated husband. The other plea was from the archbishop of Milan (Mediolanum), who had found his way through the barbarians to urge the Romans to liberate his city. Ravenna was the seat of the Gothic court, Milan the home of the revered St. Ambrose, and both seemed to be hopelessly beyond Belisarius' reach.

Under the thin screen of the truce, Belisarius flung a tight column of horsemen north with Bloody John, a nephew of the ruthless Vitalian. He bade John ride with fire and sword, taking harvests and women and towns as he went, but to keep an escape road open behind him.

John's riders sped north like a shaft from a catapult; he swung east through the mountains on the Flaminian Way; he took no heed of Belisarius' caution, and he stormed into Rimini (Ariminum) over the waters of the Adriatic. Another day's ride would have taken him to Ravenna and glory to match the fame of the lowborn Belisarius.

This blow broke the tenacity of Vitigis. In the night the

Goths burned their palisaded encampments and took the Flaminian Way, hurrying to save their farms and families and Ravenna itself—as they imagined—from the Romans.

At the first daylight Belisarius swept all his forces in pursuit. Where the Anio flows into the Tiber, he attacked savagely. The Goths were half across the rivers, and their retreat became a wild flight toward their homeland. They did not wait to discover that they were pursued by no more than a skeleton army. So Belisarius won his victory over the mind of Vitigis, and kept his promise to the populace of Rome. He was out in the open. For the first time since crossing the strait of Messina, he held the initiative, at the end of March 538.

It was a slight affair, this collision of mailed horsemen at the fords of the swollen Anio. But it marked the ending of an age. That age in which an Aetius had led his legions against Attila's Hunnish invaders would never return. Count Belisarius led liegemen of his own, and his loyalty was pledged to Justinian as that of a Count Roland would be pledged to a Charlemagne. Vitigis bore no resemblance to Attila; he was simply a German hero with a sword, as unthinking as the unfortunate Siegfried of legend. Unknown to Belisarius in this darkness of the ages another Christian leader rallied a few mailed horsemen in remote Britain to withstand the pagan Saxons. This leader of peculiar ideals may have been Arturus of a noble Roman family, but legend describes him as King Arthur, of the knights of the Round Table. Behind the legends lay the reality of feudal Europe.

As Belisarius pressed north, gathering in the small walled towns of the Apennines, he learned that John had disobeyed orders and got himself into Rimini in the path of the hurrying host of the Goths. Belisarius sent an Isaurian regiment ahead along the coast to hold Rimini, if possible, and free John's cavalry column. But he himself hung on the heels of the retreating Goths, who could be given no time to regain confidence.

Then chance served him well. Couriers came in from Ancona on the coast with vital news. A fleet had arrived at Ancona with the real strength that Justinian had promised him during the ordeal of Rome. In fact, another army was disembarking with 5,000 regular infantry and 2,000 mounted Heruls.

At once Belisarius rode west to the coast to meet it. There to his surprise he found the commander of the relief army to be Narses. The febrile eunuch, Spatharius of the palace and confidant of Theodora, had achieved his ambition to go to actual war. At their meeting Narses bowed low to the soldier, as to his superior. Yet he presented a letter of authority signed in purple ink with Justinian's name.

The letter had a curious phrase. It instructed Narses to obey Belisarius "in everything that served the welfare of the state." When reread carefully the words took on another meaning: that Narses was to obey Belisarius only so far as he served the welfare of the Empire. Belisarius thought over the words and ignored them.

Narses, the watchdog of the palace, had a simple idea how the two of them could win victory—by joining together to give battle to the host of the Goths. Belisarius knew this would be fatal. His only hope was to deceive and harry the scattered Goths until their will to resist was broken. "They must be forced to surrender," he tried to explain to Narses, "without conditions."

Narses could not understand. "Go to Rimini," he urged the Master of the Soldiers, "set free John, the nephew of Vitalian, and then by your illustrious wisdom vanquish the whole host of Vitigis."

Out of their divided counsel came misfortune.

The first calamity was the appearance of western barbarians flooding through the passes of the Alps—tribal Burgundians, sent by their masters the Franks to loot their fill in war-torn Italy. The Burgundians descended the rivers toward Milan.

In anxious Ravenna, the aging Cassiodorus wrote one of his last letters as Minister of the Gothic King. It was meant to hearten the Goths in Liguria, in the farmlands around Milan.

"Divine Providence tests our courage by adversity. Famine afflicts your province, as all the others. The Burgundians are sneaking into your territory. Yet rejoice, O Ligurians! . . . If the harvest of corn is lost to you, there will be a harvest of dead enemies. The King has seen your calamity. He has remitted one half of your taxes, and he will save you from the swords of your enemies. Like Joseph in Egypt, he will rescue his starving people. Happy age! In which a king may be likened to a prophet."

With these empty words Flavius Aurelius Cassiodorus, senator, signed off as counselor and writer to the Gothic kings. The futile Vitigis could not carry out his promises. Within two years Belisarius ended the duel between them by tricking the Goths out of Ravenna itself. And Cassiodorus sought refuge in the monastery he had founded with his wealth, to write a personal history of his time.

❀ OMEN OF THE COMET

It appeared in the midsummer sky, following the path of the sun through the sign of Capricorn. The comet kept its head toward the east, and some watchers said it trailed a flaming beard behind it, while others said it looked like a swordfish.

Justinian asked the Patriarch, Menas, the meaning of the flaming star. Menas could only tell him that God's power had balanced the firmament of the sky over the earth; quite clearly a single star had departed from its place. It must be a sign for their eyes to behold, but whether of good or evil to come, they could not know.

In giving its warning, the swordfish comet might point toward the east or to Italy. Justinian wondered if it had been wise to send Narses in command of the relief army, to keep discreet watch on Belisarius. His favored general had not been able to repeat at Rome the swift triumph of Carthage. Then, too, Belisarius had put to death a notably brave officer—Constantine, who had held Hadrian's tomb against the Goths. To be sure, the unruly Constantine had taken a pair of valuable jeweled daggers from a Roman noble escaped from Ravenna. He had refused to give back the weapons at the order of the Autocrator. But Belisarius made a fetish of protecting civilians and their property. When the enraged Constantine had tried to stab him, Belisarius had brought the case before the other officers, and Constantine had been condemned to hanging. It angered powerful relatives of Constantine—at a time when Justinian was attempting to do away with the death penalty.

His officers also reported that Belisarius was training the Italian peasantry to arms—sending some of his veterans into the northern villages to do so. The illustrious Balkan commander seemed to count on the people of the countryside to aid him to victory. Certainly he refused to fight the battle Narses demanded—to end at one stroke the increasing strain of the war. The two of them got John safely out of Rimini— by pretending to attack Vitigis from all sides and from the sea itself, until he fled again, to Ravenna. John, however, gave Belisarius no credit for this maneuver: "I have Narses to thank," he said, "for my life."

Then came the tragedy of Milan, the city isolated by swarms of Burgundians and Goths. Belisarius had ordered two of his commanders to march to the relief of the Milanese people, starving within their walls; but his commanders would take orders only from Narses, who had not acted promptly. The exhausted garrison surrendered the city; once inside the walls, the barbarians killed and carried off the inhabitants, cut-

Mosaic heads of holy women, Ravenna, sixth century.

*St. Michael Archangel, patron saint of early Constantinople.
Mosaic from St. Apollinaris, Ravenna, sixth century.*

ting the Praetorian Prefect into pieces to throw to their packs of dogs.

The men of The Silence pointed out that even in ancient Rome two commanders had never agreed on what one army should do. One must have authority over the other.

Then—when the comet flamed over Constantinople—the north of Italy was rent by a human earthquake. After the sack of Milan a horde of Franks rushed in on the heels of their Burgundian henchmen. Vitigis gathered his army into Ravenna.

That decided Justinian, who could only watch the calamities spread over a map on the wall. Narses understood the need of ending the war at once, but Belisarius was the only man capable of withstanding such odds.

Justinian dictated an order to the confidential secretary Priscus: "We do not give our purse keeper Narses the command of the army. It is our wish that Belisarius shall lead the army entire, as seems best to him."

Narses was recalled.

Even his departure left a scar for the anxious Belisarius to heal. The valuable but savage Herul regiments declared themselves to be Narses' men, and demanded to be sent back to Constantinople with him. Belisarius refused to provide them with ships and stopped their pay and rations. Whereupon the hardy Heruls deserted, to find their own way back by land, paying and feeding themselves by looting villages as they went. This march of the rebellious Heruls only added to the storm rising along the inland frontiers. As if to join the marauding Franks, the Alemanni emerged from their forests beyond the eastern Alps. Masses of Huns were seen approaching the Danube.

When he returned to the Daphne, Narses agreed with the observers of The Silence as to the cause of the storm. (Justinian soothed the pride of the sensitive eunuch by explaining that he was too valuable a mind to be spared from the palace headquarters.) Desperation had driven the stupid Vitigis to do a clever thing—to send envoys to the other barbaric nations, urging them to unite with the Goths to break the power of the Empire. However, the Alemanni merely moved down to plunder; the Long Beards (Lombards) refused to aid the defeated Vitigis, while the headstrong Franks rushed in to snatch a conquest for themselves. Throwing their axes before them, the German warriors drove the dispirited Goths out of ruined Milan. (Heedless of the eloquent proclamation of Cassiodorus.)

That summer the comet flamed over the human tides. The heat of the Po valley bred sickness among the Franks, who soaked up wine to cure themselves. They reeled back before the stand of Belisarius' disciplined regiments and disappeared into their Alps. But along the Danube gathered the Huns from the hinterland. No army remained in the Balkan heights to oppose them. Hastily Justinian recalled Germanus—who had once kept Thrace quiet—from the reconstruction of Africa. By some magic of persuasion, Germanus might hold back the barbarians at his old frontier.

Then traders came in from Palmyra, the outpost in the eastern deserts. With their loads of silk from China and incense of Arabia, they brought ominous tidings from Ctesiphon, city of the Great King of Persia. Vitigis had sent two envoys to this most powerful antagonist of the Empire. Two monks, pretending to go on pilgrimage, had slipped past the guard posts of Constantinople. At Ctesiphon's arched palace the monks had delivered the message of Vitigis—that Justinian, the Caesar of Constantinople, was waging war against innocent peoples in the West and increasing his power each year. That Justinian could do this only because he had gained a sworn peace from the Great King. He had taken his armies from the East to conquer the West. Would the Great King wait idle while the lowborn Justinian restored the power of ancient Rome, that nemesis of Persia? Or would the Great King arise in his strength and take for himself what he willed of the undefended East of the Roman Empire?

The traders did not know what the Persians might decide to do.

In The Silence, Justinian's military strategists pointed out the danger to him. They had neither the men nor the means to wage war in the East and West at the same time.

There was only one solution to their dilemma. *Belisarius must end the conflict in Italy without further delay. Vitigis and the Gothic nations must be preserved as subject-allies, to be a barrier between Rome and the menace of the hinterland. Belisarius must bring back the field army to Constantinople; in readiness to move against his old antagonists, the Persians.*

A message came from Belisarius, fifteen hundred miles away in the charred streets of Milan. Peasants in Italy had not been able to raise their crops that summer; people were seen gathering grass to eat by the streams; their yellow faces and swollen bodies pressed around the wagons bringing grain and dried meat to the soldiers. Belisarius could not give out food from the scanty army stocks. Vitigis and the Goths penned in Ravenna also began to suffer from hunger. Their stored grain had been burned—perhaps by the servants of the young queen, Matasuntha, who hated her thane-born husband. Their end was only a matter of time. Belisarius promised that.

❀ THE MEDEAN FIRE

Justinian could sense the agony in Italy for which he was responsible. He envied his cousin Germanus, who rode with patrician carelessness through human conflict as if riding ever-lastingly to a hunt. More than one horse had been killed under Germanus. Admiring friends kept him company. When Justinian made his decision as emperor he felt himself to be alone. The memory of his mistakes haunted him.

Remembering just then the envoys of Vitigis who had been kept waiting in a hostel for a year, he summoned them. In the full splendor of the Triclinium he spoke to them as the Most Sublime Autocrat, expressing fatherly sympathy for his son Vitigis and dismissing them to learn what terms the King of the Ostrogoths would offer now in submission.

As they departed through the great colonnade, they stared amazed at the image of Naples on the wall. Skilled artists were erecting mosaic vistas of conquered cities, Carthage as well as Naples, so that all passers-by might behold the glories recaptured in the West. Justinian had ordered it. He wanted to bring into the city the images of the outer world. This ceaseless rebuilding gave him a sense of accomplishment. As far off as Bethlehem the work was going on. Over the cavern of the Nativity a mighty edifice was rising, and a mosaic picture on its walls showed the Three Kings riding up to the Mother, as the song of Romanos related.

"He spares no expense," merchants said, "of any of us. He makes these monuments out of the taxes we pay."

Already Anthemius had transformed the old, leaking Church of the Apostles into a sanctuary with five small domes. Theodora had aided its building. Justinian's own inclination had created a water-palace beneath the paving, between the Augusteum and the restored portico of the Zeuxippus. In this odd palace a myriad carved columns rose from the water. Visitors sometimes fancied it was meant to allow the confined Emperor to take a boat ride without leaving his palace, but it actually stored up overflow water in case of a siege.

At times Justinian disappeared bodily underground. He took with him the trusted Priscus—who lived another life as a wealthy trader in news—and Marcellus. Still young, Marcellus had shown himself to be a reincarnated centurion, seldom speaking, rigid in his concept of duty and honor. Justinian had appointed him a swordbearer in the palace. With Marcellus leading, armed as always, the three of them passed through the underground prison of the Excubitors—empty now—into the guarded cellars of the war scientists.

"Have you—made progress?" Justinian always asked them in anxious hope.

Here beneath air vents, engineers examined captured weapons, or tested new inventions. Cartographers kept up to date the secret military maps of the new frontier fortifications and the ceaseless movements of troops. University-trained chemists labored like grimy Vulcans to improve the one secret weapon of Constantinople, the Greek fire.

"Thrice-August," the chemists answered cheerfully, "we make progress, but no discovery as yet."

It was simple enough to use what they already had—flaming liquid. Naphtha, derived from asphalt substance and bitumen, came to Constantinople from the Caucasus Mountains. This could be fired and pumped for quite a distance through bronze tubes. On the prow of a war dromond it served well enough to set fire to another vessel. But flaming liquid could damage its users as well if the pump went wrong or the wind changed.

The jolly chemists were working at a more deadly mixture. A blending of bitumen, sulphur, and lime—or perhaps the more active saltpeter—would flame up when cast into the enemy. In one experiment they had set it off by the heat of the sun; in another test, water had acted on the lime to explode the mess. All the chemists had shaved off their beards and some had scarred faces.

Their code name for the secret weapon was "Medea's fire." The name hid the nature of the experiment, but perhaps the scientists remembered how the angered Medea had slain her own children. Once they had made a demonstration of the simple naphtha flame to impress Himyarite chieftains from pagan Arabia. The awed tribesmen demanded to be told the secret of the flying fire.

"This is the secret," the astute scientists assured the Himyarites. "Hear, and remember. For an angel of Heaven brought down this liquid flame to the holy Constantine because he was the first Christian emperor. Our grandfathers bear witness that the angel gave the fire to Constantine of glorious memory, and in so doing that angel laid a curse upon any man whatsoever who gave our fire to any man who was not a Christian of this city. So take care never to touch the liquid, or the curse will be upon you and invisible flames will consume you."

The Himyarites understood how harm would come from such a curse, and when they returned to Arabia they told their fellows that the Christians were safeguarded by fire from Heaven.

Justinian wanted to believe that the chemist might succeed and the new Medean fire make Christian armies invincible in battle. But would it? He yielded to the temptation to ask his companions what they thought. Priscus answered promptly that the Most Illustrious would surely obtain the weapon, and it would be invincible. Marcellus said he did not know.

The anxious Justinian remembered that Belisarius depended upon men, not miraculous weapons. His own biscuit-eaters were clad in light chain mail invented by the Persians, and made use of the short curved bow of the Asiatic nomads. Belisarius, however, always studied the situation maps of the Strategoi. Now Justinian glanced at the huge wall maps hopefully, as if they held some inanimate strength to aid him. On them the immense and expanding frontiers were neatly traced in green. Behind the wavering green lines stood innumerable tiny blue squares. These were the *castella* upon which the strategists of Constantinople rested their hopes.

All the way from Palmyra to the deserts behind Carthage these *castella* were being built apace—stone-walled enclosures on heights with towers to defend them. They resembled eastern caravansaries combined with the old-style Roman forts. In old days the Caesars had kept frontier troops—*limitanei*—encamped behind the frontiers, but Justinian's domain no longer possessed the great strength in legions needed to do this. Constantinople armed peasantry as a kind of *limitanei* along the frontiers. These farmer guards had failed to withstand invasions of barbarian horsemen. But they could retreat with their families and herds from the villages into the fortified enclosures of the *castella*.

The barbarians, bent on snatching up captives and spoil, could not well besiege stone walls. News of the raid would reach the nearest army headquarters, and a field army would move up swiftly to relieve the *castella* and drive off the invaders. If worse befell, and the line of the strong points was lost, the strategists had provided a second line of strongly fortified cities linked together with watchtowers. These could surely hold out until the main army of Constantinople itself could arrive by sea, and speed—it consisted mostly of cavalry—to the danger point.

Such was the defense planned by the Strategoi of Constantinople against the barbarian invasions. It cost little because the single professional army was small, about 25,000 men, and the armed peasantry lived off its farms. But Justinian knew, and Narses did not suffer him to forget, that the one veteran army numbered no more than 18,000 just then, and it was far off at Ravenna, where Belisarius waited to starve the Goths into submission. Moreover, because he had been obliged to ship greater supplies to Italy that summer, the Praetorian Prefect had failed to send the yearly annona of wine, meat, and grain to the frontier forces. In another year, with more money and Belisarius back in the city, the defenses could be strengthened. Until then, Justinian used every trick of diplo-

macy to cajole and keep separated the chieftains of the hinterland who were thronging against the borders.

One year of peace his city must have, to gain safety.

On a night when the comet flamed bright, the watchers on
the beacon tower of the Daphne reported fire sighted upon a
western beacon. Warning had been relayed from the Dardanelles.

The next days brought the details of disaster. Sarmatian
Huns had crossed the middle Danube, sweeping over unpre-
pared villages, storming into the poorly guarded *castella*. The
scant field force of Macedonia disappeared under their hard-
riding masses.

One fortified city, Potidaea, had been stormed by the Huns.
Heading toward the Greek coast of the Ionian sea, they
stripped the countryside like human locusts, herding away
hosts of captives. They sacked eighty villages and bore off
with them as many thousands of humans.

Germanus arrived from Africa, but the strategists had no
armed force to give him. There remained in the city only the
Guards and Excubitors, with some Slavs learning Latin words
of command in the Strategium drill-ground. The strategists
pointed out that this was no more than a raid, and that the
Huns would retire beyond the Danube after the harvest. It
troubled Justinian most that they had overrun his homeland
on the Vardar. He resolved to rebuild Bederiana with great
walls of granite and new churches.

Of nights when his work was finished he read over a letter
of St. Basil, that sickly body with the invincible spirit.

"But what will befall us now? My brother, the tower of our
strength has not fallen. The remedies of amendment have not
been mocked. The city of refuge has not been closed."

St. Basil had been convinced of a protection greater than
castles or the Medean fire.

❊ THE ARTS AND THE SORCERERS

A boy named Agathias came to the city from Antioch. His father planned for him to study law, but Agathias had a thirst for poetry, and he followed after the aging Paul the Silentiary in silent hero worship. Long afterward, remembering those years of splendor in Constantinople, Agathias wrote: "Everything that was human had been set in motion."

Through the widened streets—the Prefect had done away with the narrow lanes of the tenements that kept out the sunlight—poured life from the Nile and the river Don; at the piers of the Golden Horn, Greek sea captains landed Spanish cattle-breeders, with Moorish silversmiths who carried their treasure of a few tools wrapped up in their hands.

With the tools arrived the skills of the immigrants. The Jewish glassmakers from Palestine—who made so many of the lamps of Hagia Sophia—knew the secret of fusing color, dark blue or even green, into the glass itself. Armenian stonecutters had a knack of chiseling patterns into the surface of flat building-blocks. (Their ancestors had studied the rock carvings of the Sassanian artists, and in Constantinople they saw the graceful figures of ancient Greek friezes in the Pheidian manner.) These artisans would have been puzzled by our conception of the word *art*. The few painters among them enriched the margins of sacred books with miniature scenes. All believed themselves to be skilled workers, members of the guilds that turned out utensils and buildings to please their patrons and pay themselves.

The ordinary citizen, who lacked rank and wealth, craved some niceties in his abode—a lion's head, perhaps, on his bronze door-knocker, or the figures of the apostles hammered out around the rim of his silver water bowl for guests. Customers and artisans shared the desire to have personal objects picture their religious faith. A housewife might envy the cloth of gold mantles of court ladies; a Persian weaver of brocades could offer her a garment in iridescent yellow, almost as impressive in the sunlight, with the symbol of Theotokos on the shoulder, instead of a badge of rank.

In this way the Constantinople manner developed. (There were hardly "schools" as yet, of the arts.) It appreciated, but departed from, the monotony of Oriental design; it turned away from the prettiness of the last Hellenistic picturing, of Pompeii, and it avoided the heavy monumental style of the ancestral Romans. (A modern critic stated that Justinian was Roman only in his building of aqueducts.)

The developing art of Constantinople resembled the Romanesque that would largely derive from it in western Europe; it was an expression of religious faith.

Fear of the Huns brought a new tide of refugees into the city. And the restlessness of the streets encouraged the devotees of the ancient mysteries. At the spring festival in the Hebdomon, unknown voices mingled a pagan chant with the Kyrie eleison. Where the statues of Constantine and his mother stood over the gilded Milliarium, a silver chain with a dangling cornucopia was hung between them. Soothsayers explained that this was the Fate of the city returning to its founder.

Superstitious souls hastened to bring a lotus blossom of Isis and a fawn-skin of Bacchus to the feet of the Fortuna above the Golden Gate. Along the Mesé, oracles spoke their warnings from the spirit world.

Justinian rarely showed anger, but now he raged against seekers of the occult who believed the messages they heard in a darkened room—whispered through a long speaking-tube by a magician. If they saw shadow shapes on a ceiling, he bade them look for the conjurer's fingers moving over a hidden lamp.

When his agents caught soothsayers at work, Justinian ordered them bound face to tail on a camel's back and paraded up the Mesé. By edict he ordered: "If a shrine of a mystery is found within a home, that house will be confiscated to our treasury."

One year a change took place, little heeded at first. Officially it was still the year 1295 since the traditional founding of the city of Rome. Now in the calendar of the churches it became Anno Domini 540. It reminded people that they lived, and would live, in a Christian world.

The next year Justinian struck at the most cherished Roman tradition. He abolished the consuls.

A murmur went through the city at this. At a forbidden seance the listeners heard the voice of Canonaris, who had confronted Constantine at the dedication of the city. "Do not raise yourself above our ancestors," Canonaris had warned the founding Emperor, "because you have made them nought."

That aging chief secretary, John of Lydia, declared openly that evil times had come upon the Roman state because only Christians were allowed to keep the records and only ordained priests might lecture in the auditoriums. Justinian retired the old man, appointing him professor in the university to lecture in Latin. Whereupon the worthy John wrote his memoirs of forty years of service to a glory that had departed, so he thought, never to return.

One evening a boy of Justinian's robing chamber slipped a sealed scroll into his hand. Evidently it had not been trusted to the hand of Priscus. With some amusement Justinian read in the message that John of Cappadocia, "your glorious praetorian prefect of the East, ex-consul, and patrician," offered sacrifice of a black she-lamb in a night of the moon to Hecate, goddess of the underworld. He kept his shrine hidden among Judas trees, and from it a screaming spirit flew up, trailing flames, and disappeared toward the moon. In this manner the pagan Cappadocian sought for evil power to exalt him to the

Emperor's throne. Was he not guilty of sacrilegious ritual and his palace forfeit to the treasury that he abused for his own ends?

As he pondered the message of the scroll, Justinian ceased to be amused. The unlettered Cappadocian was forever seeking for thaumaturgic spells to aid him. Probably a conjurer arranged the apparition of Hecate by pouring oil on a captured hawk and setting fire to it. But he could not condemn John for sorcery. In this emergency he needed all the Cappadocian's ruthless skill in raising revenues.

In the scroll he sensed Theodora's mockery. These two, who were like two hands in doing his work, hated each other. John complained fiercely that he gathered in the centenaria of silver only to watch the Despoina shine with more precious jewels. Laughing, Theodora remarked how John's purple chlamys had grown almost as long as the Emperor's, and how his bodyguards had grown into a small army able to seize Constantinople if he gave the word. Like Caligula, he rewarded his favorite cooks with noble rank—his feasts were splendid with gold, whereas Justinian used the plate captured from the Vandals and contented himself with an earthen dish of stewed herbs and bread.

If John hid treachery behind his satyr-mask of flesh and mirth, Justinian must take that risk.

Then Theodora left his side.

❊ THEODORA HIDES A PATRIARCH

Theodora never chose to explain why she departed from the women's chambers of the Daphne. Justinian had not seen fit to improve the rambling palace in which they lived—perhaps because he would not take the money from the Privy Purse. As if he had taken a monk's vows, he went from work-cell to

scriptorium. He expected to find her waiting with her women
on the terrace.

Her sleeping chamber overlooked the beacon tower and the
small palace that was kept closed. This was screened by the
gardens except for its pyramid tower of dark-red stone. Because of that stone they called it the Porphyry Palace; it was
opened only for the lying-in of imperial women, and their
children were described as born in the purple. In the fortieth
year of her age, Theodora did not expect to have another child.

The coming of the saintly Saba gave her no hope. This
shriveled anchorite from the wilderness of the Jordan, coming
on a great dromond to the Golden Horn, to be taken by the
hand by Justinian and led into the palace, where Theodora,
kneeling, begged the holy man to pray that she would bear a
child. And the aged Saba, looking down at the sheen of her
diadem, answering only: "God will preserve the glory of your
Empire." (And John of Cappadocia whispering: "God forbid
that another such as she should issue from her womb.")

Without the child, Theodora laid her protection upon her
sisters, marrying Comito, the older—an actress like herself—
to Tzitas, who had taken Belisarius' post as master of soldiers
in the East. The daughter of her younger sister Theodora wed
to the son of Hermogenes.

Even more quietly, Theodora watched the family of Germanus of noble Roman lineage. She made every effort to keep
the popular Germanus on duty far from the city. Being without illusions, she distrusted the loyalty of any men who might
find the way open to the throne of Constantinople. Justinian
was alone, without son or brother, nor was she recognized as
empress. While he trusted both Germanus and John, one of
them would surely be given the diadem if he died. He would
take no thought of that.

Perhaps the actress in her sought to play a new part. Perhaps a deeper instinct led her to make her own sanctuary
across the Bosporus.

A promontory stretched out from the wooded Bithynian shore. A lighthouse stood at its point, almost out of sight of Hagia Sophia's dome. It being far from a harbor, only fishermen resorted there. Theodora begged for a house of her own there, where she could rest.

Justinian built her no ordinary house; he ordered the wooded point terraced and walled for gardens and a mole flung out for an anchorage. On the height where Theodora could overlook the sea, his architects raised a secluded palace, with alabaster windows that veiled the inner chambers. Somehow it acquired an old Greek name, *Hieron*, the Sanctuary.

Theodora may have been responsible for that. Certainly she did not intend Hieron to be a place of rest; she transported thither all her large court, although many of her people grieved at leaving the city streets. Apparently the self-willed Despoina had removed herself from the eyes of the Augusteum. Like Nausicaa, she appeared at ceremonies, whipped by the breeze of the Bosporus in her scarlet barge. "She has trained her people to be slaves," said those who hated her, "and now she would make herself feared as empress."

Justinian did not enlighten the curious. For the first time his slight pallid wife opposed him with all her intensity. She fought his decree for persecution of the Monophysite churches. She had championed the priests of the East—and restored their churches in Antioch; she had hidden rebellious preachers like Jacob Old Clothes in her House of the Monks. (After John of Tella had been burned as a heretic.) Nor would she argue, reasonably, what they preached. "A woman has no understanding," she insisted, "of controversy in faith."

What mattered it how the Trisargion was sung in words? What mattered it if a man repeated the creed of the Nicaean Council or the words of Paul, the Apostle of the East?

Theodora had been frightened by the fanatical Saba—so Justinian thought. To Justinian's orderly mind, the words of a creed mattered much. Had there not been conflict in the city

streets over the Trisargion before his reign? If the ritual was
not the same in every diocese, how could his people be joined
in unity of faith, gathered as one congregation before the many
altars? With the great Hagia Sophia their visible shrine?

Do not interfere with the churches, Theodora begged him.
Let the people keep their shrines as of old.

When Justinian deposed the Patriarch Anthemius for agreeing in secret with the eastern confession of faith, Theodora
tried by every means to persuade him to restore Anthemius.
When a synod pronounced anathema against the old man,
Justinian ordered him into exile. It was not a harsh order, because it sentenced Anthemius only not to enter a large city.

After that Anthemius disappeared from the streets of Constantinople and Theodora fell silent. After a while the congregations ceased to wonder where the exiled Patriarch had taken
refuge, but silentiarics of the palace knew that Theodora had
hidden the old man in her women's chambers.

Soon after that Theodora moved all her people to Hieron.
And it was rumored that the vanished Anthemius served the
altar at Hieron. If so, the Emperor had been obeyed, because
the Sanctuary was not a large city.

In the letters of St. Basil, Justinian pondered the words
spoken by the Apostle Paul: *"But all these things one and the
same Spirit worketh, dividing to everyone according as he
will."*

Now Justinian did not believe that his wife had read these
words of the blessed Paul to the Corinthians. Yet her thought
had been the same—that the divine Spirit touched all alike.
Was not that the final significance of the Hagia Sophia? Still
Justinian felt convinced that if there was to be one Church
there must also be one creed within his jurisdiction. Otherwise the heretics, such as the Samaritans, Jews, and Mani-
chaeans—all of whom he had oppressed and persecuted—
might share in the communion of orthodox believers.

He remembered the words of that strange monk who came

from rebellious Severus of Antioch: "Our Empress, ordained by God," the monk had cried, lifting his pilgrim staff toward Theodora, "to aid the oppressed."

Upon Justinian alone rested the awful responsibility of a judge in these unsubstantial matters of ritual. When the new orthodox Patriarch, Menas, blessed the congregations, the robed Emperor stood beside him—not to give the blessing, but to give his authority to the act.

In the end, Justinian allowed the exiled Anthemius to remain in hiding at Hieron. And Theodora did not cease to fight him with a woman's wit and ruthlessness on behalf of her schismatic clergy of the East. This silent duel between them went on through the coming years of calamity, to a surprising ending.

Procopius of Caesarea, returning to the city, was aware of their conflict. "It is true that for a long time we supposed them to be diametrically opposed to each other in their opinions and ways of living. . . . Yet they did nothing separately in the course of their life together."

🏵 SENDING FORTH OF THE SHATTERERS

Like the glow of a sunset over the water of the Golden Horn, the light of the last year of peace lay upon the city. It had never been so fair. In that January of 540—the month of the ancient god Janus—the organs of festival were heard in the forums, even if no games drew the crowds to the hippodrome. Through the night hours the lamps of the Hagia Sophia and the new library, built upon the ruins of the Octagon, summoned the people.

In this outward aspect of tranquility, the few men of ability, but of no particular rank—except that they were all Illustrious by title—worked around the clock to hold the menace of war beyond the frontiers. By day the flicker of mirrors from the outer signal towers, like flashes of lightning in gathering clouds, brought tidings of danger along the horizon. The Sarmatian Huns were moving south again; in the west, Belisarius' commands held back the Franks in Liguria and kept the Goths within the marshes of Ravenna; in the east the armies of Persia were assembling under the Great King.

The handful of Illustrious flung trusted officers toward the dangers. Tzitas went to the troubled Armenian mountains; the son of Rufinus—that ablest of diplomats—sped along the post roads to hold back the Persians by fresh negotiations; Germanus followed him to rouse indolent Antioch to defend itself. Justinian himself dispatched two envoys to Ravenna to offer a peace that would leave Vitigis a Gothland north of the Po.

As the crisis deepened, it shifted toward Justinian's personality. He no longer had the senate to decide on means, or the Council to devise ways for him. Because he had insisted on his personal authority in shaping civilian life, there was no one else to prepare for the wars, a task for which Justinian was ill equipped.

To save money, he had done away with the largess to the armed forces every five years; he had drained the garrisons from the provincial cities even while he strengthened their walls and improved their water supply. He thinned down the post service, replacing some horse relays with the cheaper donkeys, cutting down public transport until villagers often had to pack their goods on their own backs. Now there might be immediate need of swift horses and immense wagon transport.

"Pay the taxes promptly," he urged the outer towns, "to aid us to manage the increasing expenditures for our needs."

John of Cappadocia pointed out that the one greatest lack and greatest need was gold. In John's restless fingers a bright new aureus revealed the likeness of Justinian himself mounted on a war horse and wearing the helm and breastplate of imperial Rome. The coin filled John with furious dissatisfaction. It showed Justinian as if leading to victories. But what had been obtained from the spending of all their aurei—why, monasteries in the desert, gardens for the monks atop Mount Sinai, a cathedral for poverty-ridden Bethlehem—a palace, no less, for prostitutes, and a marble summer resort for Theodora.

In this emergency John demanded that taxes be levied on all classes. "For more men live on the taxes than pay them," he declared cynically.

Then, apparently, the *Aerikon* or emergency tax was levied.

At one time in the older Rome, all citizens had been free from taxation. In Constantinople some few still enjoyed this immunity, the honorary senators, physicians, and professors, with some officers of the Guards and skilled artisans. (It had helped draw to the city master workmen in mosaics, enamel, and ivory carving—who were adding precious details to the new buildings.) Now their immunity was taken from them without pity.

But most of all, John, who had the hard duty of filling the public purse, inveighed against the "tax-free aristocracy." In Rome of the Tiber the tax system had grown pestilential for one reason; it was based on land worked by slaves, whose masters paid the revenues on the assessed value of the lands and the workers. The owners paid, that is, what they saw fit, and were free to exact what they could from the branded workers of their soil. The smell of this system still prevailed in Constantinople's empire. Every five years Censitors assessed an owner's property and held him responsible for the tax payment upon it. In the case of a village, the leading curials paid to the treasury what was due from the village. What was taken from the field worker and what was eventually paid in to the government's treasury depended very much on the integrity of the magnates.

The hated income tax on profits had been abolished before Justinian's time by Anastasius.

There was a vital difference, however, between the Rome of the Caesars and the dominion of the Constantinople emperors. The first had been based on the labor of subjects rigidly controlled; the second depended on a peasantry very loosely controlled. Especially in the eastern provinces, men worked the fields of their ancestors. In power over them rested no single patrician order, but their feudal lords. By Justinian's time his dominion bore more resemblance to that of Charlemagne than to Trajan's. His *potentiores* owed him absolute fealty, but they had the characteristics and the intransigence of European barons of a later day.

For some time, especially under the mild Anastasius, there had been a revival of town life away from the central city; barren land was coming under cultivation by the peasantry. Justinian failed to understand many matters, but he realized the importance of well-being in the provinces. In the ageless conflict between peasantry and landowners, he tried to protect the serfs.

"It is shameful," an edict to the proconsul of Cappadocia states, "to relate how the managers of great estates defy the laws. They march over the land with an army of bodyguards and throngs following, on their way to rob the common folk of everything . . . by bribes to officials, they make themselves owners of public grazing lands and herds. So land owned hitherto by the treasury has become for the most part private."

To hear the complaints of the peasantry and to call the magnates to account, Justinian organized his own corps of examiners. These were the *Discussores*, and for good reason they became known as the Shatterers. They reported directly to Justinian, and were not bound by orders of the Praetorian Prefect.

Immediately the *Discussores* pointed out the evil of rivalry in remote towns between civil and military governmental agencies.

"In certain of our provinces," Justinian's edict ran, "the civil and military governors quarrel steadily with each other. They contend not how they can benefit our subjects, but how they can more oppress them. So we have thought it right in these cases to combine the two charges in one office, and to give the old name of *praetor* to the new governor."

More than that, he called his new representative a *praetor Justinianus*. These "Justinians"—as provincials named them—uncovered time-honored habits of garrison commanders, of drawing pay for soldiers no longer on the rosters, of police and army officers defying civilian laws, of city magnates squeezing revenues to compensate them for the exactions of the military.

Then Justinian dealt drastically with the *asperiores provincias*, the farther "bitter provinces." Brigandage had reigned in fertile Cappadocia and religious strife in Palestine. Each divided province was thrown together under a duke (leader) or magistrate. Beyond the sea, Egypt, almost out of touch with Constantinople, was given a single moderator to bring the upper Nile under control of Alexandria—and to keep the grain fleets moving toward Constantinople.

Yet in the farthest provincial towns the inhabitants looked to Constantinople for their amusement. Little enough broke the monotony of labor in the fields—the arrival of a state courier, the posting of a placard, processions of the priests on festivals, the coming in of a caravan. Otherwise, there might be games in the circus, antics of mimes in the square, or gossip of a miracle, and quarrels of the youth of the demes. On the frontiers a watch was kept for barbarians coming in to raid or trade.

Along the menaced frontiers of the Danube and—now—the Euphrates, masters of soldiers held new authority. With startling vanity, the planner in the Daphne gave the new provincial groupings the epithets of a *Justiniana* or a *Theodoriada*. Yet in so doing he attempted to solve the almost insoluble problem of extending the rule of his city of the seas over the tradition-bound hinterland. He evolved the prototype of the great *theme* system that would save Byzantium at the end of the century.

His writs were nailed to church doors, to be read by congregations that had known only the orders of army officers.

Even in this ominous beginning of the year 540 Justinian would not abandon either the rebuilding of his city or his new system of government for a return to the old military state. No citizens were drafted into the army, which remained a highly trained skeleton force. (The mutinous regiments of Huns were won back to service by Narses, who gave them back pay for the time of their mutiny. Germanus went to Antioch with no more than 300 men.)

Nor is there any indication that the overstrained Emperor relaxed his efforts to safeguard individuality among his people. Their cases multiplied in the records on his table, for his judgment. An illiterate woman pleaded: her spoken testimony was written down by a *chartularius*, but the writing did not agree with what she meant to say. What must the judge decide? Mothers of children had rights as well as the fathers of families. . . . "They are to be exempted from the law . . . which requires mothers about to become guardians of their own children to swear on oath that they will not enter on a second marriage; for we have found that this oath is broken almost as often as it is given." In this Theodora's hand appears. And perhaps she decided the question: can a wife refuse to legitimize a child born out of marriage because she fears that it will shame her?

Even while Justinian writes out a rule for monastic life—after the letters of St. Basil—he can consider the case of women in remote, barbaric, and yet Christian Armenia, where Tzitas labors. "With them, women are excluded from succession. They can be sold like inanimate belongings by their husbands. The rights of the Armenian women are to be enforced."

Is this merely stubborn determination? Is Justinian by nature a bureaucrat incapable of relinquishing a detail upon which he has set his mind? Or is the man who created Hagia Sophia resolved to bring to reality a better world?

VI COMING OF THE FOUR HORSEMEN

BELISARIUS DISOBEYS AN ORDER

THERE WAS A WARNING in the Book of Revelation. When the first seals of the book were broken, four horses came forth with four riders. The first rider—of the white horse—wore a crown, and he went forth to conquer. The second rider, of the red horse, was given a great sword with power to slay. The third, upon the black horse, held a scale in his hand, on which were weighed grain and oil and wine against coins. Only the last rider, of the pale horse, bore a name and it was Death.

The readers of the scrolls of the Scriptures believed this had a meaning: after conquest followed war, and after war followed hunger—with black pestilence. Now the artists of the time who illuminated the sacred rolls with pictures to make clear the meaning drew small human figures, of a king and a helmeted soldier, of a starving man, and finally a bare skeleton. They found no mystery in the words of St. John. For misfortunes befell them much in that same order.

Early that spring, warnings multiplied within the walls of Constantinople. Tzitas, the commander in the East, was killed among the Armenians. Like a flooding river, the Sarmatian Huns poured through the thin barrier of guard troops in Thrace and reached the Dardanelles. They crossed the strait from Sestos to Abydos, at the place where the Great King Xerxes had built his bridge of boats—where Justinian's custom house stood now. From the terrace of Hieron, Theodora saw the glow of burning villages on the Asiatic shore. And far to the east the Great King Khusrau grazed his horses on the plain of the Euphrates as he advanced with his armed host, taking ransom from the Roman frontier towns on his way. The desert crossroad of Palmyra—where Zenobia had defied the soldier-emperor Aurelian—was lost to his nomad clans.

Justinian still hoped to avoid a great war in the Empire. More tangibly he gained hope from a message of his ambassadors in Ravenna. The dispirited Vitigis had agreed at once to his terms—that the Gothic treasure should be halved between them and Italy itself be divided, with Vitigis ruling north of the Po as duke of that frontier province.

But Belisarius had refused to sign or accept Justinian's peace terms. Whereupon the Gothic nobles became instantly suspicious and turned against their ineffective leader, Vitigis.

The next report was fairly amazing. The war council of the Goths had offered to submit to Belisarius, and to make him *Roman Emperor of the West*. And Belisarius had accepted the offer!

The news came like a thunderbolt upon the strategists of The Silence. They understood at once that their supreme commander needed only to step to the throne in Ravenna to become in reality master of the West. The hero-worshipping

Goths admired him; the Italian people were nursed by him, and he had defended Rome for its citizens. Sicily and the fleet were his, and Africa would hail him as Caesar if he showed himself on that coast, governed again by Solomon, his former chief of staff. Already their leader of forlorn hopes had made himself that most dangerous thing, a legend.

Justinian reminded them that Belisarius had sworn to keep faith with him. There was nothing, in any event, that The Silence could do about it now. For in the East the Persian host was advancing toward Antioch.

Outside the marshes of Ravenna—the stagnant waterways that safeguarded the city of Theodoric more than its walls —the paradoxical Belisarius was carrying out one of his feats of deception. His scattered commands patrolled the restless banks of the Po; they kept food out of the hungering city, while his envoys warned the Gothic nobles to have no more hope in the advent of those other Germans, the Franks.

Belisarius had fought a bitter war for five years. His road from Carthage to Ravenna had not been an easy one. The soldier could not bring himself to agree to Justinian's terms of half-victory that would leave his enemies still a nation strong in arms. Belisarius had driven the Gothic strength of numbers and courage into its last defense. He meant to destroy that strength.

With careful forethought he called into council his high officers—chiefly John, the friend of Narses, and Bessas, who had been born a Goth—who complained that he was disobeying the Emperor. He summoned Justinian's two envoys to hear him, and he talked quietly to all of them, asking among other things if they believed a political peace would really end the long war. Then he asked: "If you could obtain all of Italy for Caesar, with all the treasure in Ravenna, with the submission of all the Goths, would you not cast your vote to do it? If it can be done without costing the life of one man of ours?"

They had to agree that if Belisarius could accomplish this, it should be done.

Whereupon Belisarius gave them orders at once. John and Bessas and the others departed to gather provisions through the countryside and bring them by ship to the port of Ravenna. His comitatus and the veterans of Rome were to accompany him.

Now in agreeing to become their emperor of the West, Belisarius had pledged his faith to the Gothic envoys that he would protect the lives and personal property of their warriors. But he explained that he would take his oath as ruler to Vitigis and the council of nobles within Ravenna itself.

On a fair morning in May, Belisarius rode in over the causeway through the marshes. He was clad for ceremony, as if to take his place on the throne of Theodoric. His biscuit-eaters followed at ease, with lances and shields slung on their backs. Through the open gate and the massed Goths, Belisarius led his horsemen.

They passed the few monuments of Roman rule, the neglected tomb of the devout princess Galla Placidia, and the small palace where Stilicho had been murdered and the boy Romulus had put on the imperial purple for the last time. The great Church of St. Martin (that came to be St. Apollinaris') had been built by Theodoric, and in the last two generations the city had become the capital of a Gothland that was doomed to disappear like the Vandal kingdom of Africa.

Procopius watched this strange ride in, and thought that it seemed to come about by no contriving of human beings, but by the will of Fortuna herself. "For the Goths were greater in numbers, yet were being made captive by the weaker force . . . when the women sitting at the gate had seen the whole of our army, they spat in the faces of their husbands. They pointed their fingers at the Romans of such small size and called their husbands cowards."

Heedless of the women, Belisarius paused to summon

chieftains to him and assure them that they were free to return to their villages. Many started to leave with their swordsmen. This made a confused coming and going that Belisarius did not try to remedy. He set guards over the treasure. (Ever since the legendary Nibelungs, the German kings had hoarded their gold.) He set guards around the steps of Theodoric's palace, where Vitigis and the nobles waited to acknowledge him as emperor.

When he dismounted at last, Belisarius explained to his enemies that they were the captives of Justinian, the one emperor whom Belisarius himself served.

Men who have resigned themselves to make peace are not to be roused by a few words to resist. Belisarius had deceived Vitigis ruthlessly.

Very quickly Belisarius summoned into the harbor the grain ships of his officers. When they appeared up the canal the hungering families of the city rushed to get at the food.

Belisarius, however, had kept one promise. Not a Roman soldier had lost his life.

Before he could organize his bloodless conquest, Belisarius was recalled by Justinian. He obeyed the order, as he had obeyed before in Africa, against his better judgment.

❀ FALL OF ANTIOCH

There was an invisible bond between Theodora and the lovely city of Antioch. Once in her wandering Theodora had found shelter there; perhaps the Despoina believed that ancient Antioch and not new-built Constantinople should be the capital of the Empire. Certainly this Queen City of the East —as wayfarers called her—had something of the woman's nature, passionate and demanding, submitting at need to a conqueror, but never imitating his habits.

Antioch claimed the primacy of Christian faith; she had heard the voices of Paul and Barnabas. In their strange Greek patois, her people had mocked at the exhortations of the pagan Caesar, Julian. In rejecting the Rome of the Caesars, the Queen City had yielded to the influences of the East. Her artists enriched Constantinople; Anthemius copied her famous House of Gold in his eight-sided Church of Sergius and Bacchus, and her mosaic patterns of oleander blooms and confronted peacocks adorned the palaces on the Bosporus. Yet Antioch would render only lip service to the new-rich capital of Constantinople. Within the circuit of her great wall perhaps a third of a million Antiochians had thrived in peace for nearly three centuries—since the Emperor Valerian had been crushed by Persian power.

"In wealth and size," spies assured the Great King Khusrau, "Antioch is first among the cities of the East Roman Empire. Yet this city is destitute of trained soldiers. Its population cares for nothing except festivals and living in luxury; they know only the rivalries of their theaters."

The people had courage. Sheltered behind their parapets, they watched the Persian invaders appear along the banks of the Orontes River near the northern city gates. It was then June of 540. The Antiochians had heard how the enemy burned frontier towns that did not save themselves by yielding up their treasures. The Persian horsemen—two or three tens of thousands—did not seem to be dangerous; they seemed more intent on making camp under the trees across the river than in attacking the great city. A civilian who spoke Latin advanced to the Daphne gate, calling upon the excited Antiochians to earn the mercy of the Great King Khusrau by payment of ten hundredweight of gold (about $2,000,000 in mid-twentieth century money).

The bishop of the cathedral urged the citizens to pay the ransom; so did the envoy, who had been born a Roman. In fact, the strange young Khusrau was marching through Roman

Syria that summer more to satisfy his curiosity and to carry back spoil to Ctesiphon than to meet the Romans in arms.

From the parapets the Antiochians loosed arrows at the envoy, and they laughed, jeering at the name of the Great King. A few days before, some regiments of regular cavalry had reached the city from the Lebanon; youths of the hippodrome factions mustered in motley armor, ready to die in defense of their walls, and boys of every sort thronged up with stones, slings, and bows. All of them—except the regular troops—felt certain that the walls of Antioch were impregnable.

Angered by the insults, the Great King ordered the city to be stormed.

During his visit, the experienced Germanus had warned the people that the heights behind the city looked strong, but were actually a point of danger. At the last moment the citizens tried to strengthen the space along the heights with log palisades and wooden platforms.

The enemy now made a great to do down at the river. But the real attack came in the half light of dawn on the heights that had seemed to be safe. Up in the labyrinth of rocks, the civilian warriors resisted bravely, shouting: "Justinian conquers!" Before long their timber platforms broke down under the weight of the excited throngs. At the sudden crash and outcry, defenders of the parapets imagined that the wall had been broken through, and they ran back to the streets.

Within a few minutes the eager thousands became jostling mobs. No one came forward to command them. Family groups struggled to gather up their valuables and, as panic grew, to save their lives.

On the heights, the Persians climbed their ladders unopposed, to watch the bedlam below them. Khusrau gave order for his forces to withdraw from the gate leading to the gardens of Daphne and the coast. The frightened people flung open this gate. The mercenaries mounted their horses and rode headlong to escape from the disaster. The Persians were willing enough to let them go, and the townspeople began to stream after. Clumsily the militia of the factions tried to organize a street-to-street resistance, but the hysterical crowds ran into their ranks. Antioch paid for its centuries of peace.

After resistance ended, the methodical conquerors assembled the multitude of captives in bands to lead away; they set fire to the residential streets, but spared the cathedral in the great square after collecting its treasures. Then they continued their triumphal march.

Observers who visited the stricken city were amazed to find the fortifications standing intact around the charred ruin of the streets.

Envoys from Justinian reached the presence of Khusrau that summer, to offer a heavy payment in gold coin for a new peace between the empires. It is said that the adventurous Sassanian, when he arrived at the shore of the Mediterranean, put off his robes to take a bath in the Roman sea. He had a sense of the dramatic, and an appreciation of irony.

"Money cannot buy friendship," he replied to the Roman envoys. "The friendship ceases as soon as the money is spent." As if in afterthought he added: "Perhaps a payment every year would preserve the friendship you seek."

That meant payment of an annual tribute. The Roman envoys broke off negotiation to report to Constantinople. It is said also that when the captives of Antioch arrived at Ctesiphon on the Euphrates, they were given a suburb of their own. The Persians called this slave-town *Roum* (Rome). But it became known thereafter as the "Antioch of Khusrau."

The devastation of Antioch grieved and then angered Theodora. It seemed to her that her husband's generals had sacrificed the City of the East. Characteristically, she set about punishing them by intrigues not apparent to the preoccupied Justinian.

On his part he summed up the losses silently. The Gothic nation that he meant to be a guardian of the north—torn asunder. Half the population of Antioch enslaved, and the city burned because Belisarius had failed to obey him and return in time from Ravenna.

Stubbornly, Justinian gave order for rebuilding Antioch, for changing the course of the Orontes to make it a moat for the lower wall, for shrinking the walls to enclose the city and avoid the fatal heights. He refused to pay the yearly tribute to Khusrau, whereupon he faced the one thing he had sought to avoid, war in the East. To prepare for that, he summoned Belisarius home.

❊ THE CITIZENS STAGE A TRIUMPH

There was no repressing the populace when Belisarius returned to Constantinople. His fleets brought incredible cargoes, the treasure of Ravenna, almost forgotten standards of Roman legions that had fallen to the Goths in the old days— with the gold circlet of the Emperor Valens, who had died at Hadrian's City—and a captive host of stalwart warriors, their chieftains and their king, Vitigis, with his unwilling bride, Matasuntha. Beside the striking figure of Belisarius appeared philosophic Peter the Patrician, released from his cell.

Justinian bestowed an estate on the dispirited Vitigis, and he gave only cold thanks to his victorious general. He ordered the insignia and treasure to be shown only within the palace to those of senatorial rank. There would be no public triumph this time for Belisarius.

The city, however, contrived to give Belisarius a triumph of its own.

When he left his house in the morning, crowds were waiting to hail him on his ride down the Mesé. Teen-age girls ran out to throw myrtle before the hoofs of his horse. (The conqueror of Italy always showed himself in full panoply of silvered mail and plumes, with a Napoleonic bevy of officers riding at his heels.) The street was swept; incense smoke curled up from the doorways; women waved kisses from the embroidered hangings of balconies. In the forum of Constantine the circus factions massed—against the law—and their choruses resounded over the peal of their silver wind organs. *Belisarius tu vinces—semper vinceres!*

To the admiring people this man was an unquestioned hero. For he had conquered the Vandals of Gaiseric and humbled the proud Goths of Theodoric. They beheld the evidence of victory with their own eyes. Moreover the tall, bearded Belisarius was noble by any man's estimation. He pulled in his horse to greet old front-line soldiers by name, those who had fought at the Ten Mile Post or the Aelian bridge. He put gold coins in the hands of the penniless. When his admirers got drunk in celebration, Belisarius did no such thing; nor did he cast a second glance at the young wives who worshipped him with their eyes.

When he reached the Augusteum, even the beggars forsook business to acclaim him. Belisarius was an uncomplicated man who knew better than anyone else how to encounter an armed enemy; but he never managed to understand politics. During these days of adulation, warriors offered to serve in his comitatus until his personal army grew to seven thousand. The transported Goths and Vandals would have followed him against any force of Guards or city militia. He could have gained the throne of the Caesars by a spoken word, but it never entered his mind to do that. "While Justinian lives," he had told the Gothic nobles in Ravenna, "I will not take the name of a king."

Theodora foresaw danger in the stupidity of Count Belisar-

Design of affronted peacocks and matched foliage, an Oriental motif. Marble sarcophagus, Ravenna, sixth century.

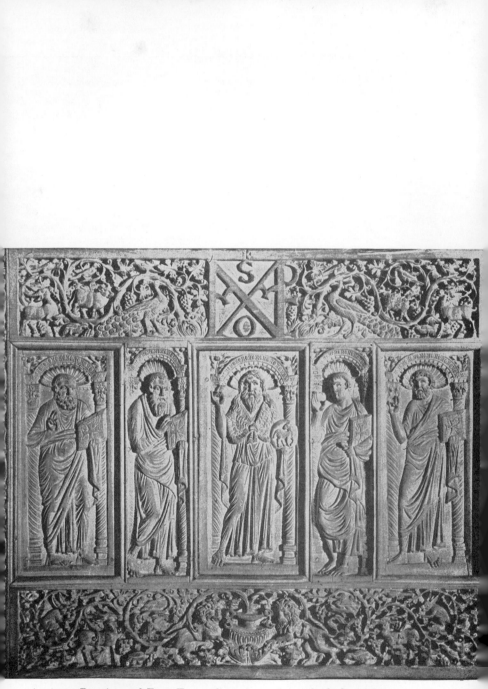

An ivory Baptist and Four Evangelists, from the cathedral of Maximian, Ravenna, early sixth century. The work of Greek artists in Constantinople, this piece shows Eastern influence in the interlaced vines, birds, and beasts of the carved framework.

ius and the adulation of the people. Justinian would not heed her.

Strategists of The Silence—Narses foremost among them— implored him to mobilize the man power of the Empire in one great army to destroy the Persian host. Justinian would not do it. He would not suspend his vast undertakings of peace to restore the military state of Diocletian. Men from the battlefields argued fiercely that he was defying destiny. They quoted the prophecy of the great Capella that when man's fame increased beyond measure retribution came upon the earth in floods, conflagrations, and plagues. Justinian did not have that particular superstition. In his mind the Four Horsemen of the Apocalypse had been loosed by war. He had watched the Vandal expedition breed mutiny and bring in the plague of the Berber folk; the Gothic war had drawn the Franks from the remote Rhineland. It was clear that when civilized powers turned to war the barbaric peoples broke out of restraint.

Then what, Narses and the others demanded, would the Emperor *do?*

Justinian did exactly what he had done before. By edict he urged the people "to make an increased effort to aid the government." Instead, the factions rioted—to be suppressed without pity. Never again was Justinian hailed as "The People's Emperor."

The crowds turned away visibly from the unimpressive man in the palace to the victorious and generous soldier riding through the streets. Justinian solved his dilemma by one simple action. He sent Belisarius to meet the Persians. For an army, he allowed the conqueror of Italy little more than his own following—his enlarged comitatus and all the captive Vandal and Gothic warriors, with some Moors of Africa and the Heruls coaxed back into service by Narses.

This time, however, there was a difference in the undertaking. Justinian made no effort to prepare the way for his general by diplomacy. Belisarius would be his own master. What passed between them at their parting is not known, except that Justinian bade his soldier halt the Persian inroad. (And for the first time Belisarius left his troublemaking wife behind.)

It may well be that Justinian was looking toward a wider horizon that Belisarius was incapable of seeing.

Because when Count Belisarius arrived in the familiar red plain of the Euphrates, he met the other commanders of the devastated eastern frontier and told them frankly: "Our mighty emperor has given us no purpose to follow because he is ignorant of what is happening here. As for me, I have come back from the West after long years, and I am only human. We are here to stop an invasion. Tell me how you think it can be done."

❈ THE WIDER HORIZON

They told him it could not be done because of Khusrau. They told him how Khusrau Anushirwan Adil—"The Just"— ruled from horseback, journeying with an armed camp, surrounded by a feudal knighthood, the *Asvaran*—the mailed horsemen who served as model to the cataphracts of Belisarius. Farseeing and impetuous, Khusrau the Just relished a barbed jest. When Belisarius was reconquering Africa, Khusrau sent word to Justinian: "Surely you owe us part of the Vandal treasure because if we had not kept hands off, you would not have got it." When he held the town of Apamea, near Antioch, to ransom, Khusrau took the jeweled encasing of a relic of the Christians, believed by them to be wood of the cross of Christ. Yet he returned the wood to them, remarking that it was precious to them, but not to him.

At Apamea, too, he ordered a chariot race to be held in the circus after the Roman manner. Hearing that Justinian favored the Blue drivers, Khusrau promptly adopted the Green. When the Green chariots lagged behind, this Great King stopped the race until they could take the lead.

Belisarius must have realized how greatly the cruel and tolerant Sassanian differed from the careful and tenacious peasant-emperor confined to his workroom in Constantinople. So, too, their domains differed. That of Constantinople clung to the seacoasts, defended itself by walled cities, sustained itself by trade, while the Persian empire, based on agriculture, extended inland to the raw materials and wealth of the continent. While Constantinople labored to get in food, the Sassanian domain was enjoying a revival. Khusrau might choose to dwell in a tent, but it was hung with cloth of gold. His arched *iwan* at Ctesiphon had the dais carpeted with green emeralds that simulated grass, patterned by streams that were strings of pearls. In that year, as in the splendid Hellenistic age, the balance of culture rested even between Justinian's imperium and the empire of the Persians. The captives of Antioch, settling down in their "Rome" on the Tigris, found their labors lightened by drawlooms that yielded the finer textiles of the East; the towers above their new homes were not merely wind towers to draw in a cooling breeze, but contained turning wheels that operated small mills beneath.

Yet of the two monarchs, Justinian had the more steadfast determination. Khusrau—"King of kings, companion of the stars, brother to the sun"—acted on impulse; Justinian could not be swerved from the course he followed. That course presents many riddles to our eyes—the insufficient army of Belisarius, the stubborn building up of the *castella* towns, the purchase of peace at almost any price from the Persians—but it was clear enough to the man in the Daphne. For one thing, there must not be another tragedy of Antioch;

for another, civilization itself must be preserved, with its laws and, above all, a single Christian Church. Once a Persian ambassador told an emperor of Constantinople: "Our two states are like two light towers that illuminate the world." Justinian may not have agreed entirely; he accepted it as a fact, and Theodora did not let him forget it. When she looked toward her homeland, it was toward the East; there, she sensed instinctively, lay the future strength of the Empire.

True, Justinian's dogged determination had recaptured the shores of the Mediterranean. But could the dominion of that inland sea survive in a conflict with the greater forces of the continent?

Once the Great King Xerxes had swept his people into the West as far as Athens, laying pontoon bridges and building the beginning of a canal (at Mt. Athos) on the way, only to lose at Salamis his battle for the mastery of the Mediterranean and its barbarous inhabitants. The Greeks of that time spoke of the routes into the continent as "the wonderful way" to the East. Alexander of Macedon led his armed people as far east as the mountains of India, attempting to plant colonies and build Alexandrias on the way. All but one of his Alexandrias succumbed to the human ebb and flow of the continent. But the art of Praxiteles followed the Macedonian's march, to grace the figures of Bactrian shrines, toward the Land of the Silk. Although Alexander failed to create his world-state of Greek-Iranian peoples—the Iranians or "Aryans" were distant racial kinsmen of the Greeks—the mingling of arts and humanities of the Hellenistic age ensued. For a splendid moment the culture of the Mediterranean region came in balance with that of the ancestral continent.

Then the Roman imperium caused a cleavage that remained. Roman Caesars sought to drive their military power into the "Orient." Lucullus, a man of wealth, forced his way east as far as the waters of Lake Van; Pompey sighted the Caspian from the heights of the Caucasus; Crassus, setting out to duplicate Alexander's triumph, got no farther than Carrhae in the plain beyond Antioch. After that, in reaction to the march of the legions, the hegemony of the eastern religions invaded the Roman world. This fusion was checked in its turn by the rise of Christianity under the Caesars. A hard frontier took shape between Christian soldiers and the pagan "fire-worshippers" of Parthian Iran—so hard that traces of it exist today, long after the crusades. Perhaps Constantine sought to move closer to that frontier when he shifted his capital eastward to Constantinople; certainly conflict intensified when the Persian kings of the Sassanian revival (from A.D. 226) moved their reign center westward to Ctesiphon.

Last of all came the flight of refugee Christian sects into the East. Schismatics like the Nestorians, treated as rebels by Constantinople, sought asylum under the protection of the Great Kings. Some of the Nestorians migrated along the caravan routes as far as the deserts on the edge of China. In so doing they influenced events more than the conquests of Alexander.

All of this had its influence on the troubled mind of Justinian. He could not escape it, from the time when he had dwelt in the small palace of the exiled Persian Hormisdas with Theodora. Did he not rely on the Christian Arab chieftain Harith and the sagacious Persarmenian Narses? When he had closed the time-hallowed schools at Athens, seven of the pagan teachers fled across the border to gain sanctuary and to debate the ethics of Aristotle with Khusrau. And one Paul, "the Persian" from the Nestorian school at Nisibis, had tutored Khusrau, translating for him portions of Aristotle's science. The same Paul, now bishop of Nisibis, journeyed to Constantinople to debate his faith publicly.

Then there was the ceaseless activity of the inmates of Theodora's "house of the monks"—the same palace of Hormisdas—that sent missionary church-builders like Jacob Old Clothes out to the eastern frontier. Justinian came to know of that only by degrees because his wife, lacking authority, carried out her intrigues in secret.

All this impelled Justinian into his baffling eastern policy that sought the "perpetual peace" with Persia. There was another overriding reason for it: the peril to both empires of invasion from the barbaric north. Beyond the natural barrier of the Euxine and the mighty Caucasus—stretching, so the geographers of Constantinople believed, along the heights of the "Taurus" range toward the Land of Silk—there had been the pressure of savage Scythians, Sarmatians, and Huns. Khusrau, better able to meet force with force than Justinian, had driven back the dangerous White Huns and had agreed to hold the passes of the Caucasus itself—until the volatile Khusrau broke the peace and rode to war against the Christian empire.

He had a reason for doing so quite apart from the urging of Vitigis. Under cover of the peace of Hermogenes, the Constantinopolitans were penetrating into the trade routes of the continent by sea and land, to the south and north of Persia. Squarely across those trade routes lay the power of Khusrau, and from them he drew profit. Persian merchants were the middlemen who sold to Roman frontier terminals the products of Asia: the silk craved by Justinian's people, the incense burned in the churches, the spices and saffron that seasoned the food, with other luxuries of life. Now the Emperor immured in his palace had heard the tale of a venturesome sea captain, Cosmas the India-voyager, that ships could round the southern coast of Arabia to voyage to the shore of India itself; Justinian was allying himself to Himyarite chieftains of the Arabian incense coast and seeking to go farther by sea. In the north likewise, Justinian built up the port of Petra as a bridgehead among the wild Lazi of the Caucasus. By rounding the Caucasus, Christian merchants might tap the caravans coming over the Road of the Silk. The Lazi complained to Khusrau that the Romans had set a praetor over them who demanded more trade, and was in fact not so much a praetor as a huckster.

So it came about that the Great King sacked Antioch. Then in the spring of 541 he led his war host up into the mountains toward the Roman stronghold of Petra.

Justinian's engineers had fortified Petra ("The Rock"). Built between the seashore and a cliff, the port seemed to be impregnable. After trying its strength by ordinary siege, however, the Persians simply tunneled under the massive wall. When a section of the wall came down, Khusrau rode into Petra.

The Lazi who had guided him thither welcomed him as a more generous master than Justinian. While Khusrau was contemplating Justinian's sea, startling news reached him. Belisarius was moving, in his absence, down the rivers upon his city of Ctesiphon. At once the Sassanian came down from his fastness of the Caucasus. He had a good deal of respect for the name of Belisarius.

The duel of wits followed between the victor of the Mediterranean, and the conquering Great King.

❀ THE CROSSROADS TO JERUSALEM

It is said that Count Belisarius lost his grip in this eastern war. Yet he had been given the almost impossible task of stopping Khusrau without an adequate army. (His sadly mixed contingents numbered some 18,000; he said himself it would take 100,000 to keep Khusrau from crossing the Euphrates.) Lacking strength, he simulated it, storming the smaller towns across the Persian frontier, parading past the stronger citadels as if hurrying to Ctesiphon. Pursuing Persians found the

Romans encamped at ease, apparently unaware of danger; but when the *Asvaran* attacked headlong, they collided with the lances of Goths in readiness for just such an attack. Belisarius started caravans of captive "fire-worshippers" back to Constantinople. But when the exasperated Great King appeared, the Roman army vanished beyond the rivers.

Then winter brought a brief truce, as Belisarius had anticipated. The Persian host, relying on horse transport, moved over these half-desert plains only when the animals could find grazing.

But in Constantinople the loss of Petra rankled. Belisarius was summoned back to explain why he could not keep the Persians in check as he had kept the Goths. To the strategists in the Daphne he gave the true picture of events: his Goths and Vandals sickening in the desert heat, the baggage carts filled with ailing soldiers, the heedless western warriors trying out their swords on Arab and Armenian villagers who relied on the Romans for protection. Belisarius himself relied on the Christian Arab, Harith, to lead his raiders. His veteran garrisons feared the Persians, but Belisarius feared most the strange fever that struck down his men.

The sickness in the camps was the first sign of the great plague. Coming out of Egypt, it was spreading, little heeded as yet, along the routes of the armies.

Then appalling news reached the Daphne. With the coming of the first grass in 542 the Persians were moving up the Euphrates again. They made no secret of their destination this time; it was Jerusalem. Khusrau had fastened on an objective that the elusive Roman army must defend.

Justinian intervened. Jerusalem, he said at once, must be saved from the fate of Antioch.

In an odd way he had himself to blame for the danger now threatening the Holy City. Under the earlier emperors, Jerusalem had been strongly held as a frontier post. Relying on his peace with the Persians, Justinian had changed that. Taking out the garrisons, he had tried to restore Palestine, raising a new edifice to the Mother of God near the site of the ancient temple, opening wells along the pilgrim routes, making Nablous (Neapolis) on its rocky height a shrine of Christ. He had erected hostels upon the hallowed sites for each people of the East, including Armenians and even the half-converted Lazi. In all this Palestine of the pilgrims there was not an armed *numerus* to defend it.

At once Belisarius sped back to the front, changing horses at the post stations through Anatolia, changing to swift chariots where the red plains opened below the forested Taurus. He may have questioned the machinations of empires—as he did later in Italy—which sent armies across the stillness of the desert. There may be truth in the report that Belisarius was no longer the man who had defended Rome. He had learned at last of the infidelity of Antonina, and had put her into a cell like any criminal.

Word from his commanders reached him on the road. At the news of Khusrau's advance, they had concentrated their garrisons in Hieropolis in the foothills. Hieropolis protected the roads to Edessa and Antioch, and they waited for him to join them there.

Belisarius kept on his way. He wrote a hasty reply to his lieutenants, admitting that they had done just the right thing to save themselves and the troops behind walls. But the Persians were making for Palestine, a province of the Emperor that had no defense, and if they stayed in Hieropolis it would be called not their safety, but their treason.

Heading south himself, he picked up troops—his comitatus and the camps of the Goths. He took them along, out of the protection of the foothills, down into the great Syrian plain. There the Persian horsemen must strike east, following the grass and watering at the streams when they left the rivers.

They would need to pass here above the dry desert to reach Jerusalem. But in the open plain his infantry could not retreat from the enemy cavalry.

The Euphrates was no longer a barrier between Belisarius and Khusrau, who had crossed to the Roman side by a pontoon bridge.

The situation being about as bad as it could be, Belisarius tried to make it appear that he was ready to give battle. He sent a column of horsemen across the river to the east bank to act as if they were moving to the rear of the advancing Persians.

This move halted Khusrau, who became very curious as to what the Romans were actually doing and what nature of man Belisarius might prove to be. To satisfy himself on these points the Great King sent a secretary, one Abandanes, to deliver a message to Belisarius, to use his eyes inside the Roman camp while he did so, and report to Khusrau what he saw.

It was a most ancient stratagem, and Belisarius seems to have taken quick advantage of it. As he had done with the emissaries of the Goths in Rome, he set a scene for the entrance of Abandanes. As actors he called in his best-appearing warriors without their weapons, instructing them to take no notice of the Persian envoy, but to keep in motion around Belisarius' pavilion as if engrossed in field sports, throwing the stone or racing their horses.

In consequence, Abandanes was led through masses of casual fighting men—who moved about so that he could not estimate their numbers—who appeared to have no interest in the splendidly robed envoy of the Great King. At the pavilion, the Roman commander seemed to be more interested in offering the envoy fruit and wine than in hearing what he had to say. Belisarius played the part of a good host at ease. When Abandanes, studying him covertly, delivered the message of Khusrau—that Khusrau had invaded the territory of Caesar (Justinian) because the Roman emperor had broken the terms of the peace—Belisarius appeared to be surprised and regretful.

"Then Choesroes [Khusrau] doesn't behave like other men," Belisarius retorted. "Usually if men have disputes with their neighbors, they sit down together to talk it over. Then, if they can't agree, they go to war. But he attacks the lands of the Romans first, and then begins to talk about peace."

By the time Abandanes explained that he had said nothing about peace, he became confused. By the time of his departure he had a strong impression that the seemingly oblivious Roman was setting a trap for his master on Roman soil. When he reported that to Khusrau, the youthful Persian stopped his advance. ("We are here," Belisarius had told his officers the year before, "to stop an invasion.")

Such is Procopius' version of the meeting between Belisarius and Khusrau. In reality, however Belisarius managed to impress him, the Persian turned back down the Euphrates because he had tidings of the spread of the plague through Syria along his route to Palestine. As he went he sacked Callinicum, a frontier town of the Romans. This was probably done to satisfy his army, but Callinicum like Antioch and Petra had reverberations in Justinian's court.

Nor did Belisarius show any sign of his old inspiration. He merely kept between Khusrau and Jerusalem as he had been ordered. Both leaders removed their commands from the plague-infected frontier—the Persian journeying up into the embattled but healthy Caucasus.

Then befell a trivial incident with serious consequences. Belisarius passed an evening chewing the fat with Buzes, his second in command, and other officers. Buzes, a veteran of the eastern front, complained because Constantinople expected them to wage a war without strength enough to attack Khusrau. The latest bit of news was that the plague had reached Constantinople. Somebody asked what they would do if the sickness carried off Justinian, and somebody else retorted that they wouldn't let Constantinople name the new emperor.

That seemed to be all. But one of the group was an informer of Theodora's, and he wrote out his version of the gossip of the generals. The Augusta did not have her husband's skepticism of the stories of spies. Very quickly Belisarius and Buzes were ordered to report back to the palace. The order had been signed by Justinian, and Theodora had persuaded him to sign it.

Belisarius never returned to the East.

❈ THE HAND OF THEODORA AUGUSTA

As the pestilence approached Constantinople, a subtle change took place in the small group of men closest to Justinian. Priscus, the confidential secretary and adroit flatterer, disappeared first. With great skill, Priscus had managed to lead a double life—ferrying himself across at night to Chalcedon, where, in the guise of a merchant, he sold his secrets to a shipping ring.

One evening Priscus stepped into the waiting caïque to find strange Greek boatmen hoisting the sail. As soon as they left the harbor lights behind, they headed down the Bosporus current toward the distant islands. Without explanation they stripped their passenger and shaved his head; they clothed him again in a coarse monk's robe and put him ashore at the stone quay of an island where monks waited to lead him into the gate of a monastery. Theodora had endowed the monastery, and there Priscus decided to stay.

Justinian had not been willing to dismiss him. Quite clearly the inarticulate Macedonian could not bring himself to part from a gifted companion in work. The best of them, who accomplished miracles—Romanos the recluse was conjuring new harmony out of human voices—kept their posts until death. And inhuman labor often shortened their years. Somehow Justinian managed to subdue their mutual antagonisms. Peter the Patrician, that ironic gentleman, bedeviled the powerful officers of the Excubitors by calling those "protectors of the palace" into active service overseas with each fresh campaign. To remain at their privileged posts the Excubitors had to forego their pay during the campaign. Justinian allowed it, never having forgotten the failure of the Excubitors to stand by him in the revolt. Anthemius the architect had a private feud with the millionaire Tribonian; living next door to the Quaestor's palatial home, Anthemius rigged up mirrors to throw the sun's glare into his neighbor's windows. When the master of the laws brought suit to end the persecution of the mirrors, Anthemius contrived an earthquake to annoy him. (One explanation of the earthquake is that Anthemius heated great sealed jars of water in the cellars until exploding steam rocked Tribonian's foundations.) When Anthemius died of overwork, the nephew of Isidore took up his task of decorating the Church of the Nativity at Bethlehem—a work that endures today because when the Persians at last overran the Holy Land, they spared this church where they recognized Magi of their own in the figures of the Three Kings of the East.

Justinian had quieted the open quarrel between Narses and Belisarius. But he could not quench the hatred of his wife for his Praetorian Prefect. John of Cappadocia soothed his own strained nerves with wine and his troupe of girls while contriving to find the money so desperately needed now. In doing so he made enemies enough and seemed to waste no regrets on them. The city had its tales to tell of him. How a certain banker had refused to produce his jewels to be assessed, and how this patrician had been escorted into the Cappadocian's guarded cellars. When released, the victim went back to his home to collect his coffers; he returned to throw the jewels at the feet of Cappadocian John without a word spoken between them. John of Lydia called his namesake "Lord High Brigand." An uglier story told of a war veteran assessed for taxes of 20 solidi, which he protested he could not pay. The Cappadocian's inspectors bore him away with them for interrogation. Then this victim explained that he would take the inspectors back to his house, to find the twenty coins, which he had mislaid. When the treasury police followed the ex-soldier they found that he had hanged himself to a beam of his house.

The talk of the market place came to the ears of the Despoina at Hieron. Alone with Justinian, Theodora explained that his most glorious Praetorian Prefect amassed his gold to pay for his treachery.

"In what way?"

"To pay those who will seize the throne."

"Who is your informant?"

"The wife of the illustrious Count Belisarius."

Theodora had a way of mimicking the titles of those she disliked, and Justinian understood her moods very well. Nor did he trust Antonina. After Theodora left him he took care to summon a friend of the Cappadocian to warn John: "Under no circumstances hold any secret talk with Antonina."

Yet within a few days, in spite of Justinian's warning, John did meet in secret with the wife of Belisarius, and his career ended as abruptly as the fall of a curtain. Not that the all-powerful Cappadocian failed to appreciate his danger from Theodora, against whom he had inveighed openly. His private army of bodyguards watched the gardens of his fantastic palace; they manned the corridors of his sleeping quarters, where lamps burned through the night. John had his own chamber searched before he entered it, and they say he woke at intervals through the night to peer out into the hall. He had the food tasted before his gargantuan feasts, and he carried a talisman of the goddess Isis to ward off the wiles of the Despoina.

Theodora, however, seems never to have made use of poison or a convenient assassin's knife. It is possible—so much came to the ears of the Augusteum—to retrace the gossamer web in which she caught John. When Belisarius departed on his last mission to Persia—"taking the hopes of the Romans with him," Procopius declares—he left Antonina behind for the first time. His ambitious wife, now more than fifty years of age, was in fact left very much alone and dissatisfied because her golden boy, Theodosius, had gone into hiding. (One of Antonina's maids and a pair of servants had revealed the secret of Theodosius' visits, and Antonina had had their tongues cut out before throwing their bodies into the Bosporus, and after that Theodosius had disappeared—as Theodora well knew.) The first step of the Most Clement Augusta was to confide in the envious Antonina how mightily had grown the power of the Praetorian John within Constantinople, even raising him above the merely popular Count Belisarius. Probably up to this point Theodora told the simple truth. And no one realized better than Antonina how helpless her husband became when facing politics. At once she appreciated to the full how, if John were removed, Count Belisarius would move by that much closer to the Sacred Palace in which the aging woman dreamed of playing the part of mistress.

With adroit dissimulation Theodora played upon the hidden eagerness of her rival. She hinted that John, although protected by Justinian, had one weakness. He could not guard his tongue. If Antonina could contrive to lead him into talk of treason, Theodora would arrange for them to be over-heard. . . .

Without scruple Antonina performed her part, fastening upon the young daughter of the Cappadocian. For all his brutality, John was devoted to the girl, who admired Antonina. She confided in her father how the distinguished wife of Count Belisarius longed to rid them all of the tyranny of the cruel Augusta—who had climbed from a brothel to the throne. (Here Antonina may have expressed her own sincere feeling.) Because she was no lawful empress, Theodora's power would cease the moment Justinian died, and if he was killed, her father—so the girl argued—could carry out his work of administering Constantinople as emperor, while Count Belisarius would be free to carry on the wars on the frontiers as Caesar.

For all his suspicions, John could not have seen the hand of Theodora in this wild project. Perhaps he thought only of protecting his daughter or wished to hear himself how far the scheming Antonina would involve herself in treason that might be the destruction of the popular Belisarius. At all events he yielded to the lure of this womanly gossip, with armed bodyguards at his back. He went at the appointed hour of night across the Bosporus to the garden of the Rufinian estate, a property of Belisarius not far from Hieron. There he found Antonina alone, apparently, and she did indeed dare to speak of ridding themselves of the Emperor.

Theodora had chosen for two witnesses men whose word Justinian would trust, Narses and Marcellus of the Guard. In this Medici-like scene they waited in hiding, with a detachment of *Spatharii* concealed in the house. They had the order of the Augusta to arrest John the Praetorian if they heard anything of treason and to kill him if he attempted to resist. In the event, when the Cappadocian heard Narses' voice, he tried to cut his way out of the trap, wounding Marcellus. Then, losing his head, big John fled alone from a peril he could not comprehend to the sanctuary of an adjacent church. Had he gone straight to Justinian, he might have saved himself. But there was no doubting the testimony of Narses, the wound of the loyal Marcellus, and the headlong flight of the Cappadocian himself.

The weary Justinian was forced to pass sentence on his favored economist. The sentence was a light one—confiscation of all the Praetorian's wealth, and exile to priesthood in a monastery outside Constantinople. There John's unquenchable spirits revived. Justinian provided him money for his comfort, and he refused to perform any office at the altar—which would have prevented his return to civilian life. Observers of events in the Augusteum wagered that John would soon exchange his priest's robe for his old praetorian's mantle.

Implacably Theodora moved to prevent that. The forces she invoked this time were never revealed. Within the monastery walls voices cried out at John. "Who bowed his head to Hecate of the underworld? Whose extortioners followed the soldier for his twenty silver coins? Why did the Ephesian girl drown herself in the swimming pool?" When John laughed at the pursuing voices, others accused him of the murder of a man who hated him, and he was scourged by the monks who cast him out clothed in a single tattered robe worth no more than a few obols according to Procopius. He was forced to beg his food from the crew of the ship that carried him to Alexandria, a derelict among strange easterners who had no particle of love for the Praetorian Prefect of the East, the squeezer of taxes.

With John disposed of, Theodora dealt after her fashion with Antonina. She induced Justinian to bestow John's city palace on Belisarius. To the delighted wife of Belisarius she confided that she had a personal gift, "a pearl so rare and indeed unique that we begrudge it you." To bestow this gem the Augusta summoned her rival to public audience. There, in the presence of her officers and the women of the propoloma, Theodora waited, her gaze intent, her small face framed in matchless pearls. Like Antonina she had come to the palace from the theater, yet there was a difference between them: Antonina had never ceased to be the daughter of a chariot-driver.

To present her gift Theodora ordered a curtain drawn back, to reveal, handsome in a court tunic embroidered with silver eagles, Theodosius, who had been Antonina's lover. No word was spoken until Antonina, perforce, uttered thanks to the Most Clement Augusta for her mercy.

In some way Theodora had tracked the unfortunate Theodosius to his hide-out and had conveyed him to her chambers in the palace. Afterwards he was allowed his liberty within the city, but died presently from the pestilence. This public spectacle of herself put an end to Antonina's ambition, although not to her hatred of Theodora. She fled from the city to Belisarius at the eastern front. (It was then that he confined her to a cell, only to release her when he was called to Constantinople.) Belisarius still would not see evil in Antonina.

And after the fall of John, the Autocrator in the East remained the only person who might be hailed as emperor by a rebellious faction. Although Belisarius had pledged his loyalty to Justinian, Theodora never trusted the pledges of men. She remembered how, ten years before, the half-unwilling Hypatius had been given the crown by the enthusiastic mob of the Nika. That could happen with Belisarius. Then, after a brief interval, she received the cryptic warning from her informer on Belisarius' staff: "The generals discuss the death of our Ever August Emperor; they say no one in our Guarded City will name his successor; they will do that themselves."

Treason could be read into the words. Justinian would have disregarded them to follow his own intuition. Theodora made instant use of them to serve her scheme of the moment. When Belisarius and Buzes landed at the Golden Horn, they were reproached harshly by Narses, serving as Grand Chamberlain. Why had the two commanders remained idle with all their

forces while the Persians wrested away Petra and despoiled
Callinicum? Stung, Belisarius gave them a soldier's answer: if
his sovereigns doubted his courage, let them send him back
to the eastern front and he would give them proof of it.

That they would not do. Unknown to the supreme Master
of Soldiers, his fate lay in the hands of Theodora, who was
considering him in the new pattern of her anxieties. Justinian
had fallen ill of the pestilence and—guarded within the doors
of the Daphne—he grew weaker daily. As if by his authority
Theodora acted; Buzes was taken away to the cellars of her
quarters at Hieron, ostensibly for questioning—there to vanish
from sight for the years of stress. Belisarius suffered no such
confinement. He was still the idol of the city, and Theodora
touched only his pride and his power.

Narses showed him the order. It confiscated his great estates
and consequently his source of wealth; it deprived him of his
comitatus. His veteran personal army was to be divided up
among different commanders, including Narses. That hurt
Belisarius deeply, yet he consented to remain at call within
the stricken city. Probably Antonina was the one to resent
leaving her palace by the Porta Aurea with its banquet hall
hung with trophies of Carthage.

Quite unnoticed, a change had taken place in the men of
The Silence. A young Syrian banker served as praetorian in
place of John. This Peter Barsymes owed much, including his
new honor, to Theodora. A little-known African, who was certainly no master of law, presided as quaestor. Peter the Patrician, Master of Offices, listened in secret to Theodora while he
puzzled the Persian ambassador by giving lavish entertain-
ments—as if stricken Constantinople were entering upon new
years of glory. These newcomers all spoke Greek, and were in
fact upflung from the melting pot of the East. The only
Roman of them all, Marcellus, held the Daphne under firm
control as Count of the Excubitors. Yet oddly enough this

disciplinarian of the guard esteemed the unpredictable Despoina as much as Narses. After many years Theodora had won the allegiance of The Silence.

For modern minds to understand the devotion of this small band of men to the sovereigns, and especially to Justinian, is not easy. He did not hold them in fear as Diocletian had done. Except in the case of Marcellus, their loyalty did not stem from tradition. Nor did Justinian, obsessed like any bureaucrat with the minutiae of government, compel the personal admiration given to the headstrong Constantine. He was in no respect a hero—"this man who seemed so good-natured," as Procopius phrased it.

Obviously they respected the peasant from the Macedonian village who tried so earnestly to play the part of Caesar. Perhaps these few who worked intimately with Justinian were aware of a courage in him unperceived by the outer world and its historians. Justinian had the unusual courage of his imagination. He would not admit defeat. What seemed to their minds impossible of accomplishment he drove them each day to create—to bring the vision of a new Rome to reality in the chaos of their age. He alone believed in such a tomorrow.

In the crisis of the plague, Theodora intrigued to protect her husband. But the fact remains that his close servants were loyal during his illness. No successor was named in the forums when physicians whispered that the Emperor was dying. In the end Justinian refused to die.

❀ "THEY SURVIVED BEYOND ALL EXPECTATION"

The bubonic plague that reached Constantinople during the festival of the city's founding in May 542 proved to be the deadliest in many centuries. It appeared almost unnoticed along the docks where vessels from Alexandria and Palestine moored.

Evidently the city "so full of good things" faced the strange scourge with some confidence. The intelligentsia trusted in their skilled physicians; the devout congregations believed their walls to be guarded by God. Moreover, illness began with only a mild fever, not hot, that brought swellings in the groin or armpits or behind the ears. It had no visible cause. (There was no knowledge, of course, of the carriers, the fleas that had fed on the infected black rats of the ships.)

Soothsayers recalled the evil omen of the swordfish comet, and explained that demons had come into the streets: "apparitions in human guise who touched men in this or that part of the body, and immediately they were seized by the disease."

Yet exorcism, the uttering of the most holy names, failed to drive the malignant demons away; people thronging into the sanctuary of St. Michael Archangel did not escape the dreaded touch. The disease actually seemed to follow a path of invisible carriers from the waterfront up to the Mesé, thence into all the districts. Physicians in the university and hospitals performed autopsies on the dead and made a great effort to analyze the conditions under which the disease appeared. It defied their understanding because it attacked persons shut up in their houses or the affluent secluded in their gardens; pregnant women often gave birth prematurely, and either the mother or the child might die, or both, or neither. The physicians could only judge that if the swelling decayed, death usually followed, and if it broke and discharged, the victim usually returned to life; they could only advise feeding those who lay in coma and restraining those in delirium from throwing themselves into water. "It was noticed of the ones who tended the sick, exhausting themselves in the task, that they survived, beyond all expectation."

As the deaths multiplied inexplicably, the trading centers and market places closed down; people began to shut themselves up in their homes. They seemed to be gripped by fear rather than hysteria. There was no general flight from the walls. Through the half-deserted streets the clergy of Hagia Sophia carried the icon of the Madonna of the Way. Religious fervor seized on the most sophisticated of the waiting populace. Awareness of approaching death makes a bitter test of civilized natures.

As the pestilence intensified in the summer heat, the populace turned for protection to its Emperor. District priests thronged into the Augusteum to beg for food. The Street of the Breadmakers used up its last grain, and ignorant folk starved behind their barred doors. Officers of the Daphne took their posts in the forums; the Referendarii of the palace took the place of the announcers in carrying messages from the streets to Justinian, and bearing back his grants of money and food. Imposing Excubitors went out in armed patrol with the white candidates. As soon as he could walk again, Justinian made a habit of going afoot in procession to the sanctuaries of the city. His presence in robes, performing accustomed ritual, helped relieve the growing fear.

In its ordeal the temperamental city showed surprising courage. Nameless groups gathered to collect the dead in the streets. At first the bodies were taken to graveyards within the walls. Then they were carted to ditches outside the land wall, and finally were borne by barges across to the towers of Sycae (Galata). Their numbers grew to several thousand a day, to 5,000 in a day. Witnesses of the disaster say that more than 300,000 perished in Constantinople out of a population of some three quarters of a million. Some who recovered showed impairment in strength or speech.

Famine took its toll, but was checked by shipments of grain and dried meat from the still-unaffected shore of the Euxine. The plague, however, entered the Balkan highlands and penetrated to Greece.

Procopius, who returned with Belisarius when conditions were worst, marveled that the plague seemed to carry off the best among the people while sparing the rogues and ribalds. He wondered also at seeing officials of the palace going through the empty streets divested of the chlamys of their rank. All men seemed to have become alike in appearance. Soldiers drove in the carts of food; beggars marched with the police patrols.

When Justinian became infected, the news was kept from the streets. The Silence arranged distractions—throwing open the hippodrome, with choral tragedies enacted for the people. After the feast days of the churches, Theodora presided over the evening refreshment in the Magnaura garden. When Avar chieftains rode into the Porta Aurea with gifts of silver for the Emperor of the Christians—expecting to be rewarded with gold for their journey—Peter the Patrician escorted them through the impressive-to-visitors colonnades and Narses bestowed the gold. If other visitors wondered at beholding Belisarius ride into the Augusteum without his showy escort, he did not enlighten them as to the reason.

Despite this façade of courage, the inmates of the Daphne were well aware of the extent of the calamity. Constantinople, the nerve center of the world-state, was crippled, and they did not know how much of it would survive. Procopius of Caesarea, who was not taken into their counsels and resented it, records his fear that summer. "It seemed as if all the human race faced annihilation."

With cold weather in the fall the daily deaths diminished from thousands to hundreds. The plague was checked in the city.

✿ THE MARCH OF THE SLEEPLESS

After the plague came the hunger.

The human mechanism by which Constantinople supplied the wants of the great domain had broken down. No shipping moved from the docks of Ephesus because no crews remained to sail them forth. Into the junction port of Alexandria the dhows of the Nile brought pepper and ivory to merchants who no longer lived to pay for them.

Money itself was changing in value because the holders of gold paid recklessly for the simplest foods, bread and oil. The new Praetorian, Peter Barsymes, requisitioned supplies. In the villages that were the mainstay of the provinces, fields lay untilled because the surviving people had fled to the hills for acorns and herbs. "Our time is accursed," a village vicar complained, "when foxes fatten in my streets while my people dig roots in the wilderness."

Trading towns that had been so prosperous fared worse than the agricultural regions. Looms in Bithynia stood abandoned for lack of wool. Potters who had clay in plenty for their wheels found no buyers for the jars that piled up in their shops.

The breakdown in human relationships could not be mended in a day or a year. Families had to survive without wage-earners and children without parents; derelict houses awaited owners. Provincial curials found it hopeless to collect taxes.

When Justinian was able to put on the imperial chlamys and meet with his officers, he found that his familiar world had altered. They were like survivors of an earthquake looking out over a country wherein landmarks had changed and habitations had been shaken from their foundations. Ironically his own innovations had been hardest hit. He had done away with the Steps and their dole of grain—even in rebellious Alexandria, where the dole dated from Diocletian's day—and now food was given out again by the Prefect's guards to the hungry crowds waiting with tokens. The pestilence had followed his new shipping; it had restored power to the magnates of the hinterland who gleaned food from their land holdings and gained more fields from hungering peasants who would sign any deed for meat. His new laws had become words on paper.

A strange Fate seemed to have favored those most remote

from Constantinople. The pestilence had spared fishermen of the islands, hermits of the desert. Famine had not touched settlements of barbarians in the forests. Where Slavs and Heruls infiltrated across the frontiers, they kept apart in their hut villages with their cattle and crops scratched from the earth, sustaining brute life as they had always sustained it.

Superstition, against which Justinian fought, stirred anew after the disaster. A witch-hunt began and found a witch in Theodora. "Surely she who hath given birth to no child," women confided to each other, "is accursed." Being accursed, she had brought the blight upon the city. Nay more, she had suckled upon evil and entrapped men by the wiles of her body. Had not the plague itself followed the course of her wandering through Asia, to enter Constantinople? And hearing this, Procopius wrote with hatred and envy in his secreted book, *The Anecdotes:* "There is no city of Asia where she did not offer her body for pay."

Out of Hieron came one rumor that fed the superstition of the streets. Secluded and guarded, Theodora's court at Hieron had escaped the pestilence; within it Buzes had disappeared; its walls concealed the aged exiled Anthemius. Now, the rumor said, a ten-year-old boy had appeared there. From the sea he came, and Theodora doted upon him, calling him by the name of an emperor, Anastasius. In reality the Augusta had sent secretly for her young grandson, born of the daughter she had left in Alexandria. Evidently she had risked bringing him to Hieron out of plague-ridden Egypt.

The rumor reached Justinian, as it was bound to reach him. He would not speak of it, nor did he go again across the water to Hieron. He kept to his work-room and his night vigils, but he did not have his old zeal for labor. Tired, his heavy shoulders drooping and his articulation thickened by the disease, he faced the defeat of his plans. He had labored for the aggrandizement of his city. When he got up to stare from his window, he beheld the gleam of unfathomable stars in mockery above the faint reflected light on the dome of Hagia Sophia with its gilt crescent.

Justinian had a way of invoking little things to aid him. That autumn at the close of All Saints' Day—long after Vespers—he returned from the prayers in the great church to his window. Removing his purple mantle, he rested a while.

There was a slight alteration, a difference in the darkness of the Mesé's end where the night patrol waited. Lights were advancing, dancing or blown by the wind. Voices rose and chimed in quick cadence. The street was still deserted at night, but many feet trod stones as if hurrying and slapping down. Justinian recognized the tread of sandals in cadence, and the voices intoning a *Jubilus*.

The brethren of The Sleepless, emerging from the Studion, were challenging the stricken city. *Jubilate Deo . . . omnis terra*. With the tapers flickering in their hands, their heads invisible in cowls, they swung past the Augusteum toward the harbor. *Jubilate Deo*.

When Justinian faced his ministers again, he had written a fresh *Novella*. As usual, it was rather naïve and surprising to the listeners. *"If these monks with blessed souls pray for the Empire, the army will be more united, the prosperity of the state greater, the agriculture and commerce more flourishing under the assured loving-kindness of God. . . ."*

By Christmas it was clear that the man in the Daphne meant to carry on his plans, as if there had been no pestilence or famine.

There would be no forgiveness for taxes. Where revenues failed, death duties would make up the correct amount. Where transport had broken down, the provincial curials would restore it, maintain the roads, and furnish food and forage to passing armies. Where old industries had failed, as in the production of silk, state monopolies would carry them on.

As for the wars, the Persian invasion must be checked, the

lost Petra recovered, and the reconquest of Italy carried to its end.

The disorder of the eastern coasts and the penetration of barbarians across the lower Danube would be met by a new Prefecture of the Isles, to operate from the seas and to have new fleets manned by the factions of impoverished coast towns. As soon as possible one fleet would voyage to Spain to capture the trading ports as far as the Gates of the ocean. In Egypt, numbed by the pestilence, new irrigation would be channeled from the flow of the Nile.

In Ravenna, ravaged by the wars—in which the Goths had taken to arms again—Justinian meant to erect a new great church. It would be, like the Hagia Sophia, a dedication of their effort, a symbol of a new Christian world. It would be dedicated, besides, to St. Vitalis.

Now, this call to achievement in Christmas of 542 is hardly the stubbornness of a stupid man. Many of his people, Procopius among them, held him to be a madman who had taken no heed of the coming of the Four Horsemen of the Apocalypse.

There was, however, a method in Justinian's seeming madness.

VII

BIRTH OF AN EMPIRE

VOYAGE INTO SPACE

I

IN THEIR RARE LEISURE many Constantinopolitans read Lucian, a satirist of ancient Rome. Apparently they gave less heed to Vergil, the panegyrist of the Augustan age. Lucian wrote while the Romans were still bent on exploration, after Trajan, but before the collapse of the third Christian century, and among his writings there was *A True Story* which relates, in Lucian's manner, a remarkable voyage of his own.

A True Story told of his venture with fifty companions in a pinnace out to the unknown western ocean. There they discovered an unusual island. In searching it, they came upon a weathered bronze plaque bearing the name of Dionysius. A footprint of the god remained visible in the sand. It led them to a river in which flowed wine instead of water—wine as refreshing as Chian. Because the explorers became intoxicated when they ate the fish of this river, they tempered the wine-fish, as it were, with fish from natural water. The source of the river proved to be a forest of grape trees, with bodies of lovely living women rising from the trunks. "All of them like Daphne turning into a tree when Apollo is just catching her. They cried out in pain when we plucked the grapes growing from their hair, yet they greeted us, some speaking Indian but most of them Greek. They actually wanted us to embrace them, and two of my comrades did so, but could not get away again."

On leaving the island of the grape-tree sirens, Lucian's vessel was suddenly picked up from the sea by a whirlwind. A stratospheric wind then bellied its sail, driving it upward for seven days and seven nights to an island in space from which they could look down on the mountains and seas of their own earth. On venturing inland they were met and arrested by the Vulture Dragoons—"men riding large vultures: you can judge of their size by the fact that the mast of a large merchantman is no longer than the smallest of their quills."

The Vulture Dragoons agreed to take care of the Romans, if they would aid these flying dragoons in their war with Phaeton, King of the Sun-people. "For the sun is inhabited as well as the moon." The war began in a quarrel over colonizing the Morning Star. The Dragoons expected allies from the Great Bear, fifty thousand Volplaners, or light infantry who used their cloaks as sails.

The hostile Sun King, however, was served by very large spiders summoned from the Zodiac. By spinning a web between the Sun and the Morning Star, these engineer spiders laid down a track for the infantry, several millions strong, of the Sun. Not to mention the dog-faces from the Dog Star.

The memorable battle that followed in space resulted in such slaughter that the blood dyed red the clouds beneath—

"as red as when the sun is setting in our country." Lucian's space allies were celebrating a glorious victory when they were beset by the Cloud Centaurs, giants upon winged horse bodies. Lucian would not tell the numbers of these Centaurs, lest his word be doubted, but they were led by the Archer of the Zodiac. Sad to relate, the Romans and their allies were overwhelmed by these winged Centaurs in the very act of setting up a monument to their victory. Lucian and his companions found themselves captives of the space half-men, bound securely by spider webs. "I have never told a lie," Lucian assured his readers, "that I know of."

Modern readers of science fiction would find something familiar in his description of the Moon-people. The inhabitants of the chill moonscape were hairless beings who nourished themselves on the smoke of cooking fires and drank only liquefied air, which sometimes fell in hail drops to our world. When Lucian's vessel was wafted down to earth at last, it came to rest in good sailing weather far out on the ocean, and it found its first mooring in the lovely Elysian Field. Anatole France might have described in much the same way this abode of the blessed whither no Stoics had found their way as yet. The veterans of the Trojan War gathered there. The immortal Homer explained to Lucian the truth of his life—that he was really a Babylonian captive (*homeros*) and not at all blind; nor had he written the *Iliad*. The peace of the Elysian Field was disturbed by Helen, who was carried off to be raped with her own consent. When Lucian wept at parting from them, the Elysians all called to him: "You'll be back again."

Now *A True Story* may be a satire upon exploration of the unknown. But its battles are realistic affairs with weapons and tactics much in evidence; the whole of it reflects mythical forces beyond Roman knowledge, an awareness of Centaurlike archers and Hyperboreans who dwell in the limbo beyond the north wind. Lucian, in that last bright age of the old

Empire, had heard of half-legendary Scythians who dwelt under the north wind.

In Constantinople nearly four centuries later there was no such illusion about the ends of the earth. From the steppes of the Caspian had come Boa, no Amazon princess, but a very real queen of the Sabirean Huns, to visit and be impressed by Justinian. Cosmas the shipmaster had fared back from Ceylon to describe not the wonders of that island, but its trade. From the headwaters of the Nile, a Brother Julian reported the baptism of the Nubian King, who wore a crown of feathers and traveled in a chair of gold on the shoulders of his slaves. Julian was one of Theodora's monks, and a fresh news bulletin was hung in the Augusteum:

> Audience with a Nubian King—Weird Etiquette of a Jungle Court.

In Constantinople those who labored at "the science of governing the barbarians" were mapping the peoples of the farthest regions. They had need of exact information.

Oddly enough, just then mystery lay thickest about the lost island of Britain. No observer seems to have found his way there to return alive. A legend arose of a Charon-like ferrying of spirits to and from *Brittia* (which might have been Brittany, on the mainland). Fishermen, the legend stated, were summoned by unseen visitors at night to row across to this shore of mystery.

"However, they see no one in their boat. When they put in to the shore of Brittia, their boats suddenly become light. They say they hear a voice on the island calling the names of the passengers. If the passenger is a woman, the voice calls the name of the husband she had during life. When they depart, the fishermen find their skiffs riding high on the waves, and they go back at speed."

Behind this tale there is a suggestion of Roman refugees stealing across the Channel from the haunts of the savage

Angles and Saxons—landing perhaps where friends waited
for them. But the truth is not to be known. Venturesome
monks, however, arrived from Ireland to visit the Egyptian
monasteries, and to carry back illuminated missals with them.
(The influence of eastern artists soon appeared in the work of
Ireland's monasteries, and the Book of Kells reveals Byzantine
design mingled with Celtic.) The informant nearest Britain
seems to have been a bishop surviving in the Rhineland, and
from him Justinian demanded the names of all peoples
subject to the Frankish kings.

Eighteen hundred miles separated the informative bishop on
the Rhine from the good Hunnish Queen Boa on the Volga.
Eighteen hundred miles, that is, as the crow flies. No wayfarer on foot, not even an Irish monk, could make the journey
from one to the other, because between them lay a welter of
savage folk, lords and despoilers of the hinterland.

That vast hinterland had been the bane of ancestral Rome.
The early Caesars had tried the "divide and rule" policy of
setting rival warlike forces against each other, while enlisting
tribal fighting men as "allies." Constantinople had barely
averted the danger of Germanizing its armies in this manner.
Justinian's immediate predecessors had been careful to enlist
barbarians only to serve under Roman officers, never under
their own kings. These emperors of Constantinople tried to
maintain a delicate counterpoise of power beyond the frontiers
by inviting strong tribal leaders to the city as allies, while
welcoming also defeated claimants to the barbaric kingships.
They tried to keep a balance between outer forces in power
and forces in revolt. Justinian himself had experimented with
this under Justin, and he realized that it was a losing game.

He brooded over it until he arrived at a simple convic-
tion. It was useless, in the end, to bring barbarians into the
Empire. But why not bring the Empire out to all the barbaric
peoples of the West? If he could no longer "divide and rule,"
he might penetrate and control.

Ivory diptych leaf of a sixth-century Emperor, in military dress (as Justinian appeared on plaques and coins) beneath religious symbols. The small figure borne at left carries the laurel wreath of Roman pagan tradition.

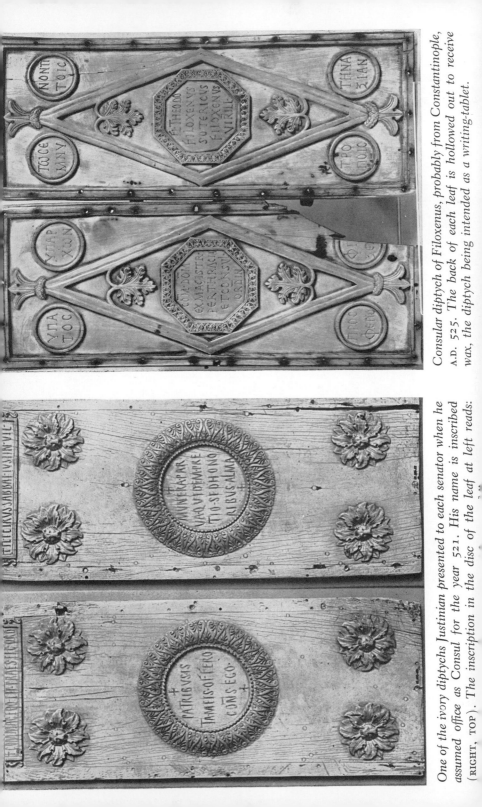

Consular diptych of Filoxenus, probably from Constantinople, A.D. 525. The back of each leaf is hollowed out to receive wax, the diptych being intended as a writing-tablet.

One of the ivory diptychs Justinian presented to each senator when he assumed office as Consul for the year 521. His name is inscribed (RIGHT, TOP). The inscription in the disc of the leaf at left reads:

❀ "THE BASILEUS UNDERSTOOD . . ."

It was one of those simple ideas that occur to many persons in ages of cultural uplift, and they talk about doing it, but actually do nothing because it appears, obviously, to be impossible. Justinian said very little about it; he merely started to do it.

Not that he abandoned the "divide" policy on occasion. The intractable Gepids were crushed by the Heruls, who were broken in due time by the Lombards. The gifted Germanus worked along the frontiers to accomplish this. But the *limitanei* defense forces had been withdrawn little by little from the frontiers.

Justinian knew it could not be accomplished by war. The historian Menander, who took up the work of the more poetic Agathias, said: "The Basileus understood that inevitably, whether the Avars were victors or vanquished, Rome would always find more of them before her."

Justinian was not content to keep the children of Hunnic or Germanic rulers at his court as hostages; he sent them to school. Mundus was a graduate of such schooling. Hermogenes served as master of offices. Belisarius himself graduated from the Strategium. The city became more of a melting pot than ever.

In abandoning the armed frontiers, Justinian meant to launch the well-being of the city far into the steppes of the nomads and the forests of the Europeans. The security of planned agriculture, the order of universal laws, the uplift of trade—all these could be transplanted from the citadel of the world-state into the wastes of the hinterland. In his *prooemium* to the *Institutes* of law, he spoke of "Africa and other provinces without number . . . *bearing witness* to our dominion."

This dominion of the visionary Justinian may well have

been described more than three centuries before him. Oddly enough the master of Constantinople was fond of reading the maxims of philosophic Marcus Aurelius. He often quoted them. Almost certainly he had read the panegyric to Marcus Aurelius by the Greek Aelius Aristides. Within it there is a description, rather imaginary, of a better world: "Now the whole world, laying aside its ancient dress of iron armor . . . keeps holiday. The cities have abandoned their old quarrels . . . they blaze with brightness. Beacon fires of friendship rise on the outer plains. The fires of war are gone as if blown out by a wind beyond the lands. . . . You have made into reality the saying of Homer that the earth belongs to all, for you have meted out benefits to the world, bridled rivers with bridges, cut carriage roads through the mountains, set outposts in the deserts, and civilized human life by bringing to it settlement and discipline."

Nothing could have appealed more to Justinian, who relished flamboyant praise. The critical part of his mind, however, realized why this world of the Antonines had failed. But could not he succeed where Marcus Aurelius had failed? He had a deep sense of his responsibility, and a new source of hope deepened the responsibility: there was Christianity. And Isaiah related: *"But they who wait for the Lord shall renew their strength."* It was Justinian's peculiarity that he took the words of the Scriptures literally, although he did not understand them very well.

Had not the sun itself stood still in the sky only on the one day when Joshua prayed? The story of Joshua, the prophet who took upon himself the responsibility of Moses, was a favorite of the time. A manuscript called the Joshua Roll adorned with most lifelike sketches has survived. In these Joshua himself appears as an ordinary Roman captain in half helmet and kilt. He meets another officer without helmet, but with wings—and he throws himself down in reverence before the strange captain of the Host of the Lord. That an angel of God should step from an ordinary gate would not have seemed remarkable to Justinian, who wrote of "victories granted by Heaven." Nor would he doubt that the dream world of the pagan Marcus Aurelius could be made real by the power of the Lord.

He set himself to achieve it, however, by very practical means. To win over a distant primitive people, the first step was to send out experienced traders from Constantinople. These pioneers carried useful tools as well as impressive luxuries and tokens from the Emperor. They brought back accurate information about the unknown folk.

Then a mission of monks or priests journeyed out. These might carry baptismal robes, but their purpose was more to make friends than to make converts. The venturesome monks carried medicine; they tilled ground in a new way for seed; out of clay they made bricks, and out of bricks they built a church. This served as medical dispensary, council hall, and beginning of communal life. The missionaries of Constantinople were instructed to work chiefly among the barbarian women, who in turn influenced the children. If they survived the pioneering stage, they stayed at their posts—reporting progress to the man in the Daphne—and often managed to persuade the local chieftain to make the journey to the city of civilization with his family. Usually the chieftain consented to leave his elder sons in the city for schooling, and if they returned to the wilderness to rule, the sons brought their people a step nearer to Constantinople.

Justinian was the first to use this missionary diplomacy. It carried the prestige of the Empire far afield. When Belisarius was occupied with the Vandals, he took care to bestow insignia from Justinian on the tribes of the Sahara, and in later years the Kabyles called themselves "slaves of the Emperor's majesty."

Missions went out to neglected peoples who had known Christian ritual. A bishop journeyed to the Crimea to build a church for the forgotten Goths and Chersonites, once allies of the Caesars. Even in the stress of the plague, the Christian Arab, Harith, was honored in Constantinople. The invisible frontier was extending beyond the outposts of the armies. In the end Menander wrote: "without war, Justinian has destroyed barbarism."

In the almost impenetrable desert of the Nejd, a certain Kayis ruled the tribes as the Emperor's man. Kayis sent his son to Constantinople and received a written set of laws which must have troubled him to carry out in that nomadic wasteland. Eventually Kayis resigned his rule to be appointed Constantinople's moderator for Palestine.

Trade followed policy into these far horizons. Friendly Abyssinians crossed the Red Sea to the coast of southern Arabia, to the Himyarites—launching their ships thence to voyage to Ceylon (described by Cosmas), the junction point of sea traffic with the unreachable Land of Silk. At Ceylon the Abyssinian merchants tried to lade precious cargoes of silk for Justinian. They were prevented by Persian agents, who bought up the silk as soon as vessels arrived from China.

But it was vital for Constantinople to open up the route of the river Nile, to Axoum, the city of the Negus in the cloudy mountains of Abyssinia. From the unknown headwaters of the river came the familiar ivory and slaves and the more important papyrus and gold. Axoum would be the junction of the hoped-for route, mainly by water, from Constantinople to India.

Yet the way to Axoum was beset by swarming, primitive peoples, by the People of the Waters above the second cataract, and the wild Blemyes in the eastern hills. The rude Christianity of early days had yielded to demon worship, and the ruins of Philae served as a shrine to Isis. It was a hard way for missioners to travel, to open the river; still Justinian sent them, with gifts, to Sitko, monarch of the People of the Waters.

John of Ephesus relates the curious happening of that year, 540. The good Bishop John was devoted to his "merciful Queen" Theodora—who was far from merciful—and his story may be colored by his loyalty to her. For this was the east of Theodora's monks, and she sent in haste one of them, Brother Julian, to overtake the mission of the Emperor. The blessed Julian and his fellows sent ahead of them a letter of the Augusta to the ruler of Thebes, the last outpost of civilization on the way up the Nile. This letter demanded that the Thebans delay the ambassadors of Justinian by pretexts until Brother Julian could pass.

Thus it happened that when the Emperor's mission arrived, the duke of Thebes explained that they must all rest while he gathered animal transport for them, with guides. When the monk Julian appeared at the guard post of Thebes, he was given forthwith the horses and escort, to speed him on his way, while the duke of Thebes explained to the ambassadors that Julian's party carried them off by force. In this manner, Julian fared beyond the cataracts to the armed followers of Sitko the king, whom Julian instructed "in many things" and baptized in the faith of "the one true God."

Theodora's touch fell as far as this wilderness of dark cliffs and isolated people. They were the converts of her Eastern Church. Justinian's embassy, however, made use of its gifts to turn Sitko against the Blemyes of the hills. A Roman detachment made a demonstration up the winding river from Thebes, but the People of the Waters drove the Blemyes far from the river. The way was open to the Christians at Axoum. In his triumph, Sitko carved a legend on the wall of the abandoned temple of the Blemyes: "*I am he who gives no rest to his foes; I am a lion to those below me on the river, and a panther to those above me.*"

On the lovely isle of Philae, the worshippers of Isis were driven out, and in the ruins a church of the Nile was consecrated.

This imperium of Justinian was a fragile thing, hardly more than one man's wish. It offered a rule by law. Its center was marked not by the Golden Milestone, but by the Hagia Sophia. Monks went out in advance of its ambassadors. It had abandoned—and forever—the concept of the *Senatus populusque Romanus*. There was no longer—and never would be again— a Roman emperor. Menander, in his summing up after Justinian's death, called him by a Greek word, *Basileus*, which means a king who is vicar of Christ.

❈ MIRACLE AT EDESSA

When the pestilence died down in Syria early in 544, Khusrau appeared from the Euphrates with his Persian army of invasion. There was no Christian army and no Belisarius to stand in his way. Unhindered, he made for Edessa.

Antioch had been the Queen City of the East, and Edessa was the fortress of the eastern frontier. Justinian had strengthened its citadel and engineered its river around it. If Edessa fell, the whole of that weak frontier would collapse. Aside from its natural strength, the city cherished a legend. Once its lord Abgar had written a letter inviting Jesus to come to Edessa. In the course of time the tradition of the letter had grown into the legend that Jesus had entered the streets of the city, thereby protecting it forever from enemies such as the Persians. Khusrau, being the personification of a victorious King of kings (*Shah-in-shah*), accepted the legend as a challenge to capture this fortress of the Christians, and there was no apparent reason why he should not do so.

At least when the elderly physician Stephen—who had tutored Khusrau as a boy—came out to ask what terms the Persian would give the Edessans, he answered in mockery. Unless the Edessans admitted armed Persians to ransack their city, he would make it into pasture for his sheep and make slaves of them. Then, instead of attacking the wall, he set his engineers to building an approach ramp to its summit, to throw his armed masses into it. The ramp rose inexorably nearer and higher. It was no mound of earth, but a broad incline of trimmed tree trunks, weighted by boulders, set with earth, and surfaced by beams roped into place. Mantlets of tough goatskins shielded the workers on the ramp from missiles, and Persian cavalry protected them from sallies by the besieged. When the Edessans, in desperation, tried to build up the parapet of their wall in front of the ramp, the Persians raised the ramp's incline quite easily.

There was something inevitable in the slow approach of the wooden roadway to the summit of the wall. The artisans and peasants of the city could not hold the parapet against an armored column pouring up the ramp. The three officers from Constantinople (two of them Persian by birth) realized this. One of them, Peter by name, ordered a tunnel to be excavated and run out beneath the ramp. The tunnel shaft advanced far before the Persian workers detected the sound of digging and began to countermine it.

Peter had to abandon the attempt to collapse the ramp. The Edessans blocked up their tunnel end with masonry. As a last resort they turned to chemicals. Swiftly they widened the end of their sap, shoring the excavation with beams. They filled up the mine with loose timbers, sacks of bitumen, and sulphur lumps. Pouring in oil of cedar, they fired this pyre beneath the earth. It flamed with intense heat, burning through the supporting beams.

The furnace ignited the framework of the ramp. Outer air penetrated the blazing pit, and sulphurous smoke rose from the surface of the ramp. To deceive the Persian engineers, the Edessans threw firepots and torches on top the work. But when Khusrau came up at daybreak to inspect the mystifying smoke and heat, he realized that the huge ramp had been fired from beneath. He summoned his army to deluge the work with water from the river. The water, however, intensified the fumes from the chemicals.

"Then was the King of kings confounded in his mind," the Edessans reported. "For a choking steam arose, driving his men away. The great work fell into charred ruins while poisonous fumes hung over it."

Enraged, Khusrau ordered the ruin bricked over and sent his people to attack the walls. "But day after day the sun-worshippers were defeated. Peasants and even women and children aided in pouring burning oil on them. After that the host of the enemy went away."

The tidings of the saving of Edessa seemed miraculous to those who waited for news in Constantinople. To the hard-pressed Justinian it appeared to vindicate his hopes. His line of *castella* had guarded the East. His chemicals of the Greek fire experiments had aided the defenders of Edessa. At once he sent envoys to discuss a truce with Khusrau, and the next year it was agreed on. For five years the Persians would preserve peace except in the Caucasus. As compensation to Khusrau's pride a yearly sum of three hundredweight of gold would be paid him by Constantinople. This small amount was no more than a token payment.

There was an odd personal incidence in the agreement between the Christian and the Sassanian monarch. Khusrau asked for the loan of Tribunus, a skilled Greek physician then in Palestine. In exchange he asked that Justinian receive back the refugee philosophers from the schools of Athens, who had grown homesick—and Khusrau requested that Justinian would treat them with mercy. To this Justinian agreed, and kept his word. It is said that the chivalrous Sassanian rewarded Tribunus for his services by a gift of the liberty of three thousand Christian captives.

Justinian had what he needed most, peace with the other

civilized state. He had never meant to challenge the strength of Persia, which served as a barrier to the westward moving hordes of Asia. And in 545 his greatest problem lay in Italy.

❀ DEEPENING OF THE DARKNESS

Perhaps the heritage guarded most jealously by Constantinople was that of the artists. Here they maintained ancient, Hellenistic standards while working in a new manner with fresh urgency. The city of course offered them a haven, with the appreciation of connoisseurs, and the stress of the time stirred them to greater efforts. Under their hands a new, Byzantine art began to take shape.

It originated in the churches, but it extended swiftly to the homes of the populace. Around the altar space of a church, stonecutters laid marble over bricks, silversmiths set screens, mosaicists brought life to the sanctuary walls; into the shrines of homes went carved ivory plaques and painted tryptiches, and mosaic miniatures—an altar in little. Pilgrims carried delicate ampullae of favorite saints incased in crystal; women girdled themselves with woven gold from which—or from pendants at their throats—hung medallion scenes of the holy figures.

For this was a Christian art, advancing from the first crude imagery, and moving away from its Hellenistic models. Before this the favorite stories, whether painted or carved, had been the adventures of Noah or Jonah or the sacrifice of Abraham. Now the populace demanded stories of deliverance, of the raising of Lazarus, and above all the image of the Theotokos, the Mother of God. In the Hagia Sophia itself, where St. Michael the Healer had dominated the walls, the figure of Mary was appearing. These simple figures were not reinforced as yet by celestial imagery. The fine likeness of St. John Chrysostom—a patron of Constantinople—seemed to be a life-portrait against a gold background. In Salonika, Demetrius stands in his church between two very human sponsors; the three are alike in reality as well as in their robes, yet the skill of the artist renders the youthful Demetrius in some way different.

In the illumination of the manuscripts—and this, with ivory carving, became a passion with the artists of Constantinople—a new vigor in drawing departs from the Greek. The full colors of the Pompeii palette yield to suggestive hues. At the same time the small sketches begin to illustrate the text rather than merely provide a decoration. The eastern custom of giving a narrative in scenes continues. A reader opening the Joshua Roll might follow the adventures of his hero without reading a word. And often in a single scene the same person performs three acts. This appeals to the popular mind, which no longer takes pleasure in the heroic poems or satires of Roman days. People turn to the earthly adventures of an Akritas or the tales of that Syrian slave, Aesop. His Wise Mouse and other marvelous animals seem to appeal more than the ancient heroes, aided by the gods, of the *Iliad*. Aesop emerged from the twilight of the ancient gods.

That twilight was deepening into night. Even in Constantinople the man in the street could no longer read the *Iliad*. A message from the palace to the streets had to be translated into the vulgar spoken Greek. John of Lydia might lecture in the eloquent Latin of Ovid, but only the law students understood him. Belisarius remarked that the recruits drilling in the square of the Strategium no longer grasped the Latin words; they answered to the cadence of commands. In the ordeal of the city its humanity found a voice in the common speech, in the jests of Aesop, in marching songs, and in the chanting of the Trisagion.

Oddly enough, just then, the learned Cassiodorus—who had

dreamed of mellowing Gothic strength by Roman wisdom—forswore his own "affected eloquence." He took refuge in monastic life on his family estate at Squillace, overlooking the Italian shore. There he kept the comfort of Roman baths and fishponds, but with a sense of urgency he gave up copying Latin manuscripts—"The Divine Letters"—to write down a simple heritage for his fellow refugees, the Psalms with his comments and the religious history of Eusebius.

Learning was dying out to the west of Cassiodorus. Some writing was done in the school of St. Martin's at Tours; there was no more than a grammar school at Massilia (Marseille) on that far coast. Where the Irish pilgrim monks went and what they did in memory of their St. Patrick, no one rightly knew. (Not yet had St. Columban brought Celtic wisdom into the mountains of the untaught Franks.) With each generation the stock of knowledge lessened; the pupils of an aged man could only repeat what he had told them. Youth turned to the stronger life of barbarism and the need of cultivating the fields. On the height of Mt. Casinum, the aging Benedict of Nursia taught his fellow refugees a rule to follow: *laborare, orare.* In their seclusion, the hours of field work must match the hours of prayer. Asceticism alone was not enough.

Few tidings from such survival centers in the West reached Constantinople. They came from the coasts; the interior of the European continent was dimming out. Monastic communities retreated to the safety of the mountains. In the decaying cities, invaders occupied the patrician halls, while the older families, half-educated half slaves, found nooks in the deserted streets. The most deadly danger was the lethargy that kept survivors from trying to repair what had been broken down. (Over this spreading stagnation the great Theodosius had sought to throw his fabric of a Christian empire. The poets said of him that his life "lay like a ruined sea wall within the barbarian tide.")

. . .

If Justinian was to extend his new empire outward, Constantinople must control all the peninsula of Italy. Without that, as he had discovered, he could not regain touch with lost Gaul and the Province. Without Sicily, his ships could not make the voyage to the coast of Spain. His unalterable decision was to win the war with the Goths.

For the war had flared up after the pestilence like windblown embers. Near-famine led the Roman commanders to take refuge in the cities, while Gothic hosts roamed the countryside. The planners in Constantinople made the decisive mistake of sending a civilian government with a praetorian prefect to administer the war-torn land. In particular the Logothete, the chief economist, was a skilled revenue-getter, Alexander, nicknamed the Scissors for his knack of clipping gold from coins. Alexander carried into Italy the tax-rolls for bygone years and an order to collect them. Failing inevitably to do this, Alexander withheld some of the army pay. Lacking money, the army commanders milked supplies from the lean citics, and their men began to desert to the Goths, who had gold. One of the generals, Constantian, wrote to Justinian that they could no longer hope to withstand the Goths. A chronicler wrote down: "What the generals had won was lost by the governors."

Far from the scene in Constantinople, Justinian could not fight the forces of disintegration in Italy. As so often before, he called on Count Belisarius to do it for him. He restored two thirds of the soldier's confiscated property and brushed aside all accusation of conspiracy. "You are the best judge of your actions in the past. Now we dismiss all charges against you. Let your actions, henceforth, show the truth of your feelings toward us."

Theodora agreed. And as usual she had the final word with Belisarius. In a meeting alone with her he agreed to betroth his half-grown daughter Joannina to her youthful grandson, Anastasius. As they had no other children, the marriage would join together two great fortunes and protect the children. For Theodora anticipated that it would earn the bitter animosity of Antonina, as in the event it did.

On his part, Justinian showed his old jealousy and his chronic begrudging of money. Belisarius' comitatus was not restored to him, nor his old rank of Autocrator. The great soldier departed with the minor rank of *Comes Stabuli*— count of the Stables (the constable of later days). He made no objection, and Justinian relaxed his rule against mobilization of the people—allowing Belisarius to recruit what men he could in the hardy Thracian and Dalmatian provinces on his way to Italy, and at his own cost. The treasury of Constantinople was almost empty.

In consequence, Belisarius arrived in Italy in 544 at the head of several thousand half-armed Balkan peasants. And he found his old enemies rejuvenated under a young leader who had all the tenacity of Vitigis without any of his failings.

❀ BELISARIUS AND TOTILA

Totila emerged from the wrack of defeat to unite and inspire the brooding Gothic warriors. He jeered at their failings and called them forth to trust in the Lord and to fight. Like Hannibal in somewhat similar circumstances, Totila kept away from the walls of Rome—and the other cities where the imperial commanders—Bessas, Constantinian, and Bloody John —shut themselves up. He did not waste his swordsmen in sieges, but led them out of the devastated north to food in the southland.

As Hannibal had done—and Belisarius tried to do—Totila showed only tolerance to the native Italians. In battle he was cruel as any barbarian king. Noblewomen taken captive at Cumae found unexpected chivalry in him. When the men of

Naples begged him for a month's truce to consider surrender, the twenty-odd-year-old Totila granted them three months— and they surrendered the city that was the vital seaport of the Romans. For the first time the Goths began building a fleet, to carry the war out to the sea lanes that supplied the Roman garrisons.

Tradition relates that the dynamic leader of the Goths visited the aged Benedict at Mt. Casinum, and heard the prophecy of Benedict, that he would go upon the sea, and enter Rome, but would reign for no more than nine years. However this may have been, Totila treated the monks with respect.

In moving up from Naples to Rome, Totila sent messages in advance. Placards appeared in the streets of the imperial city; they asked the citizens if the rule of Justinian had been as beneficial as that of the great Theodoric or the queenly Amalasuntha. Did the citizens enjoy having Greeks for overlords? Did they not pay out taxes to Alexander the Scissors and profits to the mercenary general Bessas, who sold them back requisitioned grain? (This was true enough; Bessas had commandeered the corn supply to stand a siege, but took gold from those who could still pay for grain.)

Despite this guise of a tolerant king-to-be, however, Totila waged savage warfare against Roman forces in the open country. His Gothic host became too strong to defeat, and Totila kept it in the open. In his marches an array of captured Roman standards followed him. He contented himself with closing the roads into Rome while his new warcraft blockaded the ports of the Tiber's mouth.

While he waited for hunger to take effect on the dispirited garrison and populace, Totila learned that Belisarius had appeared in the northeast at Pola. The name of Belisarius had become a legend in the land. As Khusrau had done in the East, Totila sent at once to discover what actual force followed the conqueror from Constantinople. He forged a letter, as if from a Roman officer, speeding it in the hands of trained observers to Pola. They returned to report that Belisarius was training only the fragment of an army.

To explain what followed in Italy it is said that Belisarius lacked his old mastery in command. That is not true—at least until the test of the bridge on the Tiber. He moved on to Ravenna and sent spearheads inland to relieve the hemmed-in Roman garrisons. His Balkan recruits could not hold their ground against the mounted Goths. The other generals could not, or would not, manage to unite to join him. Totila came up the ancient highways with the impact of lightning in a storm.

When Belisarius took the measure of the forces opposed to him, he wrote one of his frank appreciations to Justinian. Its very frankness showed that they understood each other as of yore. "If it was only necessary to send Belisarius to Italy, you have accomplished it. I am in the midst of it here. If you wish to overcome your enemies, more must be done. A commander must have men to give him force. Above everything I have need of my own comitatus, and next to it a really large strength in Huns and other fighting barbarians, and enough money to pay them."

He gives the reasons for Justinian to analyze. The small following he himself picked up on the way, the lack of spirit in the Roman garrisons after many defeats—"men have been seen to throw away their weapons and abandon their horses in flight"—the impossibility of raising money any longer in Italy. This matter of failure to pay the soldiers weighed heavily on Belisarius, and he explains why. "We cannot impose our orders on them now, for the debt has taken away our right to command. And you ought to know that many of them have deserted to the enemy."

He sent John with the letter to the Daphne. But John, who had ambitions of his own, lingered in the capital to make an advantageous marriage with a daughter of Germanus, who was growing in influence. Perhaps Theodora had a hand in that.

Left to his own devices, Belisarius abandoned the land for the sea. Picking up vessels on his way, he cruised down to the mouth of the Adriatic, recovered the port of Otranto (Hydruntum), and added stranded garrisons to his force. Learning that Totila had tightened the stranglehold on Rome, Belisarius crossed to Sicily and loaded a flotilla with grain. While his fighting dromonds scattered the light vessels of the Goths' blockade, Belisarius sailed his convoy into Portus at the Tiber's mouth. There he was held in check for anxious days.

Patrols sent from the port toward Rome were ambushed and slain by the Goths; sallies by the garrison from the walls of Rome were beaten back. Between the relief fleet and the beleaguered city waited the strength of the Goths and the wit of Totila. They had blocked the waterway of the Tiber with a fortified chain. Spies reported to Belisarius that above the chain stretched a bridge of boats boarded over and palisaded, the ends of the bridge being defended by strong log towers.

The spies brought rumors of desperation inside the city. The hoarded grain was exhausted; a bushel of corn sold for seven gold pieces. One man could not endure the crying of his five children, begging for food; he led them away with him, to a Tiber bridge, where he wrapped his cloak around his head and leaped into the water while his children watched. Starving families were stealing out of the gates carrying some belongings, to be tracked down, enslaved, or slain by the Goths.

Belisarius knew by experience what the situation must be within the city. Totila, wiser than Vitigis, had not molested the farmlands, and so could gain food for his armed host, paying for the supplies. There was something ironic in the well-being of the barbarians and the destitution of the forces of the Empire. Belisarius turned to his only resource, an attempt to force the passage of the river. He prepared for it hastily, but with his usual care.

Because the large dromonds could not navigate the mud flats of the river, lighter skiffs were fitted with wooden shield walls on the sides. Archers within them could use their bows through openings. Two barges were roped together, and a wooden siege tower was raised on them. The summit of the tower held an odd contrivance, a small boat mounted on a slide and filled with the combustibles of Constantinople: sulphur, pitch, and oil of turpentine.

Belisarius sent messages to warn Bessas within Rome of his move up the river, demanding that Bessas sally out to engage the Goths along the banks at the same time. The base at Portus, and his wife Antonina, he left in command of a certain Isaac the Armenian, who had brought reinforcements from Constantinople, but had never served under the Magister before. Lack of trained officers and battle-worthy troops handicapped Belisarius in his attempt.

At the start a westerly breeze favored him, aiding the motley sailing craft to breast the current. Transports and skiffs and the floating tower forged up the winding Tiber, with the grain convoy following. They reached the heavy chain and broke it apart under protection of missiles from the guard skiffs. But the Goths were swarming down to the banks, manning the bridge of boats. Here began a confused struggle. The wind drove the head of the flotilla against the barrier, and the vessels piled up from bank to bank.

However, the floating tower was towed against one of the land towers. When the two structures met, Roman engineers fired the combustibles in the tilted boat, and let go the flaming mass on the Goths defending the tower at the bridge end. The sulphurous fire killed the humans and spread through the tower. In panic the Goths on the bridge ran to the other shore.

Many things happened very quickly then. Totila himself appeared on the bank. There was no sign that the Roman army was advancing from the city. The sailing craft became

jammed against the boat bridge. While axmen severed the
ropes binding the boats, the Goths came on to attack again.
Even when cut through, the broken bridge, under the thrust
of the current, held back the ships. Some say that in his great
fatigue Belisarius suffered a stroke or wound, and could not
speak. Others insist that he had a report that behind him
Portus had fallen to the enemy and his wife was captive. (Actually Isaac the Armenian had disobeyed orders and had tried
to pillage an abandoned camp, to be slain there by the Goths.)

In the end Bessas failed to bring support from Rome, and
Totila threw new masses into the fight at the bridge. Belisarius signed for a retreat, and his flotilla made its way down the
river to the harbor.

News of the defeat broke down resistance in the city. Some
Isaurians in charge of a gate earned safety and gold by throwing it open to the Goths. The luckless Bessas gathered his
cavalry together with a few senators to break out toward the
coast. When Totila rode into the city, his warriors hunted the
inhabitants through the streets. Survivors fled to Hadrian's
bridge, to sanctuary in the basilica of St. Peter. The clanging
of the bell in the tower summoned them thither.

Totila crossed the bridge to the steps that led up to the clois-
ter. On the steps a deacon, Pelagius, awaited him holding high
the Scriptures, saying to him: "Master, spare what is now
yours. God has made us your servants. Spare the lives of your
servants."

It took courage to confront the Goth in the tumult of massacre. Pelagius had spent his wealth, and had done more than
Bessas to defend the city. His plea touched the pride or interest of the young Goth. Totila allowed his followers to plunder
as they wished, but gave order to cease the slaying and the vio-
lation of women.

A count of the survivors within the Church of Peter the
Apostle came to a little more than five hundred. "To such
fortune had fallen the Senate and the Roman People."

❀ THE DESERTED CITY

The imperial city of the past had, in fact, come to an end with the life-stream of its population. There was no longer significance, or even utility, in the dry aqueducts, the cadaverous empty baths of the Caesars, or the weed-grown Greatest Circus. A poet of another generation would speak of these "bare bones of dead pleasures." The few remaining patricians put on rough garments to join the plebeians in begging food at the doors of the Goths. Beyond reach of harm in Constantinople, Procopius sensed the change. "A very remarkable example of this change of fortune being Rusticiana [among the beggars], who had been wife to Boethius, a woman formerly accustomed to give her wealth to the poor."

The Aurelian circuit wall remained a possible fortification, or obstacle to the moving armies. Apparently Totila could not make up his mind what to do with Rome. He sent Pelagius—who had known Justinian in other years—with his Gothic envoys to Constantinople, to negotiate a peace with the open offer to swear allegiance to Justinian as emperor on the part of the kingdom of the Goths—as in the time of Theodoric—and the implied threat to destroy Rome and march on Constantinople if the war went on.

What Pelagius himself said to Justinian is not known. Justinian answered that Belisarius had the power to make war or peace; Totila must negotiate with him.

Whereupon the victorious Goth prepared to carry out his threat in full. The massive city gates were broken up, portions of the wall were torn down, and fuel was piled into the palatial structures around the Forum. Before the burning of the monuments began, a remarkable letter reached him from Belisarius, who lay ill of fever at the Tiber port. "Only men of wisdom who understand civilization can create beauty in a city," the letter related. "Only men who lack such understanding can be expected to destroy its beauty, and later generations will judge their character from their acts. Among all cities, Rome is the most notable. It was not built by the ability of one man, but by the skill of multitudes, little by little, during a long interval of time."

The letter put a question to Totila. If he was defeated in the war, would he gain any advantage from razing Rome to the ground; if he won the war, would he profit from the destruction of his greatest city? As for Totila himself: "Your acts will decide your reputation."

It seems that the monarch of the Goths reread the letter many times. Its concealed taunt may have touched his uncertain pride. More probably it merely intensified his own irresolution. Obviously he had no least wish to garrison such an amphitheater of a place, and he was needed elsewhere himself. He did not have Belisarius' patience in thinking a situation through; he could only solve a difficulty by action. He acted now by departing with his armed host to the north, leaving the unguarded city still standing within its broken wall.

Then for two years, 547–9, the aspect of Italy changed as swiftly as a moving kaleidoscope. No sooner had Totila gone than Belisarius entered Rome, inspected it, and summoned in his small force. He opened a food market for the inhabitants by ferrying supplies from Sicily.

Hearing of this, Totila's anger brought him back headlong and he drove his warriors at the gaping gates. The Goths found the breaches blocked by skillful fighting men aided by machines. Belisarius' legerdemain defeated all attack until, after days of bloodshed, Totila led his men away again to the highways where he could be master. Methodically, Belisarius fashioned new gates for Rome and dispatched the keys in evidence of victory to Constantinople.

There Justinian gathered reinforcements, a regiment at a time. He no longer refused to raise an army entire among the barbarian peoples. Through Pannonia he admitted the Lom-

bards, orthodox Christians—monks had gone among them—
but a close-knit tribal folk, dangerous in war. Narses journeyed
up to his friends the Heruls to recruit what he could. Leading
thence an uncouth host, he found the way to Italy barred by
drifting Slavic folk, and his Heruls scattered to assail these,
their tribal foes.

Yet fresh barbaric units reached Italy by water, and Totila
had no mercy for them. The records tell of a captured Hunnish officer mutilated; an Armenian who answered only two
words in a known language—*Gilakios strategos*, Gilak the general—was put to death. Bloody John, who insisted on invasion
of the countryside, led his horsemen into ambushes of the
Goths. Once Belisarius, surprised in his camp by the Goths,
had to run with his men to their vessels on the beach and sail
away to Messina. Now he used his shipping as he once ma-
neuvered his cataphracts, putting in at fortified ports, making
his orbit from Otranto to Taranto, to Sicily and Rhegium.
And now the inland cities were disappearing in the murk of
conflict; Milan lay beyond reach; the imperialists could only
hold fast to the coasts, including Ravenna, where the new
church of St. Vitalis was rising. (In another century these
Byzantine ports of call would grow into trading towns which
would become in time free maritime cities, a Genoa or a
Venice.)

Already Totila sensed the danger from the sea; he built vessels of his own by the hundred and swore to Pelagius, who had
returned to St. Peter's, that he would wrest away the island of
Sicily. He could not bring the elusive Belisarius to battle in
the open, and so could not defeat him.

The kaleidoscope of conflict made no clear pattern. Yet
new words tell of it. The antagonists of a dozen years before,
the Romans and barbarians, had become the imperialists and
Totila's henchmen.

Again Belisarius was recalled. He left an able lieutenant in
command at Rome and instructed him to seed the vacant

fields, to grow crops within the walls. Then he departed by way of Otranto on a galley. For the third time the Goths besieged Rome, and entered it by treachery.

Then, in January 550, the sagacious Totila offered mercies to the Italians who would be his subjects. The farmers would be free in cultivating their fields, paying little to their king. For Totila's warriors were liegemen, not hired soldiers; they rewarded themselves with plunder or slaves taken in battle. He tried to persuade fugitive senators to return to their homes in Rome, and as a temptation to them he ordered racing to begin again in the Greatest Circus.

Faced by the failure of his war after fourteen years, Justinian sat for long hours with his great commander in the Daphne. Inevitably he learned the only possible means of winning Italy: an army of the assembled power of the Empire, with money to pay its cost for years, a fleet to accompany its march along the coast, and an able leader to command it. The alternative was to yield to Totila's terms and accept a Gothic nation in Italy, feudal masters of St. Peter's basilica.

Justinian called upon Germanus. His carefree cousin could go as representative of the Emperor. Germanus, at home with the northern chieftains, could lead an army of Lombards, and cataphracts with Heruls added, and thread his way through the oncoming hordes to Ravenna. There was also Matasuntha of the Amal blood, granddaughter of Theodoric, who laid her spite upon Vitigis. If Germanus and Matasuntha married in their middle age, many Gothic nobles would refuse to stand against a queen of the Amal blood. They could be made allies. The way could be prepared. . . .

Justinian remembered how Theodora had opposed this marriage, for Germanus stood very near to his own throne. If the plan succeeded and Germanus brought order into Italy as he had into Africa there might be another emperor in the West.

He bade Germanus make ready to go. And he ordered the fleet of the Prefect of the Isles to make its way to Spain.

❈ AFTERMATH OF THE DESTRUCTION

The plague and famine had caused a silent revolution. We who live in the mid-twentieth century know only the effect of great wars in altering the economy and the societies of nations. A plague in the earlier centuries had an effect beyond our imagining. It shook apart any civilized society. After it strange faces and fresh beginnings appeared.

Constantinople barely withstood the shock of the plague years. Justinian had lost something of his vitality and decision. His efforts were bent on salvage, and inevitably he failed to sense the alteration taking place outside his great city on the Bosporus. Evidence of it lay concealed in the multitude of appeals for his decision.

Under the new laws an appeal could not be made to the Emperor until the higher courts, the Praetorian's or Quaestor's, had given a decision. But his subjects persisted in trying to appeal to Caesar, and Justinian read all that came to his hands. . . . Newborn infants, abandoned at monastery doors, were claimed after childhood by the parents—what should be done with them? Decision: the children to be restored to the family, but must not be sold into slavery. . . . By perversity of death, a grandmother inherits all property of her own children and grandchildren—what tax is owing to the treasury? Decision: the wealth in bulk will be taken by the treasury, and a gold solidus a day paid to the aged woman as long as she lived.

There was evidence of unrest. Justinian decreed that no arms should be carried by civilians. Black-market operators who sold for more than the fixed prices would have their shops or vessels confiscated. Artisans, laborers, and sailors were not to demand or receive increase in wages. Troops en route on the highways must not requisition private homes for quarters or fine a community for not meeting their demands; the village should provide what food and shelter it could manage.

Dwarfing these numberless details arose the need of an exhausted treasury and the danger of a sinking currency. Peter Barsymes, who had a Syrian's lack of scruples, abolished the last privileges of the senatorial order, maintained the emergency *Aerikon* tax, and levied new taxes. Wealth had shifted in the calamity, and must be sought now from the masses, in fees for marriages and burials, in raising the price of bread, and confiscating idle estates.

Peter Barsymes urged Justinian to increase the available currency by scaling down the standard gold solidus. Justinian hesitated to depreciate the currency. The great Constantine had been forced to reduce the gold content of the aureus by four sevenths. Since then the gold coinage of Constantinople had come to serve all the known world. Refugees from Britain had received the solidi as a gift and, fingering the devices on the great coins, had known that an emperor and a Christian cross endured to aid them. Across the limit of the Rhine tribesmen of the Thuringian forests "at the thin edge of darkness" had paid superstitious reverence to the shining images on the coins, saying that they were the "slaves of this lord." At the other edge of darkness in Ceylon, Cosmas the Indiafarer said that once the King had wondered whether the lord of Constantinople could be greater than the more familiar Persian Shah-in-shah—until he compared the massive gold coin of Justinian with the thin silver coin of the Sassanian. And in treaties with the Persians, Constantinople stipulated that whatever gold might be sent to Persia must be utilized for ornaments, not for coins. By now the solidus had penetrated wherever trade passed; its worth lay in its weight of gold.

Characteristically, Justinian refused the request of Peter Barsymes to devalue it, but allowed it to represent more in silver—210 obols instead of 180. (The gold coin of Constantinople remained the standard of Europe for the coming centuries, until in the later Renaissance the byzant [of Byzantium] matched the florins [of Florentine mintage] of the new age.)

As with the laws and coinage of the Empire, Justinian's answer to the paralysis of the plague's end was to force more to be accomplished. Because the African coast lacked ports, its abundant foodstuffs could not be transported to the hunger-ridden provinces of Europe. Then the harbors of Carthage and Caesarea must be enlarged. The basin of Carthage had no defense against raiding Berbers? Fortify the monastery at its point. Move the border *castella* up into the Numidian plain. The Slavs were pushing their encampments down from Macedonia into Thessaly? Wall the coastal pass at Thermopylae. The grain fleets could not enter the Dardanelles when a north wind arose? The grain rotted while the vessels beat off the strait for weeks? Build storage towers on Tenedos; unload the cargoes there, return the fleets to Africa for new shipments, while vessels from the Marmora brought in the stored, dry grain as soon as the winds ceased.

The most vital failure was that of transport. Couriers lacked post horses on the Anatolian highway. Then fast sailing sloops could take them around by the coast. Ravenna stagnated after the wartime ravaging of the countryside. New arterials must be opened up by building cart roads to Rimini and the Po. The Logothete, Alexander, would find the money. . . .

Ruthlessly the man in the Daphne denied his people the relief of inaction. If one area yielded up its almost insufferable responsibilities, the adjoining districts declined. While merchant craft of the Golden Horn reached the far outpost of the Middle Sea at Gades (Cadiz) the Lombards made Pannonia their own. Even the islands of the sea were coming into use—Tenedos and Cyprus as well as Sicily. Procopius complained of Justinian's "senseless building at the edge of the sea." It was not senseless, but it was involuntary. Unaware, Justinian was leading a retreat to the coastal regions.

Unperceived by ruler or writer, Constantinople was assuming the characteristics of ancient Byzantium, a maritime city. The Empire was returning to the Middle Sea that had given it birth.

An example of the immense work carried out by Justinian and Theodora in the aftermath of destruction exists today, in St. Vitalis. This unusual church was built rapidly and was completed in 547–8. Argentarius, who designed it, may have come, like so many other artists, from Antioch. Its octagon plan resembles that of the lost *Domus Aureus* of Antioch. The groined vaulting is certainly eastern, with the lovely detail of acanthus leaves and birds.

Archbishop Maximian, who devoted himself to its building, came to Ravenna after the capture of the city. St. Vitalis was the first Byzantine monument in the north of Italy, the other structures being Ostrogothic basilicas, simple in form and uninspired in decoration. Although plain enough on the outside, like Byzantine churches in the East, St. Vitalis develops a harmony of its own within walls. That harmony begins at the doors and rises to full orchestration within the choir space. It draws upon the imagery of East and West. The vistas of Moses, the burning bush and the receiving of the Law, are from the eastern Septuagint as surely as the miniatures of the Joshua Roll. Yet the youthful, beardless Christ and the four companions of the Evangelists are symbols of the West.

There is a story of the designing of St. Vitalis which we may never know. Did Justinian mean it to be the religious dedication of his effort in the West, as was the Hagia Sophia in Constantinople? Were the motifs from Antioch inserted deliberately? Did he intend this dedicated church to unite Latin symbols with the Greek? Or did the artists simply follow out their own imagining in those troubled years?

One detail tells a clear story. The likeness of Theodora in the mosaic portrait of the choir shows an emaciated, pallid woman. Only the intent dark eyes are lifelike in a mask of pain.

At that time Theodora was dying.

❀ TESTAMENT OF THEODORA AUGUSTA

"She sets her stubborn will to overcome things, and when she decides a matter she carries out the decision with all her energy."

So reported Procopius of Caesarea, who envied and feared the Despoina in her last years. Theodora was setting her house in order in a manner of her own. At her court in Hicron no records were kept. Seeking to wed Anastasius to Belisarius' daughter, although both were still in their teens, she brought them together in her gardens. Antonina made the journey back to Constantinople, determined to prevent the marriage of the youthful lovers.

The gossips of the Augusteum had the tale of how Theodora prevented another marriage. This was the case of Artabanes, a Persarmenian, a rising officer and an idol of women. It did not seem to have any connection with the Despoina, but in reality it concerned her. Artabanes had served Germanus well in Africa, and in so doing had rescued an impressionable young woman, Praejecta, from the hands of rebels. Justinian named the Armenian honorary master of offices, for Praejecta was his niece. Nor did Justinian object when Artabanes sought the noblewoman for wife. In Theodora's memory, however, Artabanes had been responsible for the murder of the Roman officer, Tzitas, the husband of her sister Comito. That had happened in the Caucasus, and there Theodora's agents traced back the life of the flamboyant Artabanes, to discover that he had a wife living. This peasant woman was brought to Constantinople. Furious, Artabanes was forced to give up Praejecta and take back his wife.

At the Caucasus frontier, mighty Khusrau puzzled over a letter of Theodora to a Christian Persian, urging him to work for peace between the empires. "What sort of a state is this of Rome, that it is governed by a woman?" Khusrau demanded of his Magians. "Have we anything to fear from it?"

Another letter of hers found its way to Rome, to the hand of the Pope, Vigilius, who had known her as the figure in spun gold with lappets of pearls seated in the Triclinium: "Fulfill the promise you made of your free will, to recall our father Anthemius to his office". . . . to lift the sentence of exile against the old man, honored and concealed as patriarch in Hieron.

The urgency in such letters increases with the months. When Vigilius will not lift the ban of anathema of Anthemius, he is brought unexpectedly to Constantinople—Theodora requesting it of Belisarius—and there agrees to revoke the anathema.

Seldom now does Theodora take thought for the West. Her eyes are on the homeland beyond the Bosporus, the shrines of Antioch now rebuilt by her insistence. Her implacable ambition has been for the older cities of her wanderings. Thence go the pilgrims of her House of the Monks. Thither they send their reports to her. The blessed John of Ephesus has opened the Carian mountains to the Church of her faith, that called the Monophysite. In Alexandria Jacob Old Clothes holds a secret synod of the Monophysites. In Palestine's hills the Samaritans beg for an end of persecution. If the Augusta will speak for them. . . .

Jacob Old Clothes, aging but unwearied, leaves persecution

behind to hasten through the deserts, where pillars of cloud point the way. His messages are like fragrant nard; they tell of churches rising and of deacons and priests needed to follow him. There is a bishop in Memphis; there will be a patriarch beyond that other river, the Euphrates.

She summons Peter Barsymes, hated by the populace of Constantinople. Her bidding is to protect the eastern provinces, for in them is the foundation of the new Empire of her husband. And Procopius writes in his secret history that she has bewitched Peter Barsymes by some talismanic art.

Such scraps from the records reveal only a little of her last years. Of what passed between her and Justinian nothing is known. Did the dark-eyed beauty of the theater play her part to the last, hiding her illness? No one seemed to hear of it, and perhaps Justinian was not told. She took her place by him in the audiences, hearing the murmur of greeting: "Glory of the purple. . . ."

When Antonina reached Constantinople, Theodora was dead of cancer in the throat in June 548. When her body was placed between the candles in the nave of the Apostles, an unusual incident occurred. By the body appeared the aged Patriarch Anthemius, believed by many to have been dead for a dozen years.

VIII

JUSTINIAN, FIRST EMPEROR OF THE BYZANTINES

JUSTINIAN ALONE

THEY SAY Justinian grieved too much after Theodora's death. It gave him pleasure when somebody in the audience spoke the name of "our well-loved Empress." He ordered her servants to keep the women's chambers as they were, with her belongings in place and her chamberlain presiding over the terrace court; he himself sometimes took the throne seat there, to hear those who had unfinished business with the Augusta. The religious women in gray garments with black sleeves who served the chapel of the Mother of the Light Tower maintained their prayers.

Justinian's insistence in following out Theodora's wishes had its effect far from the city. A decree ended the persecution of the Samaritans; Jacob Old Clothes carried on his missions without hindrance from the Emperor's agents. Monophysite bishops returned to their churches in Alexandria and Antioch. At last all the churches of the East were free to follow their ancient ritual.

Those who wondered in Constantinople whether the will of the Augusta had not opposed the plans of Justinian now understood that the husband and wife had been carrying out the same task in different ways. Now Justinian was deprived of the woman's gaiety and inflexible determination; nearly seventy years of age, he faced his decisions alone except for the solicitude of the more aged Narses, who had acted so long as Theodora's mentor.

There was a swift shifting of personal relationships around the throne, once Theodora's restraint had been removed. Antonina contrived to annul the marriage of the youthful lovers, Anastasius and her daughter Joannina. Their names disappeared from the public record. Artabanes, the Persarmenian noble, cast off his old wife as "distasteful to him," but the temperamental commander could no longer claim Praejecta, who was wed by then to a sound man, Marcellus, count of the Excubitors. Germanus carried out the marriage with Matasuntha, joining the Amal blood to his own ancient lineage, with a prospect that an heir might be born to the throne of Constantinople and the kingdom of Italy alike.

Almost inevitably, as personal ambitions flared, there was a plot to kill Justinian. Theodora's spies no longer watched the corridors, and he passed long hours of the night unguarded. The plot came from astute Persarmenian brains, and it fastened on grievances. A certain Arsaces, who had been convicted of treason and had escaped with light punishment from Justinian—a cudgeling and parade through the streets on a camel's back—gathered kindred spirits to confide in Artabanes, still resenting the loss of Praejecta, how their great opportunity could be seized. How they might easily slay "a man who sits without guards every night in some corridor, eagerly unrolling the Christian Scriptures in company with priests as aged as he." With Justinian dead, they would have need of a protector, to gain reward, and such they had at hand in Germanus, who nursed ill-will against the Autocrat because Justinian had taken the part of a niece against Germanus in a matter of inheritance. Surely, then, Germanus would be given the imperial purple, and they would have their reward!

Artabanes did not feel convinced of that. He was one of the many Asiatics who severed family ties to serve the Empire, eager for honors; he would not tell Germanus of the plot, but he consented to try to win over Justin, eldest son of the great commander—and Justin repeated to his father how the well-born Persians had reminded him that while he served the Emperor for little honor, Justinian gave reward to common men. Straightaway Germanus went to an officer he could trust, Marcellus. And the very integrity of the leader of the Excubitors balked him, for Marcellus would not report to Justinian a tale of conspiracy which had not been proved.

Germanus could not produce evidence simply, because Artabanes kept silence while he watched events. Some of the Persarmenians, however, were led to talk within hearing of an officer known to Marcellus, and by good luck they warned that the killing must be delayed until Belisarius returned to Constantinople. (The veteran was then on his way home from Italy.) Unless Belisarius was slain with Justinian, he might summon up an army to make an end of the conspiracy and all connected with it.

Marcellus believed this evidence. When he was alone with Justinian, he explained bluntly what he had heard.

"Germanus should have told me himself," Justinian retorted. "Why did he delay to do so?"

"He wished me to tell Your Clemency."

Belisarius was nearing the city, and there was little time to act. Brooding over the charge, Justinian followed his habit of having the accusation written down for judgment. When he

David and Goliath, seventh-century Byzantine silver plate. David rebukes Goliath (TOP); David fights Goliath (CENTER); David beheads Goliath (BOTTOM). This plate is part of the Cyprus treasure found by Greek peasants in 1902 near Kyrenia. The treasure was probably buried in the middle of the seventh century when Cyprus was invaded by the Arabs.

Part of gold girdle of medallions and coins, Byzantine, late sixth century, from the Kyrenia find. The portraits are of the Emperor Flavius Tiberius Mauricius (582–602).

Gold marriage belt, Byzantine, late sixth century.
The two large medallions represent Jesus joining the hands of the couple before him.
On the small medallions appear busts of pagan deities

ordered the conspirators arrested in their homes, all except
Artabanes implicated Germanus to protect themselves. Wea-
rily Justinian read through their evidence in the presence of
fearful senators and silent officers. By such evidence Germanus, his cousin, was guilty. And who except the popular
Germanus would dare strike at Belisarius, the idol of the
army?

Then, to the amazement of those in the judgment room,
Marcellus came forward to take the blame on himself. He
told them that he had asked Germanus to delay while he secured proof of the plot—not to incriminate Artabanes falsely.
Although this must have sounded like a clumsy fabrication,
Justinian knew the worth of the unimaginative Excubitor's
word. He dismissed all the evidence, confined his cousin and
the Persian Magister in the palace under his observation, and
then proceeded to make use of both of them—after his con-
sultation with Belisarius—to meet the great need of Constantinople.

❈ GATHERING OF THE ARMY OF THE NATIONS

"At this point in the wars," a chronicler observes of the
year 550, "the barbarians became undisputed masters of all
the West."

All, that is, except Africa. Elsewhere the military defeat of
Constantinople was written large on the master map of the
War Office. Beyond Sirmium (Mitrovica) the northern frontier of the Danube had vanished with its *castella* under the influx of drifting Slavs, Heruls, and the well-organized Lombards. Again the red Merovingian Franks had debouched from
the Alpine passes to feed themselves and watch the circus
races—of Totila's ordering—to stamp gold coins of their own
in mockery of Justinian, who had once called himself con-

queror of the Franks and Germans, and to organize a confederacy against the Empire. In Italy, where Totila reigned, the imperial garrisons held out only in a few seaports: Ancona, Otranto, and Ravenna. In vital Sicily only Syracuse and Panormus (Palermo) held out; for Totila had avenged himself on the island, building an invasion fleet of 400 sail—adding to it captured merchantmen—to ravage and burn the Roman towns, and to fare on to seize Sardinia and Corsica. Thus the trade routes across the sea were closing, and Africa itself was endangered.

Again Totila had offered terms of peace to Justinian. Justinian replied by appointing Germanus to command an army that would make a last snatch at victory before the remaining seaports fell to the Goths. It could no longer risk a voyage to Italy by sea. Instead, a fleet was fitted out and given to the Magister Artabanes—released from confinement in the palace —to descend upon Sicily.

When Artabanes landed successfully, there seemed to be hope. When Germanus raised his banner on the Dalmatian coast, chieftains led in their henchmen to serve such an illustrious general; Bloody John—now son-in-law to Germanus —brought a *numerus* of cataphracts in from Thrace; Germanus spent his own fortune to recruit more. Justinian had given him a free hand to do so, with the available gold reserve of Peter Barsymes' treasury. Matasuntha, accompanying the army, received covert messages from Gothic nobles that they would not take the field against their former queen. But the undertaking hinged entirely upon the name and ability of one man, Germanus. To move forward he was obliged to clear the Slavs from the valleys leading to Venetia.

His death from malarial fever in the summer heat put an end to the expedition. Belisarius was too wearied to take the field again. Bloody John might be capable of leading a regiment in battle, but he could not command a war between nations. The army retreated to the city of Salona for the winter, while Slavic hordes with Kutrigur Huns from the steppes pressed past it, nearing Hadrian's City. Bands of Franks appeared along the roads through the marshes of Venetia, and Totila sent ships to blockade Salona. Not much hope was left.

Justinian would not admit defeat. Scraping up forces to hold back the Huns and Slavs on the Balkan roads he strengthened Artabanes in Sicily. When the roads dried in the spring (551) he sent the seventy-five-year-old eunuch, Narses, to take Germanus' command at Salona. With Narses went the last reserves of Constantinople, the assembled veteran comitatus of Belisarius, and a contingent of Persians under a nephew of Khusrau. On the way to Dalmatia, Narses won over some wandering Gepids, and the main strength of his friends the Heruls, under their king.

It was a very strange array gathering at Salona around the brittle figure of the devoted Grand Chamberlain with the golden eagles on his long tunic, and trumpeters announcing his coming. His presence bespoke the authority of the Empire; his peculiar skill lay in winning men to wage war for him. The standard before his pavilion was a painted banner of Hagia Sophia, that of the Holy Mother. Narses proclaimed that it would bring them victory in battle.

The strength of the army of Salona lay in its three divisions of mailed cataphracts, with 5,500 armored Lombards commanded by their King Audaun. It numbered over 25,000, and it had the wealth of supplies and gold that Belisarius had never been given. In sending it forth Justinian had broken all the rules of the earlier emperors and himself—that the soldiers of Constantinople must be Christianized and Romanized, that no barbarian contingents be allowed to serve under their own chieftains. It was in actuality an army of the nations, held in restraint only by its respect for the Emperor of the western world. By that very fragile restraint and the persuasion of old Narses. . . .

The land route to Italy was blocked by the Franks clustering in the northern hills. This last-resource army of Constantinople could not turn against the Merovingian invaders without having the Gothic host of Totila on its backs. The wisdom of Narses and the experience of John—who had never been able to work well with the demanding Belisarius—found a safe route into Italy along the coast. With their fleet escorting and ferrying the soldiers over the Venetian lagoons, the army waded and floated its way around to the port of Ravenna, escaping the watch of both Franks and Goths.

As soon as Totila learned that the imperialists were in Ravenna with their strange banner, he hurried north along the Flaminian Way, calling on all his forces to join him. They say he made a splendid figure of a king, gold shining on his arms and throat, and a cloak of Roman purple on his shoulders. So he rode to the end of his fame and to his death.

With the powerful Franks at their backs, Narses and John hastened toward the Goths, throwing pontoon bridges over the small rivers in their way. They agreed to risk everything in one battle, and it fell out that way at a place called Taguinae in a wide valley from which neither army could easily escape. They agreed also to wait for the headlong attack of the Goths because if that failed their own more disciplined forces could maneuver at will.

So it happened. Although Totila had not gathered all his armed strength, he drove his horsemen straight at the center of the Roman array, which dismounted to meet the charge. The Goths used only lance and sword, while Narses' regiments used their bows, and it was much like the charge of the French chivalry at Crécy, with the same result. The Goths swept against the ironclad Lombards, stubborn in battle; their disorder was flailed by flights of arrows, until they tried to draw away, and were attacked by cataphracts on unwearied horses. Once broken, the warriors of Totila fled, to be followed fast by Narses' pursuit. In the gathering darkness a single Gepid, caught in the rush of men and animals, lunged with his spear at a rider marked by a bright helm and flying cloak, and so gave Totila his death wound.

The polished helm and bloodied cloak were sent to Constantinople to Justinian.

❋ "THE SILENCE OF A PRIMEVAL AGE"

As with the capture of Vitigis at Ravenna, the loss of their king left the Goths without cohesion. They took refuge in hill castles or trooped south to the treasure stored in Cumae. The bulk of their fleet, penned in the harbor of Naples, surrendered, and other vessels escaped to other coasts. Narses occupied Rome and left to John the task of pursuit that ended in the dark hills around Vesuvius, above the buried pleasure city of Pompeii.

It took a toll of lives, this hunting down. For two days of battle on the volcano's slopes the Gothic warriors held fast their wall of shields, until only the wounded and commoners survived. Once they threw down their swords, the Germanic folk had no more hope.

There was uncertainty and new agony in Italy the following spring (553) when multitudes of Franks poured south across the Po like wolf herds racing into a broken sheepfold. It was not an invasion so much as armed masses in quest of loot. Narses held his commands within fortifications to let the Franks pass south; then the imperialists concentrated near Rome, to protect the city and scatter the swift-marching Franks on their return. Pestilence broke out among the invaders in the heat of the south. The largest mass of them made a walled camp on the Volturno, and this Narses attacked without mercy. There is no clear account of what happened there. But few survivors escaped the Roman cavalry, and their flight carried them back to the Alps. With the departure of the

Frankish axmen, the remaining Gothic garrisons followed them or ceased resistance.

There was an anxious winter in which Narses held together his own heterogeneous command, aided the Italians to return to their homes, and kept watch to the north, where elements of Franks, Burgundians, Alemanni, and Goths surged restlessly, awaiting the coming of the Merovingian king to lead a fresh invasion. But Theudebert, monarch of the Rhineland, died and no war lord remained to take leadership of the barbaric multitudes. Thereupon the surviving Goths made a sworn peace with the aged viceroy of Justinian, agreeing to leave Italy forever. The Franks also disappeared into the mountain passes. When they did so, Narses rewarded and dismissed the Lombards, blond giants in armor who might prove as dangerous in peace as they had been invaluable during a brief hour of battle. They retired slowly through the heights to their homeland on the upper Danube. But they did not forget the fertile valley of Italy.

More than twenty years after Belisarius had landed with his comitatus in Sicily, the war in Italy was ended. "Over the land," a chronicler wrote, "lay the silence of a primeval age."

That silence after the wars was pregnant with change. Vitality had passed, with wealth, from Rome on the Tiber to such strongholds as Bologna and such refuges as the lagoons of Venetia, where traders joined the fishermen to emerge from the channel of the Rialto "like sea birds," as Cassiodorus put it. The Goths had passed from the scene forever, as the Vandal race had vanished from Africa. There was no longer a semblance of the Italian-Gothic kingdom of Theodoric the Great which Totila had sought, after his fashion, to restore and Cassiodorus had served with his pen. The aged Cassiodorus labored in his monastic retreat within the horizon of the light of a single lamp, copying out manuscripts to be preserved and "read in far places"—as indeed they were. So labored the Benedictine monks at Mount Casinum, and the link between these two scriptoria would extend to other links of the monastic centers, into the lost Province, to St. Martin's on the Loire, to the missions of the Irish wanderers, to St. Columban's and St. Gall's in the remote mountains—the life line that preserved some standards of the past for a new medieval world. But the writings were in Latin, not Greek, and the monastic rule was that of St. Benedict, not St. Basil.

The retreat of the Franks from the nearer Alps to the province that had been Gaul created a cleavage among the peoples. It was certain now that Justinian's dominion could not be extended into Gaul, as he had hoped at one time. Much less could it reach the Rhineland or isolated Britain. Beyond the barrier of the Alps, along the life line of the ancient culture, the Merovingian kingdom would mature in the barbaric empire of Charlemagne, as Anglo-Saxon Britain would emerge from darkness as the England of King Alfred.

Justinian's imperium had been restored over the Middle Sea, and it remained there, pretty much confined to the coasts and islands. Sardinia and Corsica were regained with Sicily and the way station of the Balearics. Even before the peace in Italy, a small fleet from Constantinople fared west to occupy New Carthage (Cartagena) and Corduba on the Spanish coast, as well as Gades beyond the Straits. Agathias invoked poetry to explain that beyond the Gates of Hercules, those who looked out on "the blue western sea" were still, on that sandy shore, within the borders of the wise Emperor. On his part, Procopius—who had been set to work by Justinian, after completing his books on the wars, to write an account of all the new building in the Empire—related how a garrison and fort protected Septum (Ceuta, on the African side of the Straits), where a church was built and dedicated to the Mother of God.

These far ports were guarded by a magister militum of Hispania against attack by the Visigothic state of the interior;

they developed trade with the Visigoths and provided churches for missionary work. They endured there, little noticed, for several generations. Nor would Byzantine Constantinople ever entirely lose its hold on the Middle Sea.

And for the decade of comparative peace during the 550's, Justinian managed to restore the delicate counterpoise of power with the northern barbaric elements on the land. While the Franks had left the orbit of Justinian's influence, the Lombards were fostered—and led to church service—as a check against the uncouth Alemanni and Thuringians above the Alps. East of the Lombard kingdom, the allied Heruls withstood the pressure of the Bulgar-Huns. The restless Slavs remained beyond conversion or control, pushing their forest settlements down toward the cities of Greece, but never uniting —as the Hunnic tribes were likely to do—for an armed invasion. In fact the Slavs seemed to avoid each other as much as they avoided other peoples. Farther east in the Crimea, very much as in Spain, the ports established wary trade relations with the strong Kutrigur Huns. But along the river Don the Hunnic tribes were projected inward by the advance of the more powerful Avars.

At the end of the Euxine an army of Constantinople recaptured the vital bridgehead of Petra, thus barring the Persians from this second inland sea. From Petra, roads were opened through the mountains of the Lazi, and along those roads the missionary-trader pioneers penetrated to other people of the Caucasus. In 558 a khagan of the Avars was persuaded to visit Constantinople—as a possible ally against the Huns. The nearer shores from the Dnieper to the Caspian provided the raw stuffs so badly needed for the recuperation of Constantinople—the grain, dried fish and fruits, salt, and hides. But the caravan route through the northern steppes toward China could not be opened.

Then two Nestorian monks wrought something like a miracle to aid Justinian. They found their way in from the limbo beyond Samarkand, from *Serindia* (which may have been Turkestan rather than China). These bearded monks, agents of Justinian, carried with them a cane with eggs of the silk-worm hidden in it. That was the secret of the silk, they said, the worms that spun the slight thread. Hitherto Constanti-nople had been forced to buy the woven thread from Persian markets.

Justinian sent the monks to Syria, to nourish the priceless eggs in manure on that warm coast, and—if God aided them —to feed the young worms on mulberry leaves until they could breed. Years must pass before the raw silk of Syria could feed the half-abandoned looms of Peter Barsymes' ailing silk industry. Yet the hardy Nestorians had smuggled silk itself out of the forbidden Land of the Silk.

Over this nascent structure of Justinian's rule, carried out-ward by the sails of ships and the monks, lay the hard reality of encircling dangers.

❧ THE PORTRAITS AT ST. VITALIS

When Narses dismissed most of his victorious army, he re-mained at Ravenna as Autocrator, and proved himself to be a wise moderator. Although he became, as it were, the extension of the Emperor's personality, he did not always follow out Jus-tinian's wishes. After twenty years of chaos there were too many scars on the land and its inhabitants to be healed by de-crees from distant Constantinople.

Justinian gave a prefect to Italy, and the Constitution (called the Pragmatic Sanction of 554) for its government. This was more humane than the earlier exactions of Alexan-der the Scissors—who remained, however, as Logothete and attempted to gather all revenues from Greece and Italy into one defense and renovation fund. The Sanction forgave war crimes, restored to liberty those enslaved during the twenty years, allowed provinces to elect their own bishops or magnates as governors; it restored their homes to those who had been forced to leave them. It ordered payment to teachers in surviving schools, "so that young men, trained in the sciences, may aid the Roman Empire."

Although Justinian revoked grants and contracts made by Totila, he seemed to take a lesson from the tolerant measures of the eccentric Goth—or from the advice of Belisarius. While he ordered the repairing of the aqueducts and the dredging of the Tiber to be carried out, he allowed the dole of food to be given again to the returning populace of Rome. Property must be restored to owners before taxes were collected from them. So little wealth remained, however, that Narses was able only at first to provide new gates for Rome and rebuild the bridge over the Anio destroyed in the battles of Belisarius. On its stonework he placed a grandiloquent inscription:

> In the thirty-ninth * year of the reign of Ever Triumphant Justinian, our Lord and Father of the country, Narses, late Grand Chamberlain of the Sacred Palace, Ex-Consul and Patrician, victor in open battle with marvelous celerity over the Goths, erected this bridge and cleansed the river.

So the eunuch from the Persian mountains placed his titles and achievement above a stream on the Salarian Way. There was, however, a truth behind his fantasy; as Justinian's viceroy Narses embodied the sole dignity and power in the West. Yet despite his efforts the gulf between East and West was widening; young Italians looked upon him as the creature of a strange Greek emperor.

With the departure of the last Goths, the ancient city on one side of the Tiber lost its remaining significance. The sen-

---

* As this bridge was built in 557, Narses must have given the years of Justinian's reign from the inauguration of Justin, in 518.

ate followed the patricians into oblivion. Narses did not have Belisarius' respect for the monuments; he confined his efforts to repairing some churches, and took marble from the forum of Constantine to build a new edifice, that of the Apostles. Perhaps this was more than a diplomatic gesture; he may have sensed that the Christian basilicas in this inanimate city would become the gathering places of its people. At least he took thought for the community of churches when he restrained Pelagius.

That high-spirited archdeacon wrote to the bishop of Arles in the Province begging for money and clothing to be sent to the city, "so poor and bare of everything that we cannot look upon our companions without anguish of heart." Pelagius had been named as Pope in the West by Justinian, to succeed Vigilius (who had yielded to Theodora's pleading and to the will of the Council at Constantinople), who died on his journey back to Italy with the new Constitution of government. But this was a year of evil omens, with floods devastating the fields and pestilence reappearing in the tracks of the Franks. In the popular mind these evils sprang from the advent of the Greek Emperor's rule, and Pelagius himself was tainted by them. Justinian realized that the sole authority in Italy rested in the basilica of Peter, across the river from Rome.

When the outlying bishops failed to come to St. Peter's at Pelagius' bidding, the new Pope called on Narses to use the army to enforce obedience, but Narses wisely refused, leaving the churches to make their own peace with the primate. Then Pelagius walked with him through the streets to his basilica, and there in the pulpit lifted high the Gospels in an act of purgation of evil, calling upon his followers to witness it. There was a beginning made, not of authority but of a calling to the altar of Peter the Apostle.

In the ensuing years of darkness the worship of Mary the Mother increased. The long basilica of Sta. Maria (Maggiore) was restored by the hands of workmen who had no other work.

By the empty Forum the Sta. Maria in Cosmiden gained its mosaic picturing of remote scenes of the Annunication and Crucifixion—not scenes of the older Orient, but images of the western mind. A twelve-year-old boy, Gregory, son of a noble family, must have wandered between this small edifice of Mary and the empty Colosseum where tumblers sometimes forked their legs or made bears dance for copper obols thrown to them. Surely Gregory must have read the words of prophecy carved in the weathered stone: *While stands the Colisaeus, Rome shall stand*. In this manner he lived among imagined things, in a stagnation of life that was real. And when Gregory became primate of St. Peter's, he turned to the imagination of a different world, and he spoke with authority. His voice was the first of the Rome of the popes.

Narses had his quarters in an abandoned palace on the Capitoline, but he journeyed often to Ravenna, the residence of Justinian's rule, and of the exarchs of Constantinople in the generations to come. At the entrance to St. Martin's—completed by Justinian's order, not yet dedicated to St. Apollinaris—a mosaic portrait of the Emperor stood. But the octagonal church of St. Vitalis, now finished in the last details, became the cathedral of the people. Within it Justinian had had the artists picture the Biblical story of the Septuagint, the imagery of the East.

Oddly enough, his likeness and Theodora's in St. Vitalis have nothing imperial about them except the regalia on heads and breast that they always wore. They are not enthroned; they stand with others in two groups, low in the apse. Their hands hold offerings, Theodora's being a chalice. Her purple mantle bears, in embroidery, the Three Magi. A silentiary holds back the curtain by which she has entered. The ladies attending her are as tall as she, in as richly colored robes.

Up to a point, these are life portraits. Yet they do not stand upon a visible ground. Seemingly suspended, facing the human observers, the grouped figures appear to sway in a curious motion, entirely apart from the spectators. Clustered together, in this manner they face eternity.

The mosaics of St. Vitalis dominated Italian art for this and the following century. By then they had become something strange, to Italian eyes, portraits of the Byzantines.

Two centuries later, when Charlemagne of the Rhineland visited Ravenna, he was struck by the majesty of the building, and took some of the marble facings from it to ornament his small cathedral at Aix. In planning this, he copied the design of St. Vitalis.

❃ THE LAST YEARS

For the last ten years of his life Justinian's horizon, like that of Cassiodorus, became limited to the circle of light from his work lamp. Beneath it upon his table appeared the reports from the outer regions of his world-state. By them he had to judge what had succeeded and what had failed.

In other years Theodora had been quick to urge him to take action and Narses had been as ready to warn him discreetly. But the grizzled Marcellus spoke only of matters of duty, and the wizened eunuch Callinicus who wore the robe of Grand Chamberlain, spoke in ritual sibilants: "If you please . . ."

What Justinian beheld within the city indicated that he had triumphed. The walls of the Chalké pictured Khusrau turning away from the gate of Edessa in defeat, and Totila fleeing to his death. When Justinian went out through St. Stephen's gate to open the spring festival in the circus, the new youth of the demes chanted: "Health and well-being to the Emperor of the Romans . . . and victory God-given."

The Light Tower no longer flamed in warning of invasion. When Justinian took his evening walk through the gardens, he watched scout ships hurrying in past the palace point,

their crews, active in brown kilts, pulling in the sails . . .
bringing word, perhaps, of India . . . Cosmas, the Indiafarer had taken a monk's vows in his old age and had drawn
a map of the world, in the center the sea that he called the
Roman Gulf . . . so much of the outer world seemed to
be thronging into the harbor of the Horn, seeking the portal
of the Chalké . . . a new convent for Syrian women showed
across the way, on the hill above Sycae where old Justin had
gone, more than forty years before, to meet the Huns of
Vitalian. Surely a vast change had taken place since then.

Like storms arising from the horizon, word of calamities
still came in from the provinces. Pestilence among the animal
herds—the chemists of the university had dealt with. Earthquake through the Aegean islands—the Prefect of the Isles
had turned grain fleets aside, had done what else could be
done. Torrential rains, followed by floods, in the Balkan
valleys. The man in the Daphne thought of his many *Justin-
ianas*, even while he sat with the Praetorian and his engineers,
working out designs for flood control. Curials and bishops
appeared from cities beyond the horizon, to plead with the
Emperor himself that taxes could not be met after their
disasters. "To Areobindus, Prefect of the East," Justinian
wrote, "many have come to us to plead for remission of their
taxes. But, believing it unworthy to make piece-meal exemp-
tions, we hereby decree a general remission of taxes. Yet
there shall be no refunding of payments already made." And
he added warily: "There will be certain exceptions to this."

So Justinian labored at his table to meet each need, unaware that his orders would not often be carried out in the
"bitter provinces" by the officials he never saw. When complaints reached him, he would dispatch a special agent, a
Compulsor, to the scene. A long journey distant from Constantinople, the Compulsor might find it advantageous to
share an illegal profit, while reporting—as the Shatterers had
done before him—that he had seen justice carried out.

In actuality the great reform of the government which Justinian had begun twenty years before had enduring effect only within the city. There prices were kept down and pensions limited. The gold solidi held their value. But in Cappadocia, magnates minted underweight coins of their own and forced their use; prefects often demanded revenues in grain and goods from the curials when crops were poor, and demanded payment in money during an abundant harvest. A report came to Justinian that Peter Barsymes sold off dyes and raw silk from the government monopoly at excessive prices that never showed in the accounts. Yet when Justinian questioned his Praetorian, Peter proved that silk was yielding a profit; the Keeper of the Private Purse gave evidence that 324,000 gold solidi had been accumulated in reserve, as in the reign of Anastasius.

Justinian kept Peter at work, as he had always kept those he confided in, until they broke down from strain. He had no means of realizing that while Constantinople was strengthening, his rule was little more than a dead letter in many border provinces existing in feudal fashion, forming nuclei of nationalities and churches of their own. Where the *limitanei* had been withdrawn, peasants sometimes banded together for defense; Slavs and Bulgars and Lombards now within the borders raised their own harvests and mocked at tax-collectors who did not have an escort of armed soldiers. A chronicler wrote of the frontiers that "an invasion of enemy was less terrible than the coming of the treasury agents." As for the *castella*, built as safety centers on the northern border—"not even a watchdog barks in them."

Writers of the city itself, paid by Justinian to keep the record of his time, had a habit of making one version for the old man to study and another for the amusement of their friends. John of Lydia—who never forgave the cut in his pension—worked at a *Book of Portents*—all of which, it seemed, were ominous. The more talented Procopius drew pay for writing *The Buildings* for "the Emperor Justinian who took over the state when it was disordered and not only made it greater in extent, but also more illustrious." And behind closed doors he vented his spite in the *Anecdotes*, to be shown to the eyes of a few friends of the senatorial order—a rank never gained by the industrious Procopius— which had suffered at Justinian's hands. "He never got his fill of seizing property or plundering the homes of affluent men, straightaway pouring out the gains of his robberies in presents to varied barbarians and in erecting senseless buildings."

Justinian did erect something that appears senseless enough, yet may have had precise meaning in his own mind. That was the giant bronze portrait statue of himself in the Augusteum, facing east to the gleam of the rising sun. It rivaled the statue of the city's founder, Constantine. On horseback, this bronze Justinian wore a soldier's breastplate and plumed helm (as did his image on the solidi), with a half-toga thrown over his shoulder, but without any weapons. His open right hand stretched toward the East. "And in his left hand he holds a globe, by which the sculptor signifies that the whole earth and sea are subject to him, yet he has no weapon, but a cross stands upon the globe which he carries, the emblem by which alone he has obtained both his Empire and his victory in war."

Such is the official explanation of the statue which resembles no other work of Roman or Byzantine sculpture. Justinian, with his craving for precision, must have ordered the details of his effigy that dominated the thronged Augusteum. What did he mean it to signify? There is a faint resemblance to the rock carvings of the great Sassanian monarchs who stretched their hands toward the rising sun on the cliffs of Persia. This unarmed "Christian warrior" has puzzled archeologists sorely; yet psychologists might find sense in it. It bore the legend: *Eternal Glory*. Could it express the wish-fulfillment of a vain man who conceived himself to be waging a ceaseless war without armies?

The populace of the Augusteum benches put the ears of an ass on it when exasperated by one of Justinian's edicts.

The earthquakings that had shaken the Aegean islands struck Constantinople in the week before Christmas of 557. For six days the shocks loosened buildings on their foundations, and at times during the nights panic drove the multitudes toward the city gates.

The newer buildings withstood the tremors, but the Daphne suffered, and a silentiary sleeping outside Justinian's chamber was killed by the fall of a marble slab. That was the night when the great dome of Hagia Sophia fell in.

Skeptics who had prophesied its fall were quick to say that the anger of the Lord smote those who had raised the edifice in vainglory. Anthemius, who had built it against their warnings, was dead. But the nephew of Isidore, called back from Palestine, decided that the central weight had been too great to withstand the earthquake. The dome could be restored more in the round, supported by the thrust of outer buttresses. Thus the new dome would be higher than the flattened dome of Anthemius.

Justinian ordered this to be done, and the streets were rebuilt. Meanwhile, on that Christmas Eve, he had gone in procession to the altar of St. Eirene, dedicated to peace. With the officers and silentiaries, an entire orchestra of musicians entered St. Eirene for the first time—with trumpets, cymbals, and pipes. While the choirs recited their story, a curtain was drawn back from the dais. There Justinian alone in a simple mantle with diadem, lighted the candles at the altar, and the choirs intoned: "Now Christ is born, who gave the crown to kings. . . ."

❀ FAILURE OF THE COUNCIL

Ironically, the very churches that demanded the presence of the Emperor at the altar defeated his effort to reconcile them. And that defeat came in the Council held in the secretarial chambers of the Hagia Sophia itself—before the earthquake brought down the dome.

It came as the climax of Justinian's long effort to find a single doctrine for the clergy of St. Peter's and the Monophysite churches, which, in turn, differed among themselves. (Once, in 518, he had healed the schism between East and West, and the patriarchs of the East testified: "We both follow and obey the apostolic throne.") Toward the end of her life, Theodora used all her persuasion in bringing Pope Vigilius to agree with the Patriarch, Menas, of Constantinople—after Belisarius carried Vigilius bodily from Rome, at her command (548). Then Justinian promised his wife that there would be an end of persecution of the eastern sects.

He attempted himself, even earlier, to bring the Orthodox Catholic doctrine closer to that of his Patriarchs. By an edict in 544 he attacked points in the findings of the Ecumenical Council of Chalcedon, called by Marcian and Pulcheria. He challenged—in the famous *Three Chapters*—points of Nestorian doctrine in the Chalcedon decisions. Hoping by this to bring the thought of Rome to an understanding with Alexandria and Antioch, he succeeded only in intensifying the controversy. He found that even when Pope agreed with Patriarch, their clergy and congregations held irrevocably to the oldest beliefs. The monks of the Syrian and Egyptian deserts defied the prelates, as did the Katholikos of the Armenians, and the Nestorians in Asia.

Justinian invoked his authority as Basileus. In 550 he published his own *Confession of Faith*. It stated that he was guardian of the orthodox faith in an almighty God, in a divine Christ, and in a Mother of God. He used in this almost the words of the Episcopal and Roman Catholic creeds of today. Thus Justinian sought to repair the failure of Chalcedon by an edict of his own. The Patriarch acknowledged his authority, and in fact depended on it, but kept silence as to the words of agreement; the Pope recognized the Emperor's supremacy in the state, not in the Church. The difference was so slight, and still vast as human belief.

Then Justinian attempted to bring the primates of East and West into agreement by recalling Vigilius to Constantinople. Unfortunately Vigilius did not bring with him Pelagius, who understood the thought of Constantinople. His escorting clergy were fearful of their western congregations. Again the prelates were separated by an obstacle that neither could put into words, although both, perforce, agreed with the Emperor's wishes. Justinian's stubbornness clashed with the obstinacy of Vigilius in weary months of affirmation and dissent, of threats and appeals. Belisarius was called in to serve as messenger between them, but Vigilius would send no message by him. The Pope called for a World Council, which the Emperor wished to avoid. When at last it was convened in 553 in the chambers of Hagia Sophia, Vigilius refused to attend it, and Justinian could not.

Over that Council lay the shadow of Leo the Great as advocate of St. Peter's and the shade of Chrysostom, spokesman of the eastern faith. The assembled bishops could not forget that they had been called together by Justinian's questions, which touched upon the decision of the Church, but were no cause for a great Council of the Church. They merely affirmed his edicts, as edicts. They rendered unto Caesar only the things that were Caesar's.

So Justinian failed in his supreme effort to bring his churches to a single communion.

Procopius said, with some sincerity: "He should not have

meddled with the ways of God, which he did not understand."

It seemed then to many observers that this man, seventy-six years of age, had an inhuman force in him. He went unflinching on his way through conflagration, pestilence, war, and earthquake. He took no heed of the signs of God's anger or of the human hatred he roused.

Quick-witted Procopius listened to the talk—as he had harkened avidly to the gossip about Theodora's girlhood in a brothel. "Thus they performed their fearful acts, not by human strength, but by another kind." This concept of a demon-ridden Justinian and Theodora, he wrote out in his twelfth book of the secret *Anecdotes:* "Assuming human form, they became man-demons, to harass in this manner the entire world . . . some ordinary men, of course, have shown themselves to be supremely terrible; yet these two alone co-operated to bring about calamities in all the world. In their case, however, fate assisted them by earthquakes, by pestilence, and by the overflowing of the waters of great rivers at this time."

Another year furnished Procopius with evidence of a new danger. This time it threatened Constantinople itself.

❋ INVASION OF THE KUTRIGURS

It came almost without warning. Unseen beyond the northern frontier, the counterpoise of power shifted among the barbarian peoples. The Kutrigur Huns made a truce with their tribal enemies—perhaps in the mutual fear of the advance of the Avars. Sagaciously led by a certain Zabergan Khan, they combined with leaderless Bulgars and Slavs to form the thing dreaded by Constantinople, a barbarian confederacy.

Information of the destruction caused by the earthquake

in Constantinople had percolated through to the steppes. The Kutrigurs were familiar with the roads into the Empire, and their attack was shrewdly planned. Crossing the Danube while the ice held, in March (559), and avoiding the fortified cities, they struck south across country, grazing their horses on the new grass. They swept around and over the small army of the frontier, commanded by an incompetent general, Sergius.

"There was nothing then to drive back the barbarians," Agathias relates. "No military garrisons with engines of defense and trained men to work them. For the Roman armies had dwindled to small numbers . . . no more than one hundred and fifty thousand, some in Italy, some in Africa, or Spain, others in Colchis [the Lazi country of the Caucasus] or at Alexandria or along the Nile, with a few on the Persian frontier."

In spite of the lack of man power, the planned defenses held in two places. The barbarian horde divided into three armies, the largest of them swinging down into Greece, where the fortification of the pass at Thermopylae, built by Alexander the Logothete, turned them back. Another, checked on land in Macedonia, tried to pass down the coast in makeshift barges, to be destroyed on the water by warcraft from Constantinople. The smallest column, some 7,000 strong, drove down past Hadrian's City toward Constantinople. These seemed to be all mounted Kutrigurs and Slavs, led by Zabergan Khan himself in a terrifying march that gathered the inhabitants of the villages into a growing slave train.

The Long Wall of Anastasius stood in their way. Thither Justinian had ordered the garrison-army of the city, Excubitors of the palace, students of the military academy, and the militia of the Blues and Greens. This nondescript force hardly delayed the Kutrigur horsemen. They forced breaks in the lengthy wall caused by the earthquake and not yet repaired. They rode over the camps of the militia, who scattered in flight. The forty miles to Constantinople were filled with groups of soldiery seeking refuge, trains of peasants' carts and herds of animals driven toward the safety of the city gates. Mobs pouring into the Porta Aurea infected the crowded Mesé with their fear.

All the elaborate mechanism of defense had broken down; the numbers of the oncoming Kutrigurs were not known; the dreaded horsemen appeared at Melantiadum on the coast. Watchers at the Hebdomon sighted the smoke of burning villages along the Egnatian Way. Worst of all, panic grew in the streets that had not known the approach of an enemy for eighteen years. A multitude filled the Augusteum, calling on the Emperor to give protection.

Characteristically, Justinian had ordered the altar treasures of the outlying churches to be brought to the docks and ferried across to Chrysopolis on the Asia shore. But sight of vessels departing from the harbor stirred the fear of the populace. Justinian called for the remaining palace guards, *Spatharii* and candidates, to assemble outside the Augusteum, and for senators and patrician youth to go with them to man the land wall of the city. But the populace had no faith in such an array. It would take weeks to bring trained troops from Ravenna or Carthage.

At this point Justinian called Belisarius to the palace. The name of Belisarius would serve to quiet the people, and the retired generalissimo would know what best could be done to save the city. When they met, Justinian's jealousy underlay his formal order. Belisarius, he said, was still the count of the Stables. In this emergency—until regular forces could arrive over the sea—he should take command within the city. "We give order that you do what you can to protect the city."

As he had always done, the veteran of Italy proceeded to carry out the order without discussion or delay. He put not the least faith in the great Theodosian wall manned by volunteers, but proceeded immediately to move out of the city with what force he could gather.

Belisarius called for the standards of the army. He sent these through the streets with mandators to call for all veterans who had served under him.

It made a story to be told for years—how the men who had fought at the Ten Mile and Tricamaron or the pits of Daras came out of their homes and shops when the standards passed by. They assembled in the Strategium parade-ground. Then Belisarius called for seamen and able peasants, for the spears out of the theaters, and planks and metal basins from the homes—above all for horses from the carts and the inviolable stables of the hippodrome. The veterans were armed after a fashion, the palace guards distributed among the civilians. Trumpeters led this inchoate host up the Mesé, and the standards went out to meet the Huns. Belisarius, in mail and faded cloak, joked about it, and somehow the fear in the city began to subside.

Except for a little more than three hundred mounted veterans, this was really a stage army, and no one understood that better than Belisarius. It could not withstand a charge of the Kutrigurs. But the superb tactician of the great wars could be sure that the Huns would have no understanding of what he was leading out of Constantinople. When he camped that night at Chettus, a village ten miles out, he had a great number of fires lighted, and kept his people moving around them, with a display of weapons and metal basins. From a distance it would seem that quite a host encamped there at Chettus.

Belisarius had had years of experience with Hunnic warriors, who feared very little what they saw before them, but had an instinctive fear of what might be concealed from them. They were wary of traps. So he set the stage for the next day as he had so often set it before, this time to make it appear as if Zabergan Khan's horsemen were riding into a carefully hidden trap.

That is the cream of the tale told thereafter in Constantinople—how the Huns advancing along a forest road sensed numbers in hiding on either side of them, how the head of a cavalry column (the 300 veterans) met them in headlong charge, how the dust rose from a mighty force behind them (the extra people with the props of trumpets, clanging boards, and flashing basins), how the Huns tried to turn and extricate themselves while arrows and spears struck into them from the woods, and how they left 400 dead when they fled back to open ground.

It was a magnificent scene of trickery. But without Belisarius it could not have been played.

❀ THE INVISIBLE FRONTIER

While church bells pealed throughout the city and the shout "Belisarius has conquered" passed along the Mesé, another drama began without attracting public attention. The gifted soldier had done his part, and now the strategists proceeded to dispose of the invaders.

All warcraft in the harbor were ordered out up the Bosporus to speed to the Danube. Justin, Germanus' oldest son and an able commander, also departed for the Danube by land. It was the beginning of the Easter festival in April, and the people expected Justinian to place his offering of gratitude on the altar of St. Eirene. Instead of that the aged Emperor appeared, surprisingly, on horseback to lead his court entire out of the Porta Aurea to the shambles of the Long Wall. At the end of the long ride he went into camp beyond the wall, to order it repaired under his eyes by the demes and workmen of the city.

No doubt his jealousy of Belisarius impelled him to parade out to the battlefields, to share the glory of his count of the Stables, yet Justinian had a purpose in taking the field. Negligence had left the breaks in the wall after the earthquake; they must be built up without a day's delay. The danger of invasion had not ended. Up in the Thracian valleys the Kutrigurs, licking their wounds, were joining the hordes of Bulgars and Slavs driven back from Greece and the Macedonian coast. Belisarius occupied their camp by the river at Melantiadum, gathering in what forces he could find. Justinian ordered him not to follow up the Huns. Instead envoys were sent to Zabergan Khan to offer ransom in gold for Sergius, Master of Soldiers, and all other captives in the hands of the Huns. The pagans would be tempted to dispose of their slaves so conveniently, for wealth that could be carried easily over the Danube to their homeland.

A few days more, and the first transports arrived in the small harbor of Melantiadum, bringing regular troops from Salonika. The danger was lessened by that much. But Justinian knew—and Peter the Patrician and the members of The Silence in the tents with him agreed—that a few regiments could not drive twenty thousand Huns from the wide Balkan valleys. Belisarius was recalled, and the army held at the coast while solid stonework rose in the breaches of the Long Wall.

By June the fleet from the Golden Horn reached its destination, the lower Danube. The war vessels patrolled the river, still high after the spring floods. Word of their coming brought uneasiness to the encampment of the Huns, who had no means of recrossing the Danube if warcraft opposed them. As at the forest of Chettus, they sensed a trap being set for them, and the inaction of the Empire's armies increased their foreboding. Zabergan Khan and his chieftains released their captives for the ransom money and drifted back toward the river. There Justin, waiting on events, received orders not to oppose the retreat of the Huns, but to grant them a truce. Obediently he reported to Justinian when the last of the Huns had disappeared into the steppes toward the Dnieper.

By then the wall had been repaired and the people were back in the Balkan villages. Thereupon, early in August, Justinian broke up his camp to return to his city. He made quite a parade of it, with trumpeters going before the Excubitors and the banner of Hagia Sophia rising over the army standards. The spectacle filled the Porta Aurea, and the crowds shouted at sight of the tall, stooped figure on the white horse: "May you reign for long years!" Beneath the weathered statue of the Fortune of the city, Justinian rode into the Mesé, where voices cried: "Justinian—you have conquered!"

The chronicler of that day noted that at the Amastrian Forum the Emperor turned away from the procession and rode with a few followers to the Church of the Holy Apostles. There he dismounted to go into the mausoleum, to light the two candles at the tomb of Theodora and make his prayer.

From the Daphne, Justinian then dispatched a long missive to Sandichl, ruler of the Utrigur Huns on the river Don. It explained that Zabergan Khan, the rival of Sandichl, had raided the Empire, carrying off the gold that would otherwise have been sent to Sandichl. "We might have destroyed the Kutrigurs, but we did not because we wished to make a test of your courage and your friendship to us." If the Utrigurs had courage, Justinian explained, they would take their swords in hand and take back the stolen gold. By so doing they would prove themselves to be true friends of the Emperor, their father.

The taunt and the promise stirred the Utrigurs to action. Long and savage conflict between the Huns on the Don and

those on the Dnieper exhausted their strength and ended
all chance of a confederacy. The Kutrigurs did not cross the
line of the Danube again.

The civilized state had checked by stratagem the greater
power of the barbarian peoples.

After two years the Bulgar-Huns penetrated the thinly
held frontier, but did not break through Justin's army of the
Danube. But the Bulgars had been forced south by pressure
of the Avars, who were still primitive and predatory nomads
unable to exist by agriculture. There was a danger here to
be met immediately if a greater force than Zabergan's was
to be kept from the gates of Constantinople.

For the last time Justinian manipulated the masses in
motion along the fifteen hundred miles of plains and forests.
On the highlands above Venetia the Lombards were yielding
ground to the Franks—Narses sent tidings of them. Merchants from the Don reported unknown Turks crossing the
Volga, moving south and west. But there was nothing on
the horizon that might be used to hold back the brute Avars.

Justinian gave permission to the Bulgars to settle where
they were, and dispatched traders to the Avar Khagan. The
traders persuaded Avar chieftains to journey to the wonder of
the imperial city. They passed the Danube and Justin sent
urgent warning to hold them at Justinian's side until he could
be reinforced to guard the river. So at the Daphne, Justinian
played the familiar role of imperial host while interpreters
could be found to explain the words of the Avar chieftains.
And every week *numeri* arrived from Italy to strengthen the
young Magister Justin. The envoys of Bayan, Khagan of the
Avars, desired entrance into the lands of the Heruls within
the Empire, but Justinian assured them that the Herul settlements would not provide enough grazing land for the roving
Avars. He suspected that they feared the Turks, but there
was no way of reading the minds within their broad, greased
heads; they said they feared nothing—and with his gift of

gold they bought themselves weapons of every sort in the market streets. Still, they appeared more ready to move to the West than anywhere—Peter the Patrician reached that conclusion. Accordingly they were bidden to seek the high pasture lands at the Danube headwaters in the West.

When Justin had his defenses manned, the Avars were at last dismissed, and the Magister was ordered to take all their new weapons from them at the frontier. They disappeared into the steppes, whence observers on the Dnieper reported them moving over the remnants of the Utrigurs into the West. There they found the Franks in their way, and savage strife began in the upland valleys, drawing the Franks out of the Venetian rivers.

The Lombards could make their settlements undisturbed, and along the length of the Danube there was peace.

"Justinian grew very weary," Agathias related, "and adverse from waging war."

❋ "THE FLAMES OF THE LAMPS ARE DANCING . . ."

When the water clock chimed the first hour of the day, Callinicus, who had taken Narses' place, summoned the vestiaries to bring the mantle with the dark *tablion*; he drew back the curtain of Justinian's sleeping chamber himself, peering into the faint light of the alabaster windows, to make certain that the motionless figure on the couch was breathing in sleep and not breathless in death. Then, reassured, he uttered his sibilant "If you please!" Death might well come during sleep to a man eighty years of age, and Callinicus' duty would be to report it immediately to the Count of the Excubitors.

Justinian had to be guided like a sleepwalker through the routine of the day. When seated, even in full audience on the dais of the Triclinium, he would often get up and wander away. Then Callinicus would dismiss the officials while they murmured their response: "Many years, many years, servant of the Lord." Those who spoke to him noticed that at times he did not seem to see them, and his features would change as if he followed out thoughts of his own. At night the guards found him wandering through the corridors toward closed doors. Sometimes on cold nights he put on a dark monk's robe, drawing the hood over his head. Newcomers among the guards sometimes failed to recognize the cowled figure.

When Procopius heard these rumors of the palace, he used them to add to the twelfth *Anecdote* of his imaginary demon Emperor and harlot Empress: "Men saw in the palace a sort of phantom spirit unfamiliar to them in his place. For they asserted that at times the head of Justinian would disappear while the rest of his body wandered on as if perplexed."

This was probably the last anecdote of the gifted Procopius of Caesarea. Now that he had finished his eulogy of Justinian in *The Buildings,* he was rewarded with the honorary rank of prefect of the city. That is, he drew the salary of a prefect without performing the duties, which in any case he would not have been competent to carry out.

Justinian, however, kept on with his duties, even if he had to be guided through them in the manner of a sleepwalker. His edicts became fewer during those last years, 561–5. They dealt with the oddest things—that a priest *must* know the liturgy and public prayers before officiating—that the Titians, a refugee family, should have their property in Rome restored—that the date for Christmas would be henceforth the twenty-fifth of December.

He managed to walk or ride out to be seen at the appointed time on festival days. One birthday of the city fell at a time when there was a drought and harvests had dwindled, and a new generation of the demes rioted when grain failed to arrive. Again the Blues joined with the Greens, to burn the house of Peter Barsymes, the provider of bread. With the streets in tumult, Justinian called for a procession to go through them bearing the Madonna of the Way. He called for a pilgrimage to the shrines of Jerusalem, and for Count Belisarius to attend him. His mandators explained in the streets that the grain fleet was storm-bound at the Tenedos terminal, but that its cargoes would arrive before long in the Golden Horn—as indeed they did. Yet the unrest lingered, and because Justinian himself had not been seen in public for some time, the rumor passed up the Mesé that he was dead.

Whereupon the different quarters of the city demonstrated in different ways. A few robed senators gathered at the Augusteum benches in readiness to enter their old quarters; crowds sought the Street of the Breadmakers, and through all the main streets candles appeared in the windows. The people were praying for their emperor.

Even after Justinian showed himself—he had really been ill and weak—two assassins made their way into the colonnade of the Daphne, there to be caught and disarmed by order of Marcellus. The Prefect ordered an inquiry. Servants of several magnates were arrested and questioned under torture. They gave the name of Isaac, chief steward of Belisarius, and Isaac confessed that the conspiracy sought to proclaim his master emperor and to retire Justinian to the monastery of the Studion. Thus their sworn evidence charged Belisarius with treason. It was given to the tribunal of the senate, which rendered judgment in political cases. The senators put their heads together and gave a political answer that was not a judgment. The criminals, they said, *seemed to be* guilty as charged.

That brought the evidence before Justinian for final judgment. He might have condemned the soldier he had envied and relied on. Instead, he dismissed the charge of treason. He confiscated Belisarius' wealth as a penalty, only to restore all the properties after seven months. (The legend of a Belisarius blinded by order of an evil Emperor and left to beg his food of the soldiers who had served under him, grew up later, and is entirely false. Perhaps the story came from a memory of John of Cappadocia begging food after his downfall. Belisarius was left unharmed and undisturbed; but Justinian had managed during all these years to reduce his Autocrator to the title of First Citizen.)

As for the succession, Justinian made his choice known to senators and commanders alike. After his death the rule would go to the other Justin, son of his sister Vigilantia. As Curopalatate, the likeable Justin had kept at his side; his nephew had taken to wife Sophia, daughter of the dead Tzitas and Comito, sister of Theodora. Perhaps Justinian saw in Sophia the likeness of his wife.

He made other preparations. Artists showed him the ivory bishop's throne made for St. Vitalis—carved with the lifelike people of the story of Joseph, beneath the four Evangelists. Justinian admired it greatly, and called upon expert metal casters to match the skill of the ivory carvers in making a sarcophagus for him. They were not able to do that; in the end they made for Justinian a sarcophagus of heavy bronze polished to a hue of gold, having on its lid a cross of fine gold like the great cross of the Hagia Sophia.

With the coming of winter in 563 the thing happened for which Justinian seemed to be waiting. The new dome of Hagia Sophia stood in place, ten cubits higher than the old dome of Anthemius, finished in its last details, the overhanging cross resplendent in flood of sunlight. Against that day Justinian had hoarded up happenings in his mind—the warding off of the Avar invasion, the peace of fifty years gained from Khusrau by Peter's skill and a heavy price in gold. It ended the long Lazic wars, threw open the routes of the Caucasus; it pledged immunity to Christian sects within the borders of Persia. Khusrau, the King of kings, pledged that much to his brother

—so ran the words—Justinian, Caesar of the Romans. Moreover Peter the Patrician believed that in this case Khusrau would keep his pledge.

Whereupon the aged Justinian gave order for a triumphal ceremony. He gave to a silentiary the poem of the dead Paul the Silentiary to recite. Twenty-five years before, it had voiced the joy of the first dedication of the great church. This time Justinian wished verses to be added in praise of the beauty of Theodora.

So that Christmas the procession formed again, to escort him to the dedication of the repaired church. At the end of the colonnade, the voice of the silentiary cried praise of Theodora: "The luster of her hair, the whiteness of her skin is gone. But—O—her eyes are shining."

Before the steps of the house of the Patriarch Eutychius, Justinian dismounted, and lowered the scepter he carried across his left shoulder, while the choirs chanted: "Peace has come to this Empire belonging to our Lord, all powerful. Let the spirit array of angels rejoice; rejoice, armies of the Romans, and you, Christians rejoice in praising the Lord."

And the elderly Patriarch responded in words of power: "*Attolite portas, principes, vesteras . . .*"

At the dais of the great church they helped Justinian into his throne seat opposite the Patriarch. His tall, feeble figure in shining regalia was necessary to complete the ceremony of the Nativity.

Romanos was not there to hear it, and the gallery of the Empress—as they called it now—had no woman in it. Yet there was a sense of triumph when the voices of the choirs proclaimed ". . . the flames of the lamps are dancing beneath the dome suspended in the sky."

The ceremony had an odd effect on Justinian. Without other visible reason the old man departed on a small journey. The records explain that he went across the Bosporus and rode for several days through Bithynia. For some reason of his own, he

The Riha paten, silver repoussé, late sixth century. Communion of Apostles with Jesus officiating simultaneously to two groups of Apostles. The inscription reads: "For the repose [of the souls] of Sergia, the daughter of Ioannes, and Theodosius, and the salvation of Megalos and Nonnos and their children."

Byzantine gold cup, sixth or seventh century.
The repoussé design shows symbolic
female figures representing Constantinople,
Cyprus, Rome, and Alexandria.

Cast silver bowl, early sixth century, with Bacchic motif

went forth again in the scarlet barge of state, up the Bosporus to the shrine of Michael Archangel. He seemed to want to see the places that he had held in his mind for so many years.

Yet the reality of happenings outside his walls became obscured at this time. In his imagination all the seas lay open to his ships; all peoples obeyed his law. The frontiers, the troublesome army, Narses ruling Italy from Ravenna, the cordon of missions thrust out into the barbaric peoples—all these were provided for and in order. Were not the khagans of the Turks, a new people approaching the Cimmerian Bosporus, coming into the city to be welcomed and rewarded and turned if possible against the Avars? Would not Belisarius stand with Callinicus under the two eagles to counsel him in meeting the Turks?

Then early in the spring of that year—565—Callinicus lingered after the vestiaries had robed him, to whisper that Belisarius, the First Citizen, was dead. Justinian understood the words, but did not seem to realize that Count Belisarius would no longer ride into the Chalké gate, greeting every man with a familiar face. One of them at the Stratcgium drill-ground was heard to say, "The army will do well enough without Belisarius, but what will the Emperor do?"

It was noticed then that Justinian became absorbed in the one task that had always defeated him. He did not rise willingly from his seat where the scrolls of the Scriptures, the letters of Basil, and the acts of all the ecclesiastical councils spread before him. He was obsessed with the writings of the different creeds. He was searching for the oldest of them—mysterious words of ascetics of the Egyptian desert. He sat over these writings under the lamps, seeking—so it seemed—for what had eluded everyone. As emperor, he felt the need of finding at last the words of a belief that would unite the Orthodox with the Monophysite and the Nestorian. Often he dozed in his chair after tracing meaningless words.

Then when they roused him, he would go to the window to

peer out at the dome of the church, obscure under the starlight. He would listen for the tramping and chanting of The Sleepless going by. He would listen to a street seller of candles pushing a donkey up the Mesé. As if all such goings-on of the city streets were important to him, the Emperor.

That went on until the dawn hour, when a silentiary summoned Callinicus to the sleeping chamber, and Callinicus went forth from it to announce to Marcellus, waiting at his post. "Our lord has ceased to exist as a man."

And Agathias ended his chronicle of the reign of Justinian with the words: "He was the first ruler of Byzantium. In name and deed he showed himself to be absolute master of the Romans."

AFTERWORD

JUSTINIAN'S NAME has become proverbial. So has his age. We speak of his time as naturally as we mention the age of Augustus or that of Louis XIV. Yet it is not always clear to us why we do so.

It was first of all an age of transformation. The son of Sabbatius did not, of course, enter a Constantinople of brick about the year 500 and leave it a city of marble in 565. He did leave a different city ruling over a different domain of the inland seas.

His death brought a general reaction. The suppressed factions and impoverished nobility of the city felt jubilant relief at the passing of the "absolute master" of the last thirty-seven years. His successor, Justin II, complained that he found the treasury exhausted, the frontiers unmanned, and the whole of the Empire at the mercy of barbarian invasion. Justinian's adroit manipulation of the outer peoples no longer held them in check. No sooner had Narses been recalled than the Lombards migrated (568) into northern Italy, the future Lombardy.

❀ THE POLITICAL BREAKDOWN

Justin II and his counselors—chief among them his practical wife, Sophia, niece of Theodora—turned all effort to building up the treasury, enlarging the army, and defending the Empire by active war against the invaders. Constantinople plunged into the conflict of decision with Khusrau which the unheroic Justinian had sought above all things to avoid. It drew in the nomad Turks on one side and the Hunnish peoples on the other. The Heruls disappeared as a barrier, and Justin quietly went mad (574). This "long war" of the two civilized powers went on for fifty years. At first the indomitable Sophia held the throne with the aid of Tiberius, Count of the Excubitors, thus restoring the officer-dictator of the early centuries. The new wars demanded able military leadership, and found it in Maurice (*Maurikos*) the next emperor (582–602). That ended the dynasty of Old Justin–Justinian. But it did not end the mounting conflict with the Persians, the Lombards in Italy, and the Avars surging over the Danube. It brought revolt into the city. A brutal soldier, Phocas ("Gorgon's Head") led mutinous troops to massacre Maurice, his sons, and those of his followers who remained loyal to the throne. Phocas closed the university.

Then the maelstrom of conflict obliterated the old frontiers. Slavs came in like jackals with the Avar wolf pack; the militant Persians swept over rebuilt Antioch into Anatolia, the heart of the Empire, untouched until then. In this near-eclipse of power, a fleet from Carthage—the first conquest of Justinian and Belisarius—appeared, to rouse the city and cut Phocas to pieces with his army. The Patriarch and the people entrusted the preservation of the city to Heraclius, son of the African exarch (610)—and to restrain him from fleeing back to Africa during the ordeal of the next years. Except for the city, little remained of the Empire. The Persians held the wealth of the Nile, the sanctuary of Jerusalem; they entered Theodora's Bithynia and appeared on the point of Hieron. In their longboats, Slavs of the Dnieper raided the Bosporus. The barbarian power of the north reached the Long Wall and the gates of the city itself, and in 626 the khagan of the Avars boasted: "Only a bird can escape from the city now."

Faced by destruction, Constantinople sacrificed everything for survival—taking the gold and valuables from all the churches including Hagia Sophia, drafting all men able to use weapons, enlisting slaves for the first time in the army, clearing and holding the Bosporus like a moat between the besieging foes. By a supremely daring decision Heraclius and the mobile army were sent away in the fleet to carry the war to the far Euphrates and Ctesiphon, city of the the Great King. With remarkable courage the citizens defended their great Theodosian Wall until Heraclius could gain the victory in Asia.

Although he won the last battle, the soldier-emperor Heraclius turned the university into a religious academy. In the ordeal of his time building ceased and was not resumed for generations; creative arts suffered because artisans served in the ranks. The first, glorious age of Byzantine art came to an end.

So at the end of the sixth century Constantinople became a survival center. It was a citadel besieged. Its defenses guarded its legacy of western civilization.

The ancient city-states had passed into legend. The Rome of the early Caesars had sickened to the parasite city that destroyed the Empire of the western world, the creation of those Caesars. The *Nea Roma* founded by Constantine the Great at the meeting of the inland seas was no longer a new Rome.

By the river Loire the cleric Venantius Fortunatus traced on a grave: "Orpheus and his lute are still. What of the songs of Vergil and Homer? Bare bones they are, damp in the grave!"

Constantinople had become the citadel facing east, apart from the West, and aroused to new needs. History knows it henceforth as Byzantium. And historians with a fondness for dates usually give the reign of Heraclius as the birth of Byzantium. Yet there is a newer understanding expressed by Nicolai Iorga, the Rumanian: that instead of being the last Roman emperor in the East, Justinian was the first Byzantine, and the circumstances of his life made him so.

The revolution he brought about was too great to be undone. More than the consulship, the senate, and the Roman *potentiores* and *agentes in rebus* went by the board. Slave labor yielded to a new awareness of humanity. Justinian's laws endured. His successor Tiberius responded, when Sophia protested at emptying the public treasury: "Our treasury will never be empty so long as the poor get alms and captives are brought back." His missionary expansion went on, but turned into the northeast. The melting pot of his Byzantium had effect in the western regions of Belisarius' captures; monasteries and artists pervaded the shores of Greece and southern Italy to create the cultured Magna Graecia of later centuries. The African coast prospered, largely with olive oil, and Carthage came to rival Alexandria in its overseas trade. The opening of navigation through the Mediterranean sent Syrian and Jewish traders to the moribund towns of Merovingian Gaul with such luxuries as wine and papyrus-paper. Those traders came from the markets of Justinian's city. A western visitor, late in the century, remarked with surprise that "in Byzantium everybody works." Ravenna lent its resources to St. Peter's church, and the letters of Pope Gregory reveal the growing wealth of his people; his manager of affairs was an *Argentarius*, a Byzantine treasurer.

At the same time, Justinian's stubborn attempt to unite the churches of Rome and the East failed. The clergy of St. Peter's sought contact with the outer peoples to the northwest, not to the east. Gregory the Great sent his missionary Augustine to Britain. The red Merovingians became the champions of the church of the Apostle. Under them Fortunatus wrote the hymn that is a battle cry: *Vexilla regis prodeunt—"The Standards of the King Go Forth."* The outlines took shape of a Roman Catholic Church in the West and a realm of the Greek Orthodox in the East, as far as the rivers that would be Russian. Between them arose an intangible "otherness."

Then a cataclysmic force divided the Mediterranean itself, separating Byzantium still more from the West.

❈ THE CITY SOUGHT BY THE OUTER WORLD

The end of the "long war" with the Persians (630) had seen the end of much that Justinian sought, as well as the downfall of the dynasty of Khusrau the Just, and the end of the Sassanian renaissance. It left the two empires exhausted. There followed no peace that might have brought recuperation. The Arab invasion began in 632. The rush of tribal warriors out of the Arabian desert achieved surprising success against the exhausted forces of the two civilized dominions; it routed the Byzantine army in Palestine almost on the day it overthrew the Persian chivalry on the Euphrates. The battle-torn cities of the Byzantine-Persian frontier offered little resistance. The long march of Moslem conquest from the Nile to the Loire began.

This conquest owed its strength, however, less to arms than to conversion to Islam, the new faith of Muhammad the Prophet. Islam—Acceptance—offered a lasting peace and a certain kinship in religion to the Nestorian, Koptic, and Monophysite communities of the East. (This early faith of Islam drew so much from Magian and Jewish and Christian belief that it did not appear alien to the eastern sects. The conflict of the religions came later to its climax in the crusades.) It entered Jerusalem and Alexandria without resistance. With incredible swiftness (634–47) it wrested the resources of Syria and the foodstuffs of Egypt from the Empire and took to sea to strike at the sustaining strength of the Empire. Unbelievably at the "Battle of the Masts" Arab-Egyptian warcraft drove in flight the larger Byzantine fleet (655) and the Emperor Constans, grandson of Heraclius, fled with his army and court to Sicily.

Then the city called back its own. The armed forces revolted in Sicily, killed Constans, and sailed back to the Bosporus. The land remaining to Byzantium was organized for defense into *themes*—first attempted by Justinian—governed by military *Strategoi*. The Moslem invasion mobilized the armed hosts of Asia and penetrated the inner waterways to the Sea of Marmora—to be driven back (673) by the city's fleet using the new weapon of Greek fire that burned on the sea.

The outer sea was lost when the invaders overrode Africa and the coast of Spain at the gate of the ocean. Carthage resisted until 695, and Sicily fell, while enemies closed in on Constantinople itself again—savage Bulgars from the north, the Arab-led host from the south—at the end of the seventh century.

Yet the city was never betrayed and never surrendered. It became the desire of all the outer peoples, and they gave it new names. Moslems knew it as the *Roum* (Rome) of the Christians; Slavs of the Russian rivers launched their fleets toward *Tsargrad*, Caesar's City, and then Vikings came over the long ways of the sea to the spoil of *Mickligarth*, the Great Enclosure. Crusaders came and went their way, and Venetian fleets emerged from the lagoons to carry Byzantium's trade. When the Byzantine fleet gave way to the Venetian—relying on it for defense—a Doge of Christian Venice transported an army of western crusaders across the sea to the first capture of Constantinople in 1204.

One soldier-chronicler, Ville-Hardouin, related the wonder of the crusaders at the first sight of the city from their ships. "They looked long upon Constantinople. . . . For they thought that there could not be in the world so rich a city— when they beheld these high walls and strong towers by which it was encircled and these rich palaces and lofty churches and the size of this city that was sovereign of all others in the world. And know that no man was so hardy that his flesh did not creep at the sight."

Once they broke into the sea wall these seigneurs and men-at-arms of the West plundered the city of its accumulated treasures. They felt—and were advised by their Venetian taskmasters—that the "Greeks" of the city were heretics only one degree removed from infidel "Saracens." The Venetians, being schooled in Byzantine culture, carried off the finest of the art works. They bore away the famous four bronze chariot horses of Lysippus from the hippodrome to adorn St. Mark's. Some pieces of the sacred table of Hagia Sophia may be found in the Pala d'Oro of that church.

The sanctuary of Hagia Sophia, screened by the twenty-foot iconostasis of Justinian, had been the pride of the Byzantines. The *Novgorod Chronicle* (Slavic) relates its destruction by the crusaders: "They broke down the twelve silver columns [of the ciborium] and the Holy Table [covered with gold inlaid with jewels and enamel work]; they destroyed the screen walls and the twelve crosses above the altar. They shared among them all these things of silver, and stole the Evangel used for the services, and the images and forty censers of pure gold."

Yet within three generations, the persistence of the Byzantines regained the looted city from the western conquerors. One consequence of the return of Byzantine rule to Constantinople (1261–1453) was the impulse given to the Renaissance in western Europe.

❊ THE ART OF SIXTH-CENTURY CONSTANTINOPLE

It has disappeared except for a few traces. The precious nucleus of buildings in Ravenna, however, remains almost whole. That circumstance has drawn our attention to Ravenna, and away from Constantinople, the source of the art.

There today we can find little but architectural remnants of Justinian's city. The Hagia Sophia preserves what was built into its walls; St. Eirene's is a mutilated shell, the "House of Justinian" a bare façade. The pillared cistern built by Justinian near the Great Church still serves the city, as the *Yere Batan Sarai* ("Sunken Palace"). The Daphne palace has vanished except for some foundations and mosaic floors of doubtful date.

What of the rest? The bulk of the treasures was melted down in the last-ditch defense of the city under Heraclius at the century's end; others were lost in the Moslem conquest of the eastern provinces or in the wave of iconoclasm that followed. But the greatest loss came at the hands of the heedless crusaders and avaricious Venetians in 1204—six centuries after the splendid age of Justinian.

For it was an age of splendid flowering in the arts. Until then Constantinople had been something like a museum of imported treasures. Yet the fifth century in the eastern Mediterranean had been formative. Like the city itself, a new canon of art grew from the meeting of the nations within it—Armenians bringing architectural motifs from their mountains, Greeks carrying from the Crimea the vigorous "animal style" of the ancient Graeco-Scythians, Persians imparting the delicate Sassanian designs. Master artists from Antioch and Alexandria gave new force to the old forms. Unknown minds gave simple dignity to the work. "A force and dignity," René Grousset believes, "in these golden centuries of the Christians . . . rarely equaled and never surpassed . . . [when] the tension between ancient form and new content ceased. This was the work of Justinian from the beginning of the sixth century, in the *milieu* of Constantinople."

And Charles Diehl adds: "By the end of the sixth century Christian art in the east seemed to be transformed." An example of that transformation exists in Ravenna. There the Christ under the star-flecked sky of the ceiling of the tomb of Galla Placidia (c. 450) is a shepherd and youthful, yet draped in a tunic of imperial purple, carrying a cross like a spear. The semblance of a shepherd-king still remains. In the mosaic of the Widow's Mite in St. Vitalis the Christ is still youthful, but erect in authority, and in some manner *different* from other human figures. That authority would increase in the Oriental bearded Christ, the Pantocrator, the eternal Judge of later Byzantine art.

Examples of the minor arts survive only in the spoils scattered among Western museums and church treasuries. The celebrated chalice of Antioch is now believed to date from the sixth century—like the silver Riha paten, also of Syria, now in the Dumbarton Oaks collection. This paten

reveals a scene of simple realism except that to make his
story more clear the artist has presented two Christs among
the Apostles. This same duality of the human-divine appears
in the Evangelium (Rossano, treasury of the cathedral),
where the lifelike scenes painted by the unknown miniaturist
are pointed out by the figures of Evangelists in the margins.
A splendid silver dish dug from its hiding place in Kyrenia,
Cyprus (Metropolitan Museum), shows a realistic David in
combat with a Goliath. This Goliath, little taller than David,
appears to be a young, well-armed Roman soldier, and in no
respect the monstrous giant of later European artists. Yet
the supernatural is present in this quite natural scene; a tiny
deity appears above the combatants.

The crude symbolism of the Riha paten and the Kyrenia
dish disappears in later sixth century work. The art is still
realistic, still popular in its storytelling. But the symbols have
yielded to backgrounds of otherworldness. The now-celebrated
phoenix of Antioch (the Louvre) stands solitary on a mystical rock-pyre in a space marked only by minute flower designs. In the same way the majestic Evangelists carved upon
Maximian's ivory cathedra (Ravenna) emerge from a framework of intricate Oriental design. So, in miniatures and
mosaics, backgrounds of sheer gold and deep blue emphasize
the unreality behind human forms. Other trappings disappear. Roman statues diminish to architectural decoration
or dwindle to figures in ivory carvings. Human figures blend
with an unreality that can be sensed rather than seen.

André Malraux remarks: "*Alors, Byzance règne seule. Les
siècles qui découvrent le sublime des larmes ne montrent
pas un seul visage qui pleure.*" It is the discovery of Byzantine art to suggest eternity without visible sign. Perhaps
the truest likeness of the Byzantine Mother of God is to be
found in the Virgin of Torcello, remote from all the orna-
mentation of the church, solitary with her child in the golden
obscurity of the dome overhead. Agathias wrote of the painted

likeness of an archangel: "The worshipper becomes reverent and no longer confused; yea, he trembles before the image implanted within himself as if it were the real presence."

The lost art of sixth-century Constantinople was joyous. Romanos called his accented kontakions "songs of praise." The echo of those songs survives in Beneventan chant and Ambrosian liturgy. Justinian's people moved to the melody of flute and silver organ. When the artists made the procession of the martyrs in mosaics on the walls of St. Apollinaris (Ravenna), they made a joyful procession; in festive dress the men and women carry their crowns forward against a background of palm branches. (Scenes of agony, of crucifixion, of the mortification of ascetics came later into western churches, seldom into the Byzantine.)

❊ PROTOTYPES OF THE RENAISSANCE

The majestic curtains, probably silk, that draped the altar of Hagia Sophia bore figures of the Bible on one side and on the other Justinian and Theodora making offerings of their buildings to the Eternal. They disappeared long ago. Other textiles with Christian symbols surrounded by the age-old patterns of Asia found their way to the shrines of western Europe. Two superb fragments survive in the Museo Sacro of the Vatican. The far-wandering Irish pilgrims took back vestments as well as illuminated missals with them to Kells and Clonar. Such treasures had a way of wandering— borne by missionaries or carried to safety in raids during the dark centuries that followed Justinian. The shroud of St. Columban, in the treasury of the cathedral at Sens, is Byzantine. And the designs of the textiles of Constantinople were copied by weavers in the West.

Other treasures of enameled reliquaries, delicate portraits

in gold-glass, and jeweled bindings of sacred books made by skilled hands along the Mesé became models for less skilled hands in Anglo-Saxon Britain or the Gaul of the Franks.

Charlemagne, King of the Franks—eventual conqueror of the Lombards and Avars—was as western and Germanic as the Rhine itself. Yet he made his architects try to copy the design of St. Vitalis for his small cathedral at Aix. His craftsmen imitated the gold and silver rarities of Byzantine origin, captured in the treasure-hoard of the Avars. Charlemagne himself died while planning to make his way to the Queen City of the East, and one of his shrouds was a Byzantine embroidery of stylized elephants.

After Charlemagne, Venice absorbed the arts as well as the trade of Constantinople. That sagacious mistress of the ancient Adria's sea planned her cathedral of St. Mark's after Anthemius' Church of the Holy Apostles. Venetian artists copied the illumination of a sixth-century Byzantine scripture when they decorated the narthex, and in fact all the interior of St. Mark's bears witness to the current changes in Byzantine artistry.

Until the end of the tenth century Constantinople remained the wellspring of art in the West. By then—perhaps driven forth by persecution of Iconoclasts—masters of her studios found their way beyond the frontiers. Their influence appears in the realistic murals of the eleventh century in the great church of Kiev. It shows in the simplicity and power of the contemporary murals at Ohrid, not far from Justinian's homeland. Here in Serbia-Macedonia native artists progressed from the tutelage of Constantinople to such masterpieces as the "Dormition of the Virgin" at Sopocani.

In a similar manner the artists of Sicily and southern Greece —the Magna Graecia of Byzantium—passed from the influence of the mother city to achieve the haunting magic of Mystra, and the jewel-like perfection of the Capella Palatina (Palermo).

Perhaps the last bequest of Constantinople to the West was its humanism. When humanists arose in the fifteenth-century Italian cities, they looked beyond the style of the Roman Cicero and the verses of Vergil to the dynamism of Greek thought preserved in the libraries on the Bosporus. Visitors like Chrysoloras, the envoy, and Bessarion (1395–1472), titular Patriarch of Constantinople, left pupils and their own libraries in the West. Petrarch and Boccaccio joined together in a common hunger for the Greek masters. Aldus Manutius (1450–1515) devoted his greatest effort in Venice to publishing those masters, compelling his craftsmen to speak only Greek and debate Plato while they worked. Tales of Aesop's animals journeyed with the philosophers from the manuscripts of Constantinople to the presses of Florence and Naples.

This rediscovery of Greek thought broke the bonds of medieval scholasticism in the West. Its spirit of inquiry rather than dialectic led western thought beyond Bessarion to Galileo.

❁ THE MYSTERIES

Then, too, there are mysteries still unsolved. The paintings in a small chapel at Castelseprio, near Milan, attracted no attention until 1944. They show the hand of a master at ease in his work some time between the seventh and the tenth centuries. That master knew the secret of miniature-painting in Constantinople, but he felt some influence of the West. No one can tell how or why such a masterpiece appeared in remote Castelseprio during the Dark Ages. As late as 1310 Duccio of Siena followed the tradition of the earlier illuminators of Constantinople in the pathetic realism of his "*Maesta*" (Opera del Duomo, Siena). The tie between Kiev and

Sopocani, and Palermo-Mystra and Siena was the tradition of Constantinople. That trace of the influence of his city remained along the borderlands of Justinian's Imperium.

In the full tide of the Renaissance came the rediscovery of Justinian's *Corpus Juris*. Europeans turned eagerly to this full presentation of the laws, not because it was a "codification" of ancient Roman legislation unearthed by diligent humanists in Italy, but because it served a great need. Here was an analysis of justice itself. Here the problems of the magistrates were laid down, and the needs of the individual explained. It offered laws as understandable to the individuals of fifteenth-century Florence as to those half-forgotten inhabitants of Constantinople, then lost to the Turks. The new printing presses vied with each other in turning out copies of the *Institutes* and *Pandects* and the copies spread over Europe, to influence very strongly the law of Tudor England.

Another contribution, much more obscure, came to the western printing presses. The *Geographia* of Claudius Ptolemy of Alexandria was rediscovered and studied eagerly as a masterly mapping of the known world—known, that is, to Europeans of the early Renaissance. Almost unbelievably Ptolemy's maps were engraved upon copper separately by printers in Bologna (c. 1462), Rome (1478), and Florence (1480). But where did the printers get these accurate maps of an ancient scientist who had been lost in oblivion for some thirteen centuries? Modern scholars could not answer the question. Recently one of them traced the Ptolemaic maps to a copy preserved by the Byzantines.

There still remains the mystery of the portolano sea charts. These were the deft, accurate tracing of the Mediterranean and Black Sea coasts which appeared out of nowhere in the hands of thirteenth-century European mariners—much more accurate than the efforts of the pseudo-scientists of that time. What was the prototype of the masterly portolano chart? Only recently, experts began to suspect a Byzantine origin of the charts of the coasts—not the interior of the continent—cruised so long by the ships of Constantinople.

Modern study seems destined to reveal other contributions of Byzantine science to the Europeans of the Renaissance, who were too indifferent to aid the imperial city in its last resistance to capture by the Turks.

❈ THE ILLUSION OF HISTORY

Professor John Bagnell Bury, master of East Roman history, maintains: "No Byzantine Empire ever began to exist; the Roman Empire did not come to an end until 1453." What, then, was Justinian's city? Professor Arnold J. Toynbee states in A *Study of History:* "Thus, *de facto*, the Roman Empire perished in its Central and Eastern provinces after the death of Justinian, as, after the death of Theodosius a hundred and seventy years before, it had perished *de facto* in the West." Then what endured in Constantinople for eight hundred and eighty-eight years after Justinian's death?

According to Toynbee, Byzantium lingered on as a dying universal state. It was a lifeless shell of the perished Western Empire, a ghost empire that could merely exist, incapable of creation. This ghost had become one of the great illusions of history. The pontifical Edward Gibbon in his notable *Decline and Fall of the Roman Empire* beheld only "weakness and misery" in the emperors of Constantinople who took the place of his Caesars. Gibbon's great prestige kept attention centered on the "Eternal Rome" of the Caesars and away from Constantinople, the city that preserved the eternity.

A very natural prejudice has strengthened this illusion of our western history. The "grandeur that was Rome" appeared to be in our own tradition; Byzantine Constantinople seemed to be apart from our past—something odd, and vaguely east-

ern. It was said, and often repeated, that Constantinople had
fallen under the enervating influence of the Orient. The Roman Church belonged to our tradition, the Eastern Orthodox
did not. Crusaders became the heroes of our boyhood tales,
and the strange "Greek emperors" often played the part of
villains. After Constantinople fell into the hands of the Turks,
their sultans became the antagonists of our traditions.
Western visitors to the city during the nineteenth century
described it as something exotic, drowsing over the secrets of
its past. Writers confirmed the senescent continuation of the
historians, making a proverb of the "sick man of Europe."
Few, like Pierre Loti, beheld the beauty hidden beneath the
strangeness. Keats and Browning were only two of those who
gave tribute to the magic of Rome. But they beheld the remains of the city of the Renaissance on the Tiber, the Rome
of the pilgrims and the popes, which could not have arisen if
it had not been for Constantinople.

And in Venice, how many visitors crossing the square to
St. Mark's thought of the vanished Holy Apostles in Constantinople which had been its model? How many remembered that the architecture they admired, and the luminous
mosaics, could never have been created by the artists of ancient
Rome?

André Malraux warns us, in speaking of the arts: "We cannot begin to understand the transformation [*métamorphose*]
of ancient art into Byzantine art unless we cease to see, first of
all, in the eastern Roman empire the decadence of the empire
of the west."

It is clear by now that such a transformation did take place
in the arts. Before long we will understand that it took place
also in the civilization—Cassiodorus' *civilitas*—of our ancestors. There was a great turning point in western history,
from the fourth to the sixth century, at Constantinople.
The illusion of the ghost empire that would not die cannot
last much longer. During that time our tradition lies in the

city founded by Constantine, Christianized under Theodosius the Great, transformed by Justinian the First, and saved by Heraclius. It is a great tradition.

As in the case of the city, the history of its people has been distorted. During the age of Justinian we behold them almost entirely through the writings of Chrysostom, who castigated the sins of society. To this castigation, Procopius added his innuendos until Voltaire, for one, could dismiss the time as "a silly age." It was not. Because we hear so much of the crowds at the racing and of rioting in the circus, it does not follow that they enjoyed themselves or fought only in the circus. During Justinian's life they saw very little of the hippodrome.

Today we are likely to make Voltaire's mistake in judging the people of this early Constantinople. Byzantine society may appear to us marked by its obsession with religion, its passion for amusement, and its excesses of violence. The in-inhabitants, however, lived in an atmosphere of danger. For years at a time they were confined within their walls by siege. The danger of invasion lasted for centuries. Even the estates of the great families were confined to the nearest suburbs, like Hieron, from which they could escape at a day's notice by water to the safety of the Golden Horn. The price the inhabitants paid for survival was continued nervous tension. That tension sought relief in supernatural aid; it found oblivion in games and festivals—and music as well—and it reacted often enough in emotional violence.

Perhaps discerning emperors like Anastasius and Justinian understood very well the frame of consciousness in which their people existed. At least they were remarkably tolerant of the outbreaks of the factions in the circus; they were patient under the tirades of religious fanatics; they lost no opportunity to divert popular attention to new shrines and miracle-working images. When the social history of Byzantium is written, we may gain a new appreciation of the part played by the leaders.

As in the case of the people, their problems have been magnified during Justinian's reign by writers both contemporary and modern. Charles Diehl reminds us that Justinian inherited these grim social problems from ancient Rome; he did not create them. The son of Sabbatius reached the throne to face critical weakness in his state, disorders on all sides, his capital torn by rivalry of the factions, the provinces in misery under the practices of the public administration, and growing poverty draining away the public wealth. He was a revolutionary, in setting himself against this traditional misrule.

Theodora seems to have left no record of herself. Her acts remain obscure because they were carried out necessarily by the edicts of her husband, and Theodora herself was not given to explanations. The chief source for her life lies in the wit and venom of Procopius, whose tales of a teen-age prostitute still titillate western readers. Her challenging personality has stirred the imagination of playwrights and novelists until a dozen Theodoras have appeared on the stage and in the pages of books, if not on the screen. Theodora, however, was only one woman. An Asiatic woman of her birth faced an almost impossible task in entering the palace of Constantinople. Two men who knew her better than Procopius speak bluntly of their Augusta. John of Ephesus says she was "a woman from a brothel," while Paul the Silentiary praises her as co-worker with her husband. Add to these simple facts of her life that Justinian loved her in a quite uncomplicated way. Whether her intrigues aided or harmed the state is beside the question except for historians. Theodora hardly cared. Let it be said for her that she was a match for her time.

The real Theodora did not dominate her husband, as is often said. We have seen her exert power only during his illness in the pestilence; at other times she had to get around

him. Nor was the real Justinian under the influence of a
favorite. He had an instinct for picking men who could get
things done. While he often followed where Tribonian or
Peter the Patrician led, he drove them to accomplishments
that enlarge even our modern ideas of what may be achieved
in a single lifetime.

What was the real Justinian? The writers who worked for
him, like Procopius and John of Lydia, who bring that remote
age alive before our eyes, imagined him to be a dual personality
—a bureaucrat who tore up their roots in the past. Until this
generation, historians have described him only as a paradox,
as part of the monstrous paradox of the dying state that did not
die. As late as 1949 Ernest Stein said only that his personality
reflected "the Janus-headed complexity" of his time. Others
found in him the riddle of a Balkan peasant who devoted himself to restoring the ancient Roman Empire. The real Justinian
did his best to change it, except for his own authority as
emperor.

He has been compared to that other dominant ascetic,
Philip II of Spain. There are striking similarities, yet greater
differences between the son of the Macedonian peasant and
the prince of the Hapsburgs; the builder of the Hagia Sophia
could not have imagined an Escorial. Most historians have
contented themselves with portraying Justinian merely as the
builder of that great church and the creator of the *Corpus
Juris*, without wondering why he did such things. Dr. E. L.
Woodward, however, sets the paradox squarely before us:
"Was Justinian a narrow-minded official, unable from his
exalted station to see the problems of his empire, deluded by
a subservient court into believing that the world would obey
his word? Was he in all his life the theological fanatic whom
Procopius describes as neglecting practical affairs to sit through
long nights of controversy with old priests? Or did that fierce
ascetic nature fret itself away until only imagination was left
—the gigantic imagination of an age which built the Church

of the Divine Wisdom and looked into the very eyes of the angels of famine and earthquake, fire and pestilence?"

Justinian was that recluse of imagination. In the end he failed. But few men in history have fought so hard against failure. This stubbornness in him had one consequence. It made our modern world somehow different from what it might have been.

A Note on the Afterword

These are the books quoted in the Afterword:

Bury, J. B.: *History of the Later Roman Empire. From the Death of Theodosius I to the Death of Justinian.* London, 1923.

Diehl, Charles: *Justinien et la civilisation byzantine au VI* siècle.* Paris, 1901.

Grousset, René, and van der Meer, Frédéric: *Atlas de la civilisation occidentale.* Paris-Brussels, 1952.

Iorga, Nicolai: *Histoire de la vie byzantine.* Bucharest, 1934.

Malraux, André: *Les Voix du Silence.* Paris, 1952.

Stein, Ernest: *Histoire du Bas Empire. De la disparition de l'Empire d'Occident à la mort de Justinien (476–565). Tome II.* Bruges, 1949.

Woodward, E. L.: *Christianity and Nationalism in the Later Roman Empire.* London, 1916.

The new evaluation of Byzantine life and its significance to us began in the present century, notably in the work of Charles Diehl and Nicolai Iorga. A new generation of scholars in England as well as in Russia carried forward this new interpretation. The books named below represent the modern view of Byzantine history through the centuries:

Baynes, Norman, and Moss, H. St. L. B.: *Byzantium. An Introduction to East Roman Civilization.* Oxford, 1949.

Baynes, Norman: *Hellenistic Civilization and East Rome.* Oxford, 1946.

Bréhier, Louis: *Vie et Mort de Byzance. (L'Evolution de L'Humanité).* 3 vols. Paris, 1947.

Lewis, Archibald: *Naval Power and Trade in the Mediterranean* (A.D. 500–1100). Princeton, 1951.

Lindsay, Jack: *Byzantium into Europe. The Story of Byzantium as the First Europe*. London, 1952.

Runciman, Stephen: *Byzantine Civilisation*. London, 1933.

Index

A Note on the Type

This book is set in Electra, a Linotype face designed by W. A. Dwiggins (1880–1956), who was responsible for so much that is good in contemporary book design. Although much of his early work was in advertising and he was the author of the standard volume *Layout in Advertising*, Mr. Dwiggins later devoted his prolific talents to book typography and type design, and worked with great distinction in both fields. In addition to his designs for Electra, he created the Metro, Caledonia, and Eldorado series of type faces, as well as a number of experimental cuttings that have never been issued commercially.

Electra cannot be classified as either modern or old-style. It is not based on any historical model, nor does it echo a particular period or style. It avoids the extreme contrast between thick and thin elements which marks most modern faces, and attempts to give a feeling of fluidity, power, and speed.

This book was composed, printed, and bound by Kingsport Press, Inc., Kingsport, Tenn. Designed by Harry Ford.